Constituting Communities

SUNY series in Buddhist Studies

Matthew Kapstein, Editor

CONSTITUTING COMMUNITIES

Theravāda Buddhism and the Religious Cultures of South and Southeast Asia

JOHN CLIFFORD HOLT, JACOB N. KINNARD,
JONATHAN S. WALTERS
EDITORS

STATE UNIVERSITY OF NEW YORK PRESS

Published by
State University of New York Press
Albany

Printed in the United States of America

For information, address
State University of New York Press
90 State Street, Suite 700, Albany, NY 12207

Production, Laurie Searl
Marketing, Michael Campochiaro

Library of Congress Cataloging-in-Publication Data

Constituting communities : Theravada Buddhism and the religious cultures of South and Southeast Asia / edited by John Clifford Hold, Jacob N. Kinnard and Jonathon S. Walters.
p. cm.—(SUNY series in Buddhist studies)
Includes bibliographical references and index.
ISBN 0-7914-5691-9 (alk. paper)—ISBN 0-7914-5692-7 (pbk. : alk. paper)
1. Buddhism—Social aspects—Asia, Southeastern. 2. Buddhism—Social aspects—South Asia. 3. Monastic and religious life (Buddhism) 4. Theravāda—Buddhism—History—20th century. I. Holt, John, 1948– II. Kinnard, Jacob N. III. Walters, Jonathan S. IV. Series.

BQ4570.S6 C66 2003
294.3'91'095—dc21

2002075877

10 9 8 7 6 5 4 3 2 1

This book

is inspirited by and dedicated to

Frank E. Reynolds

Contents

Introduction — 1
John Clifford Holt and Jacob N. Kinnard

One — Communal Karma and Karmic Community in Theravāda Buddhist History — 9
Jonathan S. Walters

Two — Toward a Theory of Buddhist Queenship: The Legend of Asandhimittā — 41
John S. Strong

Three — Beggars Can Be Choosers: Mahākassapa as a Selective Eater of Offerings — 57
Liz Wilson

Four — The Insight Guide to Hell: Mahāmoggallāna and Theravāda Buddhist Cosmology — 71
Julie Gifford

Five — When the Buddha Sued Viṣṇu — 85
Jacob N. Kinnard

Six — Minister of Defense? The Viṣṇu Controversy in Contemporary Sri Lanka — 107
John Clifford Holt

Seven — Localizing Lineage: Importing Higher Ordination in Theravādin South and Southeast Asia — 131
Anne M. Blackburn

EIGHT PREACHER AS A POET: POETIC PREACHING AS A MONASTIC STRATEGY IN CONSTITUTING BUDDHIST COMMUNITIES IN MODERN SRI LANKA AND THAILAND 151
Mahinda Deegalle

NINE "FOR THOSE WHO ARE IGNORANT": A STUDY OF THE *BAUDDHA ÄDAHILLA* 171
Carol S. Anderson

TEN INTERPRETIVE STRATEGIES FOR SEEING THE BODY OF THE BUDDHA 189
James R. Egge

LIST OF CONTRIBUTORS 209

INDEX 211

Introduction

John Clifford Holt and Jacob N. Kinnard

Religious experience is, by definition, a profoundly personal and individual matter; it is, however, always also a communal experience. There is no escape from this fundamental recognition. On the one hand, even the most private, contemplative, esoteric, or otherwordly mystical religious experiences are necessarily temporally conditioned; that is, they occur within historical and, therefore, cultural contexts. On the other hand, all normative social constructions of reality are, ultimately, individually mediated; that is, all culturally shared conceptions of religion are apprehended as instances of personal consciousness. Thus, the personal and social natures of religion and religious experience are inextricably intertwined. Taking this as a fundamental premise, the essays in this volume address the topic of how community functions within Theravāda Buddhist culture by focusing on the ways in which the historical, social, and philosophical dynamics of various Buddhist communities have helped to forge particular apprehensions and conceptions of personal religious meaning and identity that are, at the same time, collective and social.

Although many historians and anthropologists of religion have from both the theoretical and the culture-specific perspectives explicitly addressed the question of what makes a religious community, the issue remains a vexing one. We frequently talk, for instance, of *the* Buddhist tradition, in the singular, to describe an entity that transcends doctrinal differences and cuts across both physical and temporal borders. In contrast, it is almost nonsensical to talk about a single Buddhist community; how, for instance, could we meaningfully talk about a community that encompasses the Sri Lankan fire walker, the Thai collector of amulets, and the Californian meditator? However, we do talk about *Buddhist* communities, as the smaller entities that make up *the* Tradition. But what about these groups makes them specifically Buddhist? How do different and often disparate communities constitute themselves as Buddhist? And despite their disparities, in what ways are they linked by one shared tradition? How do they communicate this shared identity?

The basic premise of this volume is that communities are not organically occurring entities, but that they are, as Benedict Anderson has persuasively argued about all communities, imagined; as such, they are in a constant state of flux, being rethought and reformed—reconstituted—in response to the flow of specific historical events. The essays in this volume, then, explore the dynamics of this imagining, by looking at who has produced Theravāda discourses and practices in South and Southeast Asia, and why and how the discourses and practices have shaped the identities and characters of the communities of Buddhists in this region. Certainly, the most obvious Buddhist community is the sangha, but this book attempts to push beyond the confines of the monastic community, and to consider a variety of communities—both lay and monastic, and their varied interactions.

Thus, from a variety of perspectives—historical, doctrinal and philosophical, social and anthropological—the authors of the chapters that make up this volume explore the types of issues that have proven important and definitive for identifying what it has meant, individually and socially, to be Buddhist in a plethora of ways within a variety of contexts in South and Southeast Asia. Each individual essay, and the volume as a whole, is informed by a single basic question: how have various Buddhists in South and Southeast Asian cultural contexts constituted communities within which explicitly Buddhist qualities and values have been personally affirmed?

Jonathan Walters's lead chapter in this volume addresses this central question by drawing our attention to how perceived dynamics of karma, a bedrock assumption operating creatively in the lives of all Buddhist adherents, are thought to sustain and alter the nature of specific social relations between given individuals over several lifetimes. That is, he points out how it is not uncommon for the Buddhists he has known in contemporary, village Sri Lanka to assert that karma is responsible for why and how they are related to their siblings, parents, or friends, and how their actions in the present will determine the nature of these same relations in future lives. What Walters is pointing out is that karma need not be understood exclusively as an inexorable cosmic law that works only on the level of determining an individual person's present and future state of conditioning. Karma, moreover, is also thought to function socially or collectively among or between various individuals. The karma of one individual may affect, or be in confluence with, the karma of another. Further, families, castes, villages, and even nations may have collective karma. Walters refers to these phenomena as "sociokarma." While reviewing the work of an earlier scholar who had previously examined the idea of collective karma and had come to the conclusion that it was a modern aberration of Buddhist doctrine and culture, Walters proceeds to analytical studies of the *Jātakas,* the *Buddhavaṃsa,* the *Anāgatavaṃsa,* and the *Apadāna* to find that instances of several different types of sociokarma are clearly instantiated. The essay is extremely rich in its implications. For instance, it has been held that Buddhists believe that consciousness is what transmigrates as a result of karma from one rebirth to another. Usually this is taken to explain how an individual's identity and conditioned context has arisen. But Walters's essay makes it clear that there is a particular strain of Buddhist thought that understands that the very nature of social relations, or the very condition of a particular community, can transmigrate. That is, communities are constituted by karma.

John Strong's essay focuses on a neglected aspect of Buddhist community: queenship. He argues that in ancient India, kingsghip was really something of a family affair with the chief queen playing key roles in a type of power-sharing arrangement with the king. That is, her role of leadership with the community was part and parcel of a sociopolitical dynamic in which "her rule and authority [was] part of a greater symbiosis of power and performance." By examining the profile of Asandhimittā, the chief queen of Aśoka, as it can be gleaned through a study of a the extended Cambodian *Mahāvaṃsa,* the Pāli *Dasavaṭṭhuppakaraṇa,* and the Thai *Trai Phum* (translated by Frank and Mani Reynolds), Strong points out that just like kingship, queenship must be earned through the generation of karmic merit, that it may be constituted by a dual nature ("righteous" yet "fierce"), that a queen's karmic merit must also be accompanied by the cultivation of wisdom, and that, just like kings, queens were very active in the public promulgation of the Buddha's dharma. What he finds in this study, therefore, is that not only are the nature of kingship and queenship co-extensive, but that they are consubstantial, symbiotic, and mutually dependent as well.

Liz Wilson has focused on Pāli and *Mūlasarvāstivādin* literature which depicts how the *dhūtaṇga* master of asceticism, Mahākassapa (Sanskrit Mahākasyapa) was especially inclined to receive alms from impoverished and unfortunate lay donors who were in dire need of merit to transform their conditions. She argues that in consuming the "bio-moral" status of depraved givers, Mahākassapa, as a highly desirable field of merit, has engaged in a form of sacrifice, or in "monastic begging as a means of unburdening others of negative karmic conditions." Historically, this dynamic between desperate laity and highly virtuous monk appears to be a transformation of the Vedic pattern constituting the patron/priest relation, a kind of "Buddhist moral sacrificial altar in the post Vedic age." Moreover, she argues, it is really a form of "demerit transfer," a religious practice reflecting socioreligious relations constitutive of "karmic communities of interdependence."

Julie Gifford's study strikes a similar chord in showing how the religious practice of a Buddhist saint is seen to benefit the spiritual conditions of a needy laity. In focusing on one of the Buddha's most venerated disciplines, Mahāmoggallāna, she demonstrates how Theravāda cosmology can be regarded as the product of particular visionary experiences. That is, Mahāmoggallāna's "meditation facilitates the deployment of supernatural powers" which become the basis for his knowledge used in constructing "a cosmological map of samsara." According to the *Vimānavatthu* commentary, Mahāmoggallāna relates his visionary experiences of the various realms of the cosmos to the Buddha, who, in turn, incorporates them into his teachings about suffering, karmic retribution, and the transformative power of the dharma. Gifford argues that karma is understood in this context as inherently social, insofar as the karma of one person affects the totality of all members of the community. It is for this reason alone that the Mahāmoggallāna's cosmological insights, derived from his meditative attainments, are made available compassionately through the teaching of the Buddha's dharma. Everyone has a stake in the spiritual quality of the community as a whole.

Jacob Kinnard's essay answers the question of how the worshiping community at Bodhgayā (Bihar, India), the historical pilgrimage site associated with the Buddha's enlightenment experience, has been transformed over the past century from being a cultic community comprised almost exclusively of *Vaiṣṇava* and *Śaiva* Hindus to its present polyvalent constituency of Buddhists from all over Asia. Kinnard reviews the fascinating legal history of how Buddhists demanded, in colonial courts under British imperial rule, that Hindus "return" the "Buddhist Jersuslam" to its "rightful" Buddhist heritage. This Buddhist demand, headed by the Sinhala Buddhist Anagarika Dharmapala, occurred only after at least a four hundred year occupancy by *Śaiva* brahmins who regularly conducted rites in the Bodhgayā temple for *Vaiṣṇava* pilgrims who regarded the Buddha as Viṣṇu's ninth avatar. Kinnard's study registers how *Śaivas,* Buddhists, *Vaiṣṇavas,* and "All-Indian nationalists" have attempted to constitute their respective communities in staking their rival claims to this sacred site. It is a classic study of the manner in which communities define themselves in relation to each other.

John Holt's study of the contemporary Viṣṇu controversy in Sri Lanka analyzes the processes by which aspects (worship of Viṣṇu) of one religious tradition (Hindu) have been assimilated, subordinated, and legitimated by another (Sinhala Theravāda Buddhist). He argues that assimilations of this nature are often the product of political expediency rather than the result of doctrinal innovations, the latter of which are usually post hoc formulations. He finds the same processes at work in the current monastic-led drive to purge Sinhala Buddhist culture of deity propitiation, especially deities of Hindu origin. While this attempt to extract veneration of deities is made publicly on doctrinal grounds, Holt finds that political pressures brought about by rising ethnic consciousness within the context of Sri Lanka's protracted civil war between Tamils and Sinhalese has been a salient factor in pumping the impulse for reform. That is, ethnicity, rather than doctrinal purity, is sometimes a driving force in the process of reconstituting the substance of religious community.

Anne Blackburn's chapter "addresses questions about the processes through which new Buddhist communities come to be localized and accepted as natural." Specifically, she illustrates how an eighteenth-century Theravāda monastic lineage from Thailand was imported to Sri Lanka and legitimated by various strategies, including the translation of important Pāli texts into the Sinhala vernacular and by emphasizing monastic forest-dwelling legacies regarded with great respect by the Buddhist laity. She then briefly looks at similar patterns of localization strategies in twelfth-century Pagan (Burma) and in sixteenth-century northern Thailand.

Mahinda Deegalle's contribution is concerned with the emergence of new forms of monastic sermonizing in Sri Lanka and Thailand in the late twentieth century. In particular, he notes how *baṇa kavi* (poetic sermons) have become a popular means of preaching the dharma to the laity by innovative monks who are trying to present the dharma in new, culturally attractive fashions suitable to the contemporary age, especially youth. One of the important issues that he raises is that music and song have been regarded traditionally in the Theravāda *Vinaya* monastic disciplinary code as offences to be avoided. Therefore, the monks who have engaged in this new form of preaching are now trying "to constitute a sense of community and religious affiliation as they struggle against the established normative monastic authorities." In his sketch of how two monks (one Sinhalese and one Thai) have mounted their campaigns, Deegalle argues that the roots of *baṇa kavi* are actually founded upon an existing medieval Sinhala literary poetic tradition from the fifteenth-century Kōṭṭē period.

Carol Anderson has studied the significance of the *Bauddha Äahilla,* a practical and popular guide or compendium of instructions for how Buddhists should engage in cultic activities such as *sil,* the chanting of *pirit, bodhi pūjas,* or other forms of religious activity at Buddhist *vihārayas.* She points out that the text has a definite iconic value for many lay Buddhists, is often presented as a gift to adolescent Buddhists on *Vesak poya* days, and has remained a standard handbook since it originally appeared in the late nineteenth century. Since the *Bauddha Ädahilla,* in its many recensions, constitutes a practical liturgical guide for engaging in traditional forms of lay ritual, Anderson rejects categorizing the text as part of the "Protestant Buddhism" type of religiosity which other scholars have declared as the dominant form of lay Buddhist religious piety during this particular historical time frame. Whatever the origins of its inspiration, the *Bauddha Ädahilla* has iconic value not only to nostalgic Buddhists, but for students of Buddhism seeking to gain a profile of how the Buddhist community has understood the form and function of "congregational" life in modern Sri Lanka.

James Egge's chapter examines "how Buddhists view the qualities of the Buddha that are mundane, physical, impermanent, royal and auspicious in relation to those that are transcendent, immaterial, permanent, ascetic and pure." His method is to consider the nature of the sacred marks of the Buddha body as "signs capable of pointing to both mundane and transcendent aspects." By "signs," Egge is referring to the heuristic devices deployed by Charles S. Peirce as icon, index, and symbol. He adopts them here for the purpose of his own analysis. In his study, Egge concludes that these signs actually mean nothing in and of themselves, but are dependent upon "interpretive communities" for the meanings they acquire. He points out, that is, that "a text is meaningless without an interpretive community, and without imagined interpretive communities, there are no historical meanings."

The discerning reader will find the spirit and intellectual orientations of Frank Reynolds throughout the contents of the various essays constituting this volume. That is hardly a surprising fact: all of the contributors to this collection were, at one time, students of Frank Reynolds at the Divinity School of the University of Chicago. All of these essays are reflective of Reynolds's various buddhalogical, theoretical, and methodological interests. Reynolds's approach has been almost always dialogic or collaborative in nature; his method has usually been one of conversation, and his wide interests have spanned concerns for the self on the one hand to concerns of the cosmic dimension of religion on the other, from the classical to the popular, and from the political to the contemplative. His vision has always been to seek a plurality of voices speaking to a common problem of importance. It is therefore fitting that this collection of essays dedicated to him is thoroughly a collaborative work containing a plurality of voices focused on a common problem of fundamental importance to the understanding of Buddhism per se and the history of religions in general.

The essays comprising this volume were originally formulated for a conference held July 21 through 23, 2000, at the Breckenridge Center of Bowdoin

College in York, Maine, to honor Frank Reynolds as our teacher extraordinaire and to thank him warmly and genuinely for the great compassionate influence he has exercised upon all of our professional and personal lives.

On behalf of the contributors to this volume, the editors acknowledge and thank Clark Gilpin, former Dean of the Divinity School of the University of Chicago, and Craig McEwen, Dean for Academic Affairs of Bowdoin College, for their very generous financial support.

ONE

COMMUNAL KARMA AND KARMIC COMMUNITY IN THERAVĀDA BUDDHIST HISTORY

Jonathan S. Walters

INTRODUCTION: SOCIOKARMA IN CONTEMPORARY SRI LANKA

THIS ESSAY BEGINS with my experience studying and living in a rural Sri Lankan Theravāda Buddhist village on and off since 1984. On numerous occasions my deep affection for this village and its environs has been given a karmic explanation by my village friends, who consider it obvious that during previous lives I have lived there and experienced parallel social relationships with the rebirth precursors of these same villagers. Thus, for example, my university friend's mother very quickly decided that I must be a son of hers who died shortly before my own birth, come back to her in this unlikely form, a belief she instantiated by calling me "son" and teaching me to refer to everyone else in her extended family and indeed in "our" village at large according to the kinship terms that would be appropriate were I in fact her own son. Likewise, my friends often have tried to make sense of our friendships—sometimes an odd meeting of worlds, to say the least—as the karmic result of having been friends during previous lifetimes *(pera ātma mitrayo)*.

More striking still is the commonplace expression of an aspiration or hopeful intention (called *prārthanāwa*) for the constitution or continuance of specific social relationships during future lives. Typical is this aspiration, which I happened to receive in the mail while composing the present essay: "I think that you really are as it were my very own brother," writes the wife of a village friend, "We make the aspiration, 'definitely during the next life, may you be born in our very own family.'"[1] Such aspirations, expressed in person or in letters, may include different social relationships (be my friend, father, son, husband), different specifications as regards time (in the next life, in some future life, in many future lives, in every life until we meet Maitreya Buddha and attain *nibbāna*), and as regards space (in this village, here in Sri Lanka, in America, in a Buddhist home). But the underlying assumption that karma constitutes present and future social relationships is clear throughout the variation. Family, friendship, and village community itself are constituted, at least in part, by previous karma, and will be constituted in the future by present karma. And it is important to remember that such *prārthanāwas,* far from being merely descriptive or informative, are themselves mental actions (karma) believed efficacious in bringing about desired sociokarmic results.

I should be clear from the outset that I do not take karma to be a mere proposition, idea, doctrine, concept, or hypothesis. The ordinary way it comes up in discussion is instead as an assumption, presupposition, starting point, perspective, orientation, or category of the imagination. Karma is like temperature; no one asks whether temperature exists, but rather whether this particular object is hot or cold, or how to act in response to its temperature. Likewise, I have never heard my village friends debate *whether* there is karma and rebirth, but I have often heard them debate what this particular karma *might be*. In terms of the present discussion, I have not in fact ever heard anyone doubt that I (and they) do have karmic connections to that village community, but rather have heard and participated in lively and sometimes very entertaining reflections on just how it all plays out. And whatever one may consider their epistemological value, these sorts of discussions have very real social effects in the present life, expressing and deepening the bonds of affection and loyalty that characterize social relationships, and implying various rights and responsibilities within the larger community.

It makes perfect sense that community should have a karmic dimension, given the social dimension of virtually all karma. The classic acts of both *puñña* (merit) and *pāpa* (sin) almost always are social affairs. *Dāna* (giving) is always a gift to someone else (or to a group of others), and like other acts of merit (*pūjā, poya, baṇa,* pilgrimage) is regularly performed in groups; it is almost *de rigueur* to dedicate the merit of such acts to other humans (the stock phrase is *jñātimitrādi*, "family, friends, etc."), to the dead, and/or to deities. Likewise, most demeritorious acts also occur in communal settings: various types of killing, theft, sexual impropriety, falsehood, and intoxicated excess would be impossible for the isolated individual, who nevertheless usually remains the predicate of scholarship on karma. So too, karma as result *(vipāka, phala)* inevitably has social dimensions because the goodness or badness of a good or bad rebirth is largely conceived according to social categories such as family, status, wealth, caste, power, and/or political situation. Even birth among the gods, animals, or hell-beings has its social dimensions.

Indeed, it might seem unnecessary to argue that karma has social dimensions and society has karmic dimensions, an overlap that for convenience I dub "sociokarma." But as I shall now proceed to suggest it is actually astonishing how little this conjunction of karma and community has been recognized in the scholarship to date.

SOCIOKARMA IN THERAVĀDA STUDIES AND IN THERAVĀDA HISTORY

To the best of my knowledge the only scholarly study of the phenomenon I call sociokarma has been made by James P. McDermott, who treats it under the designation "group karma."[2] Drawing on the writings of twentieth-century Thai, Burmese, and Sri Lankan Theravāda Buddhists, he identifies three sorts of notions of "group karma," which he designates "overflow karma," "the karma of communal relationship," and "national karma."[3] His project being to "analyze some of the contemporary discussion of 'group karma,' and then to attempt to determine whether there are canonical precedents for such notions,"[4] McDermott proceeds to discuss early Buddhist texts relevant to each of these types.

McDermott takes the term *overflow karma* from a 1956 tract on karma by Bhikkhu Sīlācāra of Ceylon; it refers to the effects of one person's karma upon the karma of others. This phenomenon is especially evident in the case of famous people, whose deeds whether good (the Buddha, Gandhi) or bad (Hitler, Alexander the Great) have had an enormous impact on millions around them.[5] Another variant on this theme is the well-known idea that a righteous king's righteousness brings prosperity and safety to the entire kingdom, the reverse also being true; McDermott quotes a 1918 declaration by the Thai Supreme Patriarch Prince Vajiranana (Wachirayan) that "the king's acts of piety merit not only himself but the people and the guardian spirits of the kingdom" as well.[6] More pervasive still is the overflow of all karma, even that produced by ordinary people, which inevitably affects others within one's community.[7] McDermott finds "canonical precedent" for such a notion of overflow karma in the *Kurudhamma* and *Maṇicora Jātakas,* where a perspective very similar to Prince Wachirayan's is clearly articulated,[8] and in a *sutta* of the *Anguttara Nikāya* (III.172–73), where the Buddha enumerates among the benefits of a well-given gift the inability of thieves, kings, or impious heirs (in addition to fire and water) to destroy one's property in future lives. McDermott writes, "This suggests the recognition that no saṃsāric stream of existence is completely independent. Although each individual is heir to his deeds alone, the ripening of his karma has consequences that reach beyond himself."[9]

"The karma of communal relationship" follows directly from this sense of the interconnection of the karma of individual participants in any given social situation: as defined by McDermott, "in any given situation the karma of each individual must be in confluence with that of every other participant in that situation."[10] Drawing on a book by Thai physician Dr. Luang Suriyabongs, McDermott includes within this categorization the similarity in karma that must underlie birth in a single family, or for that matter within any group. He finds "canonical precedent" for the view not only in the *Anguttara* passage referred to above, but also in the story of the murder of Mahāmoggallāna as recorded in the *Dhammapadaṭṭhakathā,* where "the karma of the sectaries and of the highwaymen had to be in confluence with that of Moggallāna before they could injure him, for they are all executed shortly thereafter."[11]

McDermott includes in his category "national karma" a wide range of sociokarmic phenomena that seem to be linked together, and distinguished from the first two types, by their shared political bent: the overflow karma of pious or impious kings (as suggested above by Prince Wachirayan); "family karma" conceived on a national scale (as suggested by Dr. Suriyabongs); the idea that national groups might suffer karmic punishments or enjoy karmic rewards together as groups in the future (or be suffering or enjoying such results as national groups in the present), a view McDermott traces to Egerton C. Baptist of Ceylon; and a variety of group karma perspectives that emerged in Burma during the 1950s and 1960s, including the idea that the meritorious deeds of the state are the actions (karma) of the entire populace, and plans for "state-aided karma" in which the poor would receive the dole as "karmic boosts."[12] For his "canonical precedent," McDermott follows Baptist's lead in examining the story of King Viḍūḍabha's slaughter of the Śākyans as reported in the *Dhammapadaṭṭhakathā (Viḍūḍabhavatthu)* and in the *Jātakaṭṭhakathā (Bhaddasāla Jātaka),* where the Buddha explains: "Monks, if you regard only this present existence it was indeed unjust that the Sākiyas should die in such wise. What they received, however, was entirely just, considering the sin they committed in a previous state of existence . . . [when] they conspired together and threw poison into the river."[13]

Oddly, having surveyed so much evidence of thinking about "group karma" in both modern and ancient Theravāda, McDermott nevertheless consistently tries to dismiss it as aberrant, atypical, and/or merely modern. Thus, in the case of overflow karma, he simply dismisses as "unorthodox" two extensions of the argument made by Bhikkhu Sīlācāra, namely that there may be unintentional transference of merit and that there may be transference of demerit. Likewise, the portrayal of the king's righteousness affecting the prosperity of the people, in the *Kurudhamma* and *Maṇicora Jātakas,* is dismissed as "not a common one in the Pāli canon," while in the instance of the *Anguttara* list of sociological benefits of individual merit, "it is not necessary, nor even very likely that this notion implies a concept of overflow karma, however. Rather, the point may be simply that in any given situation the karma of each individual must be in confluence with that of every other . . ."[14]

In this quotation the second type of group karma, "the karma of communal relationship," appears to be fully accepted by McDermott, but here too he will not accept the implications drawn from it by Dr. Suriyabongs that

> although man creates his own individual Karma, whatever he does will have its effect on his environment too. Thus, he at the same time has a common family-Karma, a racial, or national Karma or a group-Karma. The good he does will not only benefit himself but all others who live with and around him, that is, all sentient beings. And vice versa, evil will not be suffered by himself alone.[15]

Shying away from such conclusions, McDermott reduces the idea of karmic confluence to a mere extension of his staunchly individualist perspective: "[I]t is simply the common aspects in the action of certain individuals which lead them into membership in a group, the communal experiences of which are due to each individual member as a result of his own individual past."[16]

All of these strategies are brought to bear against the evidence of the third type of "group karma," "national karma." Thus, the straightforward treatment of sociokarma in the Viḍūḍabha story is written off as a "rare exception."[17] Another text of the same cycle cited by Baptist, in which the slaughter of an innocent Bandhula the Mallian and his thirty-two sons is justified as "the fruit of their misdeeds in previous states of existence," has according to McDermott "nothing . . . to suggest that this is anything other than the fruition of personal misdeeds of each individual member of the group. To read into this or similar accounts [of which there are many] a developed concept of national karma is to go beyond what is even implicitly warranted by the text. Nevertheless, the fact that Egerton Baptist cites this as an example of national karma is significant, for it points to the shaky character of the foundations on which any case for a classical precedent for a concept of group karma must be built."[18] Taking up an argument by Rev. Nyanaponika, McDermott further undermines the notion of group results for national misdeeds by pointing out that the same beings will not necessarily be reborn into the same national group during the next life, even though in the same breath he recognizes that none of the authors he discusses shares Rev. Nyanaponika's assumption that such national continuity need be the case.[19] McDermott concludes his article with the judgment that "[a]lthough isolated cases analogous to . . . overflow karma, the karma of communal relationship, and national karma are to be found in the *Tipiṭaka* and early commentaries, their nature and infrequency in this literature make it clear that a systematic concept of group karma was in no sense operative in early Theravāda. . . . It is only in this century, then, that one finds a conscious effort to split with this tradition."[20]

But McDermott is actually more generous in allowing sociokarma *some* discursive space than are the Western scholars upon whom he in turn draws, for example Winston King, whose *In the Hope of Nibbana,* though the source of McDermott's knowledge of Burmese "state-aided kamma," treats karma as positively antisocial, productive only of social passivity and indifference to others.[21] And King in turn sees more scope for *any* discussion of karmic society than does the primary scholar upon whom he in turn draws, Max Weber, who considered early Buddhism in general so thoroughly "asocial" as to render contradictory the very existence of Buddhist community, even the community of monks and nuns.[22] Yet in his discussion of Buddhist art Weber, like McDermott, presents excellent evidence of the importance of sociokarma in the Theravāda tradition.[23]

It may be a question of half empty or half full, but especially in light of the fact that sociokarmic thinking is so utterly commonplace in contemporary Theravāda societies the premodern examples provided (against himself) by McDermott, King, or Weber are alone sufficient to convince me that sociokarma needs to be taken more seriously than McDermott's dismissals would suggest. I say this not merely because sociokarmic thinking is commonplace today, but also because I think McDermott vastly underestimates the significance of the very sources he uses.

Thus, the *Jātaka* as a whole represents an unmistakable monument to sociokarmic thinking in its portrayal of the constantly intersecting previous lives of the same group of people who dominate the Buddha's final/present life. Yasodharā, Rāhula, Sāriputta and Moggallāna, Ānanda, Devadatta, and a whole cast of other characters are reborn together, life after life, developing the social relationships they will have with the Buddha in the present, when the soteriological aspect of those sociokarmic connections comes to the fore. In many *jātakas* this implicit claim that the early Buddhist community was constituted through karmic connections to the person of the Buddha is made explicit by treating the early Buddhist community writ large (sometimes "the present followers of Buddha," sometimes "the five hundred monks") as the Bodhisatta's entire community during countless previous lives human, animal and divine. In the *Jātaka,* the Buddhist community is one huge interconnected karmic web transmigrating together across time toward a group fruition of all the good karma combined, realized in salvific participation in the Buddha's own intimate community.[24]

This group transmigration clustering around the Bodhisatta is charted out and further expanded in two additional texts which McDermott and the other scholars I have mentioned do not consider at all, the *Buddhavaṃsa* and the *Apadāna*. The *Buddhavaṃsa* lays out a temporal grid across which the future Buddha, meeting up with previous Buddhas, develops his present Buddhahood; in the *Apadāna* the entire early Buddhist community is charted according to that same grid. All the arahants enlightened by Gotama Buddha turn out to be reaping the fruit of actions (karma) they performed in the same festivals, the same kingdoms, the same communities—often the same families—in which the future Buddha himself was performing his own Buddha-becoming actions. The prediction of future Buddhahood bestowed upon the Bodhisatta by each previous Buddha in the *Buddhavaṃsa* is echoed in similar predictions given by those same previous Buddhas to the rebirth precursors of the various ranking relatives and followers of Gotama Buddha, as reported in the *Apadāna*. And the *Apadāna* further enriches the picture of that particular mass of beings transmigrating together in the hope of attaining nirvana in the dispensation of Gotama Buddha, a hope that was not in vain except for Devadatta and his five hundred followers and their families (note the sociokarma) who are sucked into hell along with him. The *Apadāna* does this by drawing all sorts of different sociokarmic links among various subgroups such as married couples repeatedly reborn to marry again (the Buddha and Yasodharā, Mahākassapa and Bhaddā-Kāpilāni), nuclear families whose members meet up again and again as they progress along the Path (the Buddha and Mahāpajāpatī Gotamī, Rāhula and his sister, the seven daughters of Kiki King of Kāsi, numerous groups of monks), and so forth.[25] In these *Khuddaka* and related texts, taken as a whole, we not only find an extraordinary picture of karmic confluence, but also, given the consistent centrality of the Bodhisatta himself in this transmigrating mass, an idea closely approximating "overflow karma." And given that most *jātakas* involve kings and kingdoms, there is far more "national karma" here than McDermott has realized, too.

I would suggest further that ideas of group karma are more common in the *sutta*s themselves than McDermott wants to allow. Thus, I would argue that all the *sutta*s that describe the effects of good and bad karma imply karmic confluence, given that they involve social status, wealth, and so forth.[26] Even if most *sutta*s are not as explicit about the synchrony with others' karma as is the *Anguttara* text McDermott cites, we nevertheless have reason to see the developed sociokarmic thinking of the *Jātaka* or the *Apadāna* as a playing out of ideas already there in the *sutta*s, rather than as some sort of major deviation from them (which anyway would have occurred long before the twentieth century!). Indeed, in a famous *sutta* of the *Saṃyutta-nikāya* which is quoted not only in Theravāda but also in Mahāyāna sources,[27] and which Buddhaghosa treats as exemplary of "the *sutta*s," the Buddha is reported to have declared that "it is not easy to find a being who has not formerly been your mother . . . your father . . . your brother . . . your sister . . . your son . . . [or] your daughter."[28] This being the case, the question becomes what social relationship does *not* have some karmic precursor? At any rate, I obviously do not find an empirical basis for McDermott's claim that a systematic concept of "group karma" became operative in the Theravāda only during the twentieth century. What we find in the full *Jātaka* or the *Apadāna* collections is considerably more ancient than that, and more developed than either the contemporary perspectives cited by McDermott or the warm aspirations of my village friends.

Yet sociokarma remains underdetermined in the scholarship; McDermott, despite his dismissals, is the only scholar who has dealt with it in any depth at all. Thus, John Garrett Jones's well-known 1979 study of the *Jātakas* does not notice this dimension of the collection at all; he includes a chapter on "Karma and Rebirth" that does not mention society, and a chapter on "Social Teachings" that does not mention karma.[29] Charles Keyes and Val Daniel's 1983 collection of anthropological studies of karma, even the learned introduction and summary by the editors, respectively, never moves beyond the recognition that karma can effect social status, and that karma itself is a cultural construct that can vary from community to community (both very important points to be sure, but points that fall short of a recognition of karma as constitutive of community, and vice versa).[30] By the same token, karma plays almost no role in such seminal collections on Theravāda Buddhist society as the edited volumes on *Religion and Legitimation of Power in Sri Lanka, Religion and Legitimation of Power in Burma, Thailand and Laos,* and *The Two Wheels of Dhamma,* nor in such narratives of Theravāda Buddhist social history as Gombrich's *Theravāda Buddhism: a social history from ancient Benares to modern Colombo*[31] or Chakravarti's *The Social Dimensions of Early Buddhism.*[32] Melford Spiro's *Buddhism in Society,* which makes its explicit project to determine the relationship between "kammatic Buddhism" and society, fails to recognize any but mundane (type 1) sociokarma and therefore can portray karma as at best an obstacle to economic development and public charity.[33]

The only exceptions to these generalizations that I have been able to find in Western scholarship appear in a volume of essays that in many ways is the precursor of this present volume, and which is similarly inspired by Frank Reynolds's work, namely *Sacred Biography in the Buddhist Traditions of South and Southeast Asia,* edited by Juliane Schober. Reynolds's own leadoff essay in that volume calls attention to the social dimensions of the *Jātaka* identification of "rebirth precursors" of the Buddha and "of particular members of his family, of particular disciples, or of other contemporaries."[34] It also highlights the several *Paññ āsa Jātaka* versions of one of the richest sources of sociokarmic speculation, the story of the romantic co-transmigrations of the rebirth precursors of the Buddha and his wife.[35] John Strong's contribution to Schober's volume takes up precisely this "family affair" in the biography of the Buddha, and remarks significantly that "[k]arma is not only individual, it is collective as well, and as a result, karmic biographies treat not only of the 'histories' of identifiable karmic continua over a series of lives, but also of ongoing karmic nexuses."[36] Likewise, Mark Woodward's contribution to the *Sacred Biography* volume highlights the significance of the "cohorts of the Buddhas" who populate the *Jātaka* tradition, stating, "Bodhisattvas do not journey to *nibbāna* alone. Every Buddha has parents, a wife, a son, disciples, chief disciples, a personal servitor, and chief male and female lay donors who follow him on the path to enlightenment. These communities begin to form as the bodhisattva practices the perfection. . . . Future Buddhas will have similar communities. Presumably, they have already begun to form."[37] And my own contribution to that volume spells out some initial thoughts about what I call "the co-transmigration of social units" in the *Apadāna* narratives and about the correspondence of that literary trope to a social fact of the early post-Aśokan Period when it was composed, the fact that acts of good karma were in many instances performed jointly by large social groups including families, towns, guilds, and religious associations.[38]

Thus, my claim *that* there is sociokarma in Theravāda Buddhist tradition is not an especially original one. In its admitted multiplicity the perspective is old, ubiquitous, and fairly obvious. But recent trends in Theravāda Studies—shifts from "early Buddhism" to "Theravāda Tradition," from the ever-decaying original core to the ever-enlarging Buddhist civilization, from the arahant in solitude to the monk as social leader, from a hyper-rational philosophy to a living religion with its own cosmology, soteriology, mythology, and communitas—have made it increasingly important that we *do* recognize sociokarma. And given the standing scholarly tradition that would minimize, ignore, or actively deny the presence of sociokarma in Theravāda Buddhist history, I hope it has been a worthwhile exercise to review in these general terms some of the evidence of its significance.

THE TYPES OF SOCIOKARMA

All the examples of sociokarma that I have been able to find fall into seven general categories: (1) social context, (2) overflow karma, (3) karmic confluence, (4) co-transmigration of social units, (5) sociokarmic aspiration, (6) political karma, and (7) the karma of social institutions. Though these obviously overlap, each can be clearly distinguished from the others. I have listed the types in a sort of order, with the degree to which society is explicitly karmic, and karma explicitly social, increasing as the numbers grow larger. In the present section I describe and discuss these seven types, use them to organize the many examples of sociokarma already given above, and introduce a few further examples. This should help bring some clarity to my so far rather haphazard survey of this important topic, thereby increasing its usefulness as a tool in the study and teaching of the cultures that have presupposed the truth of sociokarmic phenomena. By way of conclusion I provide a couple of examples of how "thinking with sociokarma" can benefit both scholars and practitioners of the Theravāda.

1. The first of my categories, "social context," refers to the most basic social dimensions of karma, without implying anything beyond the fact that karma can be performed and/or bear results within specifically social situations. With perhaps the exception of purely private acts of merit such as meditation or worship in solitude, or purely self-harming sins such as suicide, all karma occurs in a social context and therefore has inherently social dimensions. Even in my hypothetical counterinstances, the kind of person one becomes through private merit affects his or her community in all sorts of ways, not to mention the social dimensions of suicide. The same social dimensions are of course characteristic of most karmic effects, too, given that most people do belong to and experience their lives within communities. Just as one's social background, status, wealth, power, gender, age, and other social factors will shape an individual's actions, so the results of actions are regularly conceived according to those same factors.

   The inherently social nature of karma as both action and as result becomes especially clear when a social group undertakes to perform some joint act of merit or sin. Thus, in the *Apadāna* narratives the past-life karmic seed *(kammabīja)* or original act of piety which finally bears fruit in any given arahant's present-life arahantship often turns out to have been a group act, such as participation in a royally sponsored festival, worshipping a *stūpa* "while tagging along with father," or meeting a previous Buddha in a large assembly, while the ultimate fruit of merit is itself participation in the uniquely salvific, karma-transcending society, a Buddha's own intimate community. In the *Buddhavaṃsa* staggering numbers of people reportedly gain entry into the Path on single occasions during the times of previous Buddhas. "Our" (*amhākam,* note the sociokarmically charged pronoun) Gotama Buddha likewise usually preached his sermons to large groups; those in the present who are moving toward arahantship in the future have very likely earned some merit in those very group situations, and will realize its result in the future society that is the intimate community of Maitreya or some further future Buddha still.[39] As mentioned, "the five hundred monks" or just "the followers" who constitute the Buddha's intimate community turn out in the *Jātaka* to have perfected themselves through group actions performed in countless previous lives, and in the *Apadāna* the same turns out to be true of "the five hundred nuns" who formed Mahāpajāpatī Gotami's most intimate community. Likewise, the Śākyans who are slaughtered by Viḍūḍabha, the five hundred followers and their families sucked into hell with Devadatta, Bandhula the Mallian and his thirty-two sons, and other groups perform *pāpa* karma as a group in the past and/or suffer karmic effects as a group in the present, clarifying the sometimes social context for all action and result of action, evil as well as good.

2. The second type of sociokarma, overflow karma, has already been discussed at some length above. This type differs from "social context" in two ways. First, it is not necessarily the case that overflow karma would bear its results in a shared social time-space; the effects of Gotama's preaching (or Hitler's Holocaust) continue to overflow beyond the time-space that Gotama or Hitler occupied. Second, whereas "social context" implies no more than the fact that some karma and results of karma occur within specific social situations, overflow karma implies further that within such a situation one person's karma directly affects that of others. The directness of this effect in the case of a good king's overflow karma is clear in the 1345 *Trai Phum,* where the Great *Cakkavatti* King states in his "Sermon of Victory" that "[i]f any ruler or king, while he reigns, acts righteously, and does righteous things, the common people, slaves and free men, will live peacefully and happily, will have stability and balance, and will enjoy good fortune and prosperity; and this is because of the accumulation of the merit of the one who is the Lord above all."[40] In his mythic continent of Utturukuru, all the ranking people are born with beautiful bodies and, should they exhibit any flaw, or the common people any affliction, the merit of the *Cakkavatti* is enough to remove them.[41]

   The overflow karma of Gotama Buddha is paradigmatic of this type because people in the present moving on toward future *nibbāna* in the time of Maitreya or some future Buddha are doing so as part of the ongoing result of their karmic connection(s) with Gotama Buddha during previous lives, which were inadequate to warrant rebirth in his intimate community and *nibbāna* in his *sāsana,* but nevertheless remain soteriologically charged. According to the *Buddhavaṃsa*, all Buddhas create such soteriologically charged "overflow" karmic connections with "countless crores" of beings who meet them but do not attain one of the four stages of the Path then and there.[42] Woodward recognizes the teleology implicit in this vision of karmically constituted Buddhist community when he speculates that future Buddhas are already constituting sociokarmic connections with members of their future intimate communities in the here and now. These bodhisattas and those with whom they forge their connections are in turn already linked together as ongoing overflow karma of Gotama and other previous Buddhas, whom all have met during previous lives, as becomes explicit in the *Anāgatavaṃsa.*[43]

   I would also categorize as "overflow karma" various doctrines and practices surrounding the so-called transference of merit, in which many beings somehow share the merit of one individual's piety, through physical actions (such as touching offerings) and verbal expressions (uttering "sādhu!," inviting the deities or the dead to mentally share the merit, dedicating merit to friends, family and relatives) and the ideas upon which these practices are based (about the mechanism by which *anumodanā* works, what non-human beings can and cannot do karmically, etc.). Moreover, and still within this same rubric, it would appear despite McDermott's protestations that, as Bhikkhu Sīlācāra maintained, demerit also can be "shared" or "overflow" in this same way. Thus, for example, the originary sin of the Bodhisatta together with his companions *(sahāgatā)* who eventually are massacred as the Śākyans (the final result for the Buddha himself was the headache he once suffered) is said in the *Apadānaṭṭhakathā* to be the mental pleasure they experienced when watching a fishmonger kill fish (*somanassaṃ uppādayiṃsu,* note the collective verb). Though the *pāpa* belongs most properly to the fishmonger rather than to the boys, it is shared collectively by the Bodhisatta and his compatriots in precisely the same way that a deity or *preta* is said to share in merit; it brings them together again in a future life when they do something even worse, namely poison a river, and together again to suffer the effects of that, as the hapless victims of Viḍūḍabha whose collective trickery brings on their own demise.[44]

3. The third type, "karmic confluence," refers to instances when the members of a social group such as a family or neighborhood come into their social relationships on the basis of extremely similar karmic tracks, which, through what Baptist calls a "conspiracy of circumstances," all lead to that same place and time where they find themselves, the shared motivations and predilections that drive them as a group, and so forth. This type is to be distinguished from type 1 (social context) in that, like type 2, it implies a karmic basis for the fact of social context. It is however distinguished from type 2 (overflow karma) because it does not imply a direct karmic relationship *between* anyone, merely individual karmic paths so strikingly similar as to lead different beings to the same time and place. The *Anguttara* text cited above, and indeed all the *anisaṃsa* texts from the *suttas* to the present that proclaim sociological effects of merit, depend upon this sort of "conspiracy of circumstances": not meeting with bad people implies a negative coincidence with their karma, meeting with good people implies a positive coincidence with their karma, wealth and popularity and position and power are all at least in part social things that must find a niche amidst the sociokarmic circumstances of all others within one's community.[45]

The somewhat common trope of co-birth clearly bespeaks a developed idea of karmic confluence. Most famously, the Buddha is said to have been born at the same instant as his seven "Co-Borns," or in Miss Horner's rendering "Connatal ones" *(Sahājātā)*[46] who would play key roles in his own final karma-produced existence: Yasodharā, Ānanda, Channa, Kāḷudāyi, Kanthaka, the Bodhi Tree, and the group of four treasure urns all arose at that same instant on that Vesak day long ago. While the first four appear from the *Jātakas* and the *Apadāna* to have had more than coincidental karmic relationships with the Bodhisatta, and therefore to better fit the fourth and more sociokarmically determined category, "co-transmigration of social units," Kanthaka the horse and of course the Bodhi Tree and the treasure urns play no previous life role in the *Jātaka* and therefore would best fit within the rubric of this category. Because karmic confluence accounts for all karmic dimensions of society that cannot be explained by the other types, and therefore must be a vast and unfathomable thing as universal as the complete range of everyone's social interactions, everyone with whom any single individual has social interactions throughout her or his entire life is in some general sense a "co-born." Thus, karmic confluence closely overlaps with Sri Lankan trust in horoscopes; because karma determines birth and asterisms encode what is thus determined, the comparison of horoscopes in arranging a marriage is precisely a search for an appropriate karmic confluence. And as John Strong provocatively suggested at the conference where this essay was first presented, there is also room here for thinking about "karmic dispersal," the disjoining of karmic associations.

4. The fourth type of sociokarma is what I consider to be sociokarma proper, namely, the co-transmigration of social units. I believe this is also what John Strong means by "ongoing karmic nexuses." Here society is seen as an explicitly karma-constituted entity, while the social dimensions of karma are explicitly emphasized. Though social context is highlighted, type 4 differs from type 1 in assuming a karmic basis for social relationships. Though the overflow karma of previous and future Buddhas no doubt fuels co-transmigration of social units, especially the co-transmigration of their paradigmatic own intimate communities, unlike type 2, type 4 does not imply one primary actor affecting secondary actors but rather the group as such proceeding together in basic equality (or more precisely, in rotating inequality), and it does require (an extended series of) shared time-places. Likewise, the co-transmigration of social units certainly represents a karmic confluence, realized in lifetime after lifetime, but unlike type 3 that confluence is no mere coincidence in individual karmic streams: the karma itself produces what could awkwardly be called "resociety," the interval between rebirth and its necessary complement, redeath.

   Here as in everything, the Buddha's own life and community are paradigmatic. Yasodharā is successively reborn as the Bodhisatta's life-partner through those myriads of *kalpas*; Mahāmāyā and her sister Mahāpajāpatī Gotamī share motherhood of him over and over; Rāhula is his son, Suddhodana his father, and Devadatta his nemesis. Though the exact social relationship also changes from birth to birth—Devadatta may be the leader, Sāriputta the father—the raw fact of social relationship does not change. And as mentioned the unit that co-transmigrates with the Bodhisatta is further universalized until the constituent members of the entire early Buddhist community turn out to be all the Bodhisatta's close associates from previous lives, in ongoing social relationships (of discipleship, enmity, slander, parental or sexual love, friendship) with him and with each other which develop as karmic patterns unto themselves through these lifetimes, sometimes in very complex ways that have occasioned the speculation of later Theravāda thinkers.[47]

Summing up the importance of this nexus of co-transmigrating cohorts of the Bodhisatta (and Buddha), at the conclusion of a lengthy reflection on the comparative superiority and inferiority of the rebirth precursors of the Buddha and Devadatta, Nāgasena tells King Milinda that:

> Devadatta and the Bodisat accompanied one another in the passage from birth to birth [and] that meeting together of theirs took place not only at the end of a hundred, or a thousand, or a hundred thousand births, but was in fact constantly and frequently taking place through an immeasurable period of time. . . . And it was not only with Devadatta that such union took place. Sāriputta the Elder also . . . was through thousands of births the father, or the grandfather, or the uncle, or the brother, or the son, or the nephew, or the friend of the Bodisat; and the Bodisat was the father, or the grandfather, or the uncle, or the brother, or the son, or the nephew, or the friend of Sāriputta the Elder.[48]

And universalizing the trope further still, the co-transmigration of social units is by no means limited to the paradigmatic biography of the Founder and his most intimate disciples.[49] Such co-transmigration of social units is generalized further into ordinary society at large. I have already mentioned the ways in which sociokarma is taken to constitute village society in Sri Lanka. Ian Stevenson's *Cases of the Reincarnation Type* relates numerous modern Sri Lankan, Thai, and Burmese examples of rebirth successors recognizing and/or entering into relationships with the families and friends of their rebirth precursors. And of course if we take literally the Buddha's statement that it will be hard to meet someone who has *not* been a member of one's immediate family in some previous life, it will be clear that there is room to conceive of literally all society, like its homologue the *Jātaka,* as one big web of co-transmigrating social units. Nāgasena continues from the passage above about the Buddha's constant co-transmigration with his cohorts to inform King Milinda that "[a]ll beings in fact . . . who, in various forms as creatures, are carried down the stream of transmigration, meet, as they are whirled along in it, both with pleasant companions and with disagreeable ones."[50] And so indeed does this category also include the negative examples mentioned above of groups transmigrating together around bad group deeds, including the Śākyans who are destroyed by Viḍūḍabha for having once jointly enjoyed the killing of fish and later for jointly poisoning a river, the five hundred followers of Devadatta and their families who are sucked into Avīci hell together after repeated lifetimes as Devadatta's minions,[51] Bandhula and his thirty-two sons,[52] and families tragically wiped out in bus wrecks in Sri Lanka.

5. The fifth type, "sociokarmic aspiration," flows directly from the fourth. It refers to the means by which Theravāda Buddhists attempt to act upon the presupposition that social groups are karmically produced and productive in the process of co-transmigration. Thus, for example, Milinda and Nāgasena are born together in their appointed roles as the result of such aspirations made by these men's rebirth precursors.[53] The paradigmatic aspiration to be born in the kingdom of Maitreya Buddha is itself fundamentally social, predicated upon being *with him* in his intimate community and often including the wish for others in one's present community to be part of that future community as well.

   It will be clear that sociokarmic aspirations can take many forms. These variations on the basic theme can be categorized into two broad subtypes: (a) the aspiration that oneself or another be reborn in some particular social status, regardless of the other beings who constitute the particular society within which that status is enjoyed; and (b) the aspiration for continuity in some particular present social relationship, that is, the aspiration that the transmigrating individuals who constitute it meet up with each other in future transmigrations too.

   Under the rubric of the first subdivision (a) we could include explicitly selfish sociokarmic aspirations such as the Burmese inscriptional wishes for high status, wealth, or pretty wives, mentioned by Weber,[54] as well as more altruistic but still individually framed aspirations such as the Bodhisatta's aspiration for Buddhahood, or the typical person's aspiration to play a role in the intimate community of a future Buddha such as Maitreya. In the *Apadāna* the rebirth precursors of most of the disciples in Gotama Buddha's intimate community singled out for their special talents or relationship to the Buddha—Sāriputta as chief among those with wisdom, Moggallāna as master of psychic powers, Kāḷudāyi as best "pleaser" *(pasādaka)* of the people, Ānanda as best servitor, and so forth[55]—aspire to that social status as the culmination of their seed-pieties during previous lives. Thus, after a rebirth precursor of Mahāpajāpatī Gotamī witnesses a previous Buddha praising his own combination aunt, step-mother, foster-mother, and leader of the nuns' order she, feeling a surge of mental pleasure *(pasāda, pasanna)* aspires to that peculiar social status (*taṃ ṭhānaṃ*, lit. "that place"). This is not an aspiration to be Siddhartha's aunt-of-all-trades, but to be *any* Buddha's aunt-of-all-trades; the social status itself is what her karma is directed toward. In fact, the rebirth precursor only learns the identity of the Buddha whose aunt she does in fact become during her final life, after the previous Buddha intuits her aspiration and provides her a prediction of its eventual fulfillment when "in one hundred thousand eons, born into Ikshvāku's clan the one whose name is Gotama will be the master in the land."[56] Precisely the same pattern is followed in the *apadānas* of various other early disciples singled out for their "special talents," who similarly are portrayed enjoying their then-present status in the intimate community of Gotama Buddha as a result of a specific sociokarmic aspiration for it during the time of a previous Buddha. I do not know of any Theravādin examples of individuals consciously aspiring to a *bad* future status, but the Bodhisattvas of some Mahāyāna texts who aspire to birth in hell in order to assist hell beings would certainly fit that bill. This subtype would also embrace sociokarmic aspirations for birth in a specific locale (such as the aspirations of contemporary Sri Lankans or occasional odd foreign scholars who want to be reborn in their same villages during future lives), or for a more generalized social status (such as the Burmese prayers, cited by Weber, to be reborn as a Buddhist).[57]

In addition to these more individual sorts of sociokarmic aspirations, those in the other subtype (b) represent aspirations for the continuity of social relationships with particular individuals, paying less regard to one's own specific status or circumstance and more to the identity of one's companions. Most of the examples of this subtype, too, are aspirations for continual rebirth with people whom one holds dear, such as the Burmese prayers for rebirth with the members of one's own present family, or with friends or lovers, or with particular Bodhisattvas (say, particularly noble kings claiming to be such).[58] But other apirations in this subtype are instead despicable ones for rebirth with enemies whom one will attack or revile perpetually, such as the former aspirations in this life and in many previous lives of Ciñcamānavikā, Sundarī the Slanderer, and most of all Devadatta to harass the Bodhisatta throughout his *Jātaka*s and final existence.[59] There is also a middle ground here, in which aspirations to harass are for the good of the victim, such as the aspiration by Nāgasena's rebirth precursor to be reborn as King Milinda's gadfly.[60] Following from John Strong's idea of "karmic dispersal," it is also easy to conceive of aspirations *not* to be born with bad people in general and/or the particular bad people whom one suffers in this lifetime.

6. I am uncertain that my sixth type, "political karma," ought to be a type at all, because, unlike the examples of the first five types, and of the seventh, which I shall mention momentarily, all the examples of this sixth type could be absorbed under the other headings. Put differently, sociokarma, which is specifically political, or what we could call "politicokarma," is no more than a specific and particularly large version of one of the other types. Thus, notions that karma and its results can occur in a specifically political context—that the state can act as a group entity, or that cakkavattihood is a karmic result of previous merit, or the Burmese plans for "state-aided karma" surveyed by McDermott—are subsumed under type 1, social context; notions about the ability of the king's merit (or demerit) to affect everyone in his kingdom exemplify type 2, overflow karma; conceiving of the polity as a confluence of the karmic paths of its citizens obviously belongs to type 3; the state as a co-transmigrating social unit (as in the *Jātaka*s when the Bod-

hisatta and his five hundred are the king and his men, or the historical Śākyans reborn together as a political unit) exemplifies the co-transmigration of social units, type 4; aspirations such as Aśoka's to be overlord of all India clearly belong to type 5, sociokarmic aspiration; ideas that the polity itself has a karmic destiny outside the individuals who constitute it in any particular instance, such as mentioned below, exemplify the final type I have identified, the karma of social institutions (type 7).

Yet all of these types of politicokarma cannot be fit into a single one of the other categories, and for the overlapping reasons that political or "national" karma has already been treated as a separate type by others; that the polity is obviously of special centrality in any study of society; and that the examples of politicokarma are especially rich ones, I do treat it as a separate type here. I treat it *here,* at this point in the list, both because in its scope it pushes to the upper limits of the other types, and because it begins to anticipate the seventh type, the karma of social institutions. Though in most of the examples I know the various sorts of politicokarma all presume that the karmic connections and dimensions in the polity inhere in its constituents as individuals or as a group, but not in the institution itself, the polity has occasionally been considered to have a sort of karmic life of its own. It is precisely because the nation will not be populated by the same individuals in future lives that Rev. Nyanaponika throws out the whole notion of sociokarma, but to the extent that one's nation's reputation, wealth, power, military situation, and so forth are dimensions of the goodness or badness of one's birth in it, that is, are karmically constituted, it is at least possible that, say, the populations of imperialist or genocidal polities should be reborn into the populations of postcolonial societies where they experience the poverty and other forms of suffering they created during previous lives, and sometimes repeat and/or experience the terror they used in creating it. In this vein I have heard interesting ideas about the connections between the players during World War II and those in contemporary Sri Lanka.

7. The distinguishing characteristic of the seventh and final type of sociokarma, the karma of social institutions, is that the institution, whatever it may be, takes on a life of its own quite apart from the individuals who participate in it. Thus, for example, it appears from the *Buddhavaṃsa,* the *Anāgatavaṃsa* and similar texts that intimate communities of Buddhas share a structure unto themselves—with the Buddha (himself a type) at the top, two chief disciples and a servitor, orders of monks and nuns living according to the same vinaya and laypeople observing the same precepts, various specified relatives of the (every) Buddha, etc.—which roles the Buddha and arahants become karmically prepared to fill but which, like the office of God, exist outside the individuals who fill them. The karmic independence, as it were, of social institutions from the individuals who constitute them is especially clear in the Mahāvihāran *vaṃsas*, in which for example Arahant Mahinda declares that the Sri Lankan Sangha of monks and nuns, a number

of the most famous religious monuments of Anurādhapura and indeed the kingdom of Anurādhapura itself, and its kingship, are merely the this-Buddha-era versions of social institutions that existed as such (only the names and certain details vary) during the times of three previous Buddhas as well.[61] The "resociety" of these institutions, like the succession of Buddhas and their intimate communities, cannot be effected by precisely the same masses of people, given that at least some among them became arahants who escaped karma and rebirth altogether.

CONCLUSION: SOCIOKARMA AS A HEURISTIC DEVICE

In terms of scholarship and teaching, perhaps the best justification for paying attention to sociokarma is the raw fact of its presence in Theravāda tradition. While I do not want to overstate sociokarma's significance—karma is only one dimension of society, and society only one dimension of karma—I do think that any study of or class about Theravāda society, or karma, would be incomplete without a recognition of the ways in which these two intersect. Even if it *were* the case that no Theravādins before the twentieth century ever contemplated the social dimensions of karma, and the karmic dimensions of society, surely today, at least some Theravādins take sociokarma very seriously indeed. That alone is reason to give it some attention in thinking about both society and karma.

But knowing *that* sociokarma represents one part of Theravāda tradition is only a preliminary step in really making use of the typology; the payoff comes in learning to see sociokarma in the thick of the Theravāda histories we study. By way of example, I want to suggest—and for the sake of brevity merely suggest—that sociokarma opens up interesting new angles on the *Jātaka* stories as ethical paradigms.

The role of sociokarma in the *Jātaka* has already been spelled out in some detail above, and recognized by Reynolds and Woodward. But while reflecting on the various layers of sociokarma in the *Jātaka* in order to compose this essay, I have come to question an assumption that I think has been made universally, certainly by me, in readings of the *Jātaka* as key transmitter of basic ethical paradigms. That assumption is that ordinary Buddhists would read or listen to or look at a *jātaka* identifying themselves with or taking the subject-position of the Bodhisatta.[62] Even if the twenty-five Buddhas of the *Buddhavaṃsa* narrative, which only covers a period of one hundred thousand plus four incalculable kalpas, should be extended into the past or into the future to produce vaster Theravādin visions of the Buddhas of the universe, like the Kandyan "Thousand Buddha Motif" studied by John Holt,[63] still, as far as I know all Theravādins insist that Buddhas are extremely rare, that as Nāgasena proves to Milinda only one can exist at a time, and that the achievement of Buddhahood requires an effort which in every birth across that vast expanse of time is beyond the capability of any but the most exceptional being.[64] These dogmas underlie the historical record that at least publicly none but a tiny handful of Theravādins has considered himself or herself a Bodhisatta, or has been so considered by others. Instead, the vast majority of Theravādins in literature and in fact have aspired to become arahants in the dispensation of such a Buddha, and in the meantime to develop foundations for such salvific participation in his intimate community. From the beginning Theravādins have vehemently rejected the Mahāyāna claim that all Buddhists should and in fact do aspire to the Buddha-vehicle (emulate the Bodhisatta, Skt. Bodhisattva).

Yet when we treat the *Jātaka* as an ethical text, we always seem to assume that Theravādins do just that. Though I do I think there is clear basis in the *Jātaka* and related texts for considering the Ten Perfections *(dasa-pāramitā)* to be a set of general ethical guidelines intended for imitation by all Buddhists,[65] the manner in which the Bodhisatta himself fulfills them is always extreme, going beyond how even a really good person (or buffalo, or god, or rabbit) could be expected to act in such a situation. The extremes to which the Bodhisatta goes in perfecting himself have been especially glaring to commentators both in the tradition and in the academy in the case of the *Vessantarajātaka,* where the Bodhisatta's commitment to *dāna* plays out in giving away his own kingdom, children, and wife; the ethical tension, the gut reaction that I could never do that, has been widely noted.[66] But this invites the questions, who then does imagine himself or herself Vessantara, capable of such extreme sacrifices? And if it is not with Vessantara himself, then identifying with whom can Buddhist audiences of this widely popular tale take away moral and ethical values?

John Holt's study of the "visual liturgy" of the eighteenth-century Kandyan king Kīrti Śrī Rājasiṃha provides an excellent foundation for answering those questions. Holt's study demonstrates that Kīrti Śrī himself emulated Vessantara and attempted to portray this self-identification as an all-giving bodhisatta to his people.[67] Holt makes most clear the ethical—and political and economic and military—tension embodied in this self-identification; Kīrti Śrī faced real challenges, but by all rights does indeed appear to have possessed exceptional qualities that made successful his bid to be among that handful of Theravādin Sri Lankan kings self-identified and identified by others as bodhisattas or at least as the sorts of cakkavattins who could become the same. And Holt demonstrates the many ways in which Kīrti Śrī did in fact read in the story of Vessantara his own "precarious situation."

Holt also provides a basis for answering the second question when he points out that in the Kandyan paintings, King Vessantara and the other characters in the story—indeed, the characters in all the *Jātaka*s that Kīrti Śrī chose to depict—are dressed like (maybe even portraits of?) the Kandyans of the day.[68] The Kandyans under Kīrti Śrī could certainly have imagined themselves in the scene, participants in the story of a Vessantara as their own king—but not *as* Vessantara. They would be participants as Vessantara's family members, sharing in the sacrifices and rebukes; or as Vessantara's ministers, trying in vain to get him to steer a more prudent economic and political course; or as Vessantara's subjects, angered at the expense and confused about the reasons. For them, from the sociokarmic perspective, the story would have different morals to convey, about the reasons to stop being angry with such a Bodhisatta husband, father, or king, or about how to share in the merit of such a being with whom one is lucky enough to be co-transmigrating, and/or about how to deepen sociokarmic connections with him.

Many further examples of the positive benefits of "thinking with sociokarma" could be adduced, but such benefits go beyond scholarly ones. In practice, to express friendship or kinship in such religious terms deepens social bonds, providing society and the relationships that constitute it a transcendent foundation intimately bound up with Theravāda conceptualizations of the Path and soteriology. Moreover, as with all Buddhist teachings on karma, so sociokarma carries with it profound ethical implications, inculcating a sense of responsibility, obligation, and/or gratitude to other actors whom one encounters in life. The *Saṃyutta* claim that virtually everyone we meet in this life has been a close relative during previous lives is interpreted by Buddhaghosa as a method for cultivating the sublime virtue of loving-kindness *(metta):*

> [An angry person] should think about that person [at whom he is angry] thus: this person, it seems, as my mother in the past carried me in her womb for ten months and removed from me without disgust as if it were yellow sandalwood my urine, excrement, spittle, snot, etc., and played with me in her lap, and nourished me, carrying me about at her hip. And this person as father went by goat paths and paths set on piles, etc., to pursue the trade of merchant, and he risked his life for me by going into battle in double array, by sailing on the great ocean in ships and doing other difficult things and he nourished me by bringing back wealth by one means or another thinking to feed his children. And as my brother, sister, son, daughter, this person gave me such and such help. So it is unbecoming for me to harbour hate for him in my mind.[69]

On a larger scale, inculcating ethical responsibility for the evil deeds of the group or nation, of the sort implied by Egerton Baptist and the *Viḍūḍabhavatthu,* and the cultivation of such anger-killing sociokarmic sympathies for opposing groups or nations, no doubt have more place today than ever in various Theravādin societies.

In a different vein, the varieties of sociokarma always serve the fundamental Buddhist purpose of undermining self-centered visions, in this case of karma and the Path, by helping one recognize that the acts and fruits of merit occur in a social context, that one's merit overflows to others in the same community (and vice versa), that all karmic fruition requires a confluence with the karma of others, that people co-transmigrate with those who play roles both good and bad in their lives, that people can act to deepen such connections with those whom they hold most dear, that even political communities have karmic dimensions (or that even karma has a political dimension), or finally, that some communities complete with their social hierarchies persist karmically independent of the individuals who in any particular birth occupy them. Any of these types of sociokarmic reflection or aspiration serves to dislocate attachment to one's own individual karma and its results, promoting in its place the kinds of altruistic compassion exemplified and advocated by the Buddha himself. After all, in the end, all karma and attachment, including that karma we call community, must be left behind.

NOTES

1. *Mage ma sahodarayek wage kiyā tamayi hitenne. Labana ātmaye nam oyā ape pawule ma ipadewā kiyā api prārthanā karanawā.*

2. James Paul McDermott, *Development in the Early Buddhist Concept of Kamma/Karma* (New Delhi: Munshiram Manoharlal, 1984), esp. 151–56; id., "Karma and Rebirth in Early Buddhism," in *Karma and Rebirth in Classical Indian Traditions,* ed. Wendy Doniger O'Flaherty (Berkeley: University of California Press, 1980), esp. 175; id., "Is There Group Karma in Theravāda Buddhism?" *Numen* XXIII, 1 (1976):67–80. These heavily overlapping works all draw on the author's 1971 Princeton dissertation.

3. McDermott, "Group Karma," 80.

4. Ibid., "Group Karma," 67.

5. Taking up the overflow karma of the Buddha as his example, Bhikkhu Sīlācāra reasons that "countless millions of beings . . . have had their Kamma completely changed for the good through the 'overflow Kamma' of Gotama, the Buddha. And that Kamma has not yet exhausted itself. It is still flowing on; and in its flow fertilizing the minds and enriching the hearts of many even today in the spiritually dullard West . . ." Bhikkhu Sīlācāra, *Kamma (Karma),* ed. Bhikkhu Kassapa (Colombo: Bauddha Sāhitya Sabhā, 1956), 20–21, cited in McDermott, "Group Karma," 68–69 and id., *Development,* 152.

6. Cited in McDermott, "Group Karma," 69, where he is citing Robert C. Lester, *Theravada Buddhism in Southeast Asia* (Ann Arbor: University of Michigan Press, 1973),

77, who in turn is citing the original source: Prince Vajiranana (Wachirayan) in *Right is Right* (Bangkok: Bangkok Daily Mail, 1918). The idea goes back to the very beginnings of Thai Theravāda history, as it is explicit in the mid-fourteenth-century *Trai Phum:* "If any ruler or king, while he reigns, acts righteously, and does righteous things, the common people, slaves and free men, will live peacefully and happily, will have stability and balance, and will enjoy good fortune and prosperity: and this is because of the accumulation of the merit of the one who is the Lord above all." Frank E. Reynolds and Mani B. Reynolds, tr., *Three Worlds According to King Ruang: A Thai Buddhist Cosmology* (Berkeley: Asian Humanities Press/Motilal Banarsidass, 1982), 153.

7. Bhikkhu Sīlācāra continues: "The little thread of Kamma which we call 'ours,' is thus not exclusively ours—how can it be, when, in ultimate truth and fact, there is no 'us'?—but in its course through the fabric of our national, and our world-Kamma, imparts something of its colouring to its neighboring threads. . . . We do not live, and cannot live, to ourselves, even if we want to. The many living threads of the so-called individual's Kamma twine and intertwine with other threads, and change the course and colouring of these other threads for the good or ill, according as our own particular thread is a good or an ill one." Bhikkhu Sīlācāra, *Kamma,* 21, cited in McDermott, "Group Karma," 69 and id., *Development,* 152.

8. Ibid., 76 and id., *Development,* 155.

9. Ibid., "Group Karma," 77.

10. Ibid., "Group Karma," 77.

11. Ibid., pp. 77–78.

12. McDermott draws on Winston King and Donald Eugene Smith for these latter points; see McDermott, "Group Karma," 72–73 and id., *Development*, 154–55. Here Baptist's views are emblematic: "[I]f a people or a group of people—the largeness of this group may even constitute the inhabitants of a single country or many countries—get together and perpetrate a wrong, will they as a group, suffer for their evil deed? Though *Kamma* is individual to each being, we cannot overlook the fact that in such circumstances, all the beings involved in the perpetration of the evil deed, have, with common consent, done so of their own freely expressed 'volition.' Accordingly, they may at some future time, by a conspiracy of circumstances, as it were, be drawn into a pool of anguish and bitterness together, all at once." Egerton C. Baptist, *The Buddhist Doctrine of Kamma* (Colombo: n.p., 1972), 32–33, cited in McDermott, "Group Karma," 72. In a footnote (n. 19) McDermott quotes Baptist quoting W. Y. Evans-Wentz in his Public Debates in Sri Lanka during the year 1921, worth repeating here: Evans-Wentz "pointed out how even religions must reap, as religions, what they sow. This he called *'Religious Karma'*: 'We see now,' he [Dr. Evans-Wentz] said, 'how the whole of Christendom is just beginning to reap the harvest which was sowed in the Dark Ages. Religious Karma will see to it that if a religion has been upheld through the shedding of blood in religious persecution, as in the days of the Inquisition, or if it has propagated itself by the sword, it will be destroyed in like manner.' "

13. DhA i.360, trans. Burlingame, *Buddhist Legends* II:45–46; cited in McDermott, "Group Karma," 79. My brackets and small elision. Another version of the cycle is found at E. B. Cowell, ed., *The Jātaka or Stories of the Buddha's Famous Births,* Vol. IV, tr. W. H. D. Rouse (Delhi: Motilal Banarsidass, 1990 repr. of Cambridge University Press 1895 original), 91–98 (#465, Bhadda-Sāla-Jātaka). Cf. also n. 51 and n. 52, below.

14. McDermott, "Group Karma," 77.

15. Ibid., 67, citing Luang Suriyabongs, *Buddhism in the Light of Modern Scientific Ideas* (Bangkok: Mahamakuta-Raja-Vidyalaya Press, 1954), 72.

16. Ibid., 71, cf. id., "Karma and Rebirth," 175.

17. McDermott, "Karma and Rebirth in Early Buddhism," 175.

18. McDermott, "Group Karma," 80, my brackets.

19. Ibid., 73–75 and id., *Development,* 153–54. I have heard people speculate that the L.T.T.E. are reincarnated Nazis, who are jointly suffering and will continue suffering karmic repetition and results of their actions as Nazis even though they are not born together as Germans in the present.

20. Ibid., 80. Elsewhere McDermott portrays the "development of a notion of communal or group karma of various sorts" as one of the ways in which "contemporary Buddhists continue to extend the notion of karma in new directions," and dates its invention to a 1925 article in *The Maha Bodhi* (McDermott, *Development,* 151; cf. id., "Group Karma," 67)!

21. See Winston L. King, *In the Hope of Nibbana: The Ethics of Theravada Buddhism* (LaSalle, IL: Open Court, 1964), 55 ("overflowing the strict doctrine of kammic merit for the better," Burmese people are generous—note that throughout, King has trouble reconciling his overly individualistic take on karma with the active concern for and kindness to others he repeatedly experienced in Burma), 148 ("Why, again, should anyone waste his precious merit-making power upon another whose destiny he can so little affect?"), 176 (lack of social theory: "is there any?"), 177 ("no real *salvation* to be found in the socio-historical context"), 180–81 ("basic social axiom of Buddhism" is that only the individual matters!), 231 ("*Kamma* doctrine . . . which especially connotes pessimistic fatalism and social passivity . . ."). King appears to be the source of McDermott's view that any inkling of sociokarma must be a modern phenomenon, a new development in the doctrine of karma (e.g., King, 230–34).

22. Max Weber, *The Religion of India: The Sociology of Hinduism and Buddhism,* tr. Hans H. Gerth and Don Martindale (New York: The Free Press, 1958), 213, 218.

23. "In Burma as elsewhere the religious interests of the correct Buddhistic laity were oriented primarily to rebirth opportunities as indicated by source inscriptions of recent times [from late premodern Burma]. The queen mother prays always *to be born again as a high personage. . . .* [A]gain the prayer is expressed that when the future Buddha Maitreya comes, to be permitted to *go to nirvana with him.* Some wish to *escape rebirth in a*

base family. There is the wish to be born again always as a *rich man and adherent to Buddha*. . . . Still another would like to be born again and again *together with his present family (parents, brothers, children)*. And another wishes in a future life *to possess a particular woman as a wife*. In case they should be reborn as lay persons, monks often wished, in any case, to have *pretty wives*. And besides such hopes is the prayer that good works be *conferred on dead persons*, especially those who are in hell . . ." Weber, *The Religion of India*, 262–63, my emphases and brackets. For a parallel and especially remarkable example by the queen mother of Sukhothai in 1399 see Forest McGill, "Painting the Great Life," in *Sacred Biography in the Buddhist Traditions of South and Southeast Asia*, ed. Juliane Schober (Honolulu: University of Hawai'i Press, 1997), 208–209.

24. Mark Woodward has done some of the initial work in charting out just how regularized these sociokarmic connections become in the *Jātaka*, providing numbers of appearances (out of about 547 discrete *jātakas*) of Sāriputta (90), Moggallāna (57), Ānanda (147), and Devadatta (67). See Mark R. Woodward, "The Biographical Imperative in Theravāda Buddhism," in Schober, *Sacred Biography*, 54. T. W. Rhys Davids, tr., *The Questions of King Milinda* (Delhi: Motilal Banarsidass, 1982 reprint of Oxford University Press 1890 original), Part One includes an interesting appendix (pp. 303–304) of births where the Bodhisatta and Devadatta met; his list only contains sixty-four *jātakas*, but at that point (see p. 304) the proofs of Fausböll's original edition of the Pāli had only been completed up to number 513! A complete reckoning of all the rebirth "connections" *(samodhāna)* in the *Jātaka*, not just of Devadatta and other "stars" but also of all the major and minor characters, would show how thoroughly the early Buddhist community is considered here to be karmically constituted.

25. For references to these examples see Jonathan S. Walters, "Stupa, Story, and Empire: Constructions of the Buddha Biography in Early Post-Aśokan India," in Schober, *Sacred Biography*, 175–76, and corresponding notes on 191.

26. Thus, for example, the stereotyped sermon which the Buddha delivers to the laity throughout the *Mahāparinibbānasutta* (e.g., T. W. and C. A. F. Rhys Davids, *Dialogues of the Buddha* [London: P.T.S., 1959, 4th edition of 1910 original], Part II, 91), on the fivefold loss to the wrongdoer and fivefold gain to the doer of good, though it treats mostly of karmic fruition in this life, does indicate in its social categories (poverty or wealth, bad or good reputation, confused or confident in "whatever society he enters," respectively) what also characterizes the fourth and fifth categories (mental state at death, station in the next life) whether bad or good. The fourteenth-century Thai compendium *Trai Phum* is very explicit that both a king's status *qua* king and the ability of the people to follow his lead are effected entirely by their respective accumulated merit (Reynolds and Reynolds, *Three Worlds*, 148, 154). Cf. Charles Hallisey, "The Advice to Layman Tuṇḍila," in *Buddhism in Practice*, ed. Donald S. Lopez Jr. (Princeton: Princeton University Press, 1995), 302–13, for a late medieval "apocryphal" *sutta* that contains numerous specific examples of social results of merit including wealth, family, gender, and political power.

27. The text is taken up by Buddhaghosa as emblematic of "the *suttas*," see n. 28, below. It is also quoted, in very much the same perspective as Buddhaghosa's but put in

the mouth of the Buddha himself as in the *Saṃyutta* original, in the mid-sixth c., A.D. Chinese apocryphal *sūtra Book of Resolving Doubts Concerning the Semblance Dharma (Xiangfa jueyi jing),* tr. Kyoko Tokuno in Lopez, *Buddhism in Practice,* 269 ("In future generations when all types of evil have arisen, all the clergy and laity should cultivate and train themselves in great loving-kindness and great compassion. Patiently accepting the vexation of others, one should think, 'Since time immemorial, all sentient beings have been my brother, sister, wife, children, and relatives. This being the case, I will have loving-kindness and compassion toward all sentient beings, whom I will succor according to my ability. If I see being who are suffering, I will devise various contrivances [in order to save them], without concern for my own body and life"). As Charles Hallisey has pointed out to me, ironically enough the Buddha makes this statement in the *Saṃyutta* text in order to persuade his interlocutor *not* to be attached to his own family as some uniquely constituted social form.

28. *Saṃyutta-nikāya* II. 189-90, cited in *Visuddhimagga* 305–307 (translated by Bhikkhu Nanamoli as *Path of Purification,* 331–32), reproduced at length and contextualized in Gunapala Dharmasiri, *Fundamentals of Buddhist Ethics* (Singapore: Buddhist Research Society, 1986), 58–61.

29. John Garrett Jones, *Tales and Teachings of the Buddha: The Jātaka Stories in relation to the Pāli Canon* (London: George Allen & Unwin, 1979), ch. 3 and ch. 6, respectively.

30. Charles F. Keyes and E. Valentine Daniel, eds., *Karma: An Anthropological Inquiry* (Berkeley: University of California Press, 1983), especially "Introduction: The Study of Popular Ideas of Karma" (by Keyes, 1–26) and "Conclusion: Karma, the Uses of an Idea" (by Daniel, 287–300). For social status see also Keyes's article in the collection, "Kammic Theory of Popular Theravada Buddhism," 261–86 esp. 263–64; Keyes is, however, so convinced of karmic individualism that he enters into some real intellectual gymnastics, jumping around the idea of merit-transference, in order to link the karmic individual into Buddhist community at all. This same inconsistency between presuppositions about strict karmic individualism and the ethnographic reality of Buddhist community-mindedness similarly vexed King (see above, n. 21).

31. See Richard F. Gombrich, *Theravāda Buddhism: A Social History from Ancient Benares to Modern Colombo* (London and New York: Routledge & Kegan Paul, 1988), which treats Buddhism as "Religious Individualism" (67–69, 72) despite seeing, for example, that "if *kamma* is completely ethicized, the whole universe becomes an ethical arena, because everywhere all beings are placed according to their deserts," (69), which is a good description of type 3 sociokarma discussed below, "karmic confluence." Gombrich seems to intuit that a social history of Theravāda Buddhism would for a Buddhist have to be predicated on karma as much as a social history of Christianity would for a Christian have to be predicated on God, but he dismisses such a view at the outset on methodological grounds: "[A] social account of religion cannot command general attention unless its author aims for a certain metaphysical neutrality. If his apparatus of causal explanation depends on a particular metaphysic, so that, for example, he explains all misfortunes such as famine, disease and war as merely the results of bad *karma* or God's punishment of sinners,

he cannot command credence among those who do not accept the metaphysic" (8). Fair enough as a methodological move, but taking the "metaphysically neutral" stance is no reason to ignore the existence of the idea altogether, which in fact Gombrich proceeds here to do, comparable to a social history of Christianity written as though God had not been a concern *of the Christians whose history is being narrated.*

32. Uma Chakravarti, *The Social Dimensions of Early Buddhism* (Delhi: Oxford University Press, 1987). This despite the fact that her major textual and inscriptional sources are all concerned with aspects of karma and rebirth, including sociokarmic phenomena, which clearly were part of the real-world motivation/ideology that she otherwise so carefully and provocatively recovers.

33. Melford E. Spiro, *Buddhism and Society: A Great Tradition and its Burmese Vicissitudes* (New York: Harper and Row, 1970). Spiro's explicit search for how "the members of a social group identify with each other," which he says determines "the extent [to which] the group is characterized by social integration" (476–77), is taken up in terms of karma/rebirth in an extensive chapter (438–77) that does indicate numerous type 1 examples of sociokarma (social control through fear of bad karmic results, karmic legitimation of power, social cooperation in merit-making festivals, sharedness of the belief as foundation for social solidarity) but reduces more substantial examples of sociokarma (e.g., on p. 451) to individualistic/psychological terms and ultimately sees the karma/rebirth model as socially "dysfunctional" in terms of economic development and charity (461–63); implicitly, development in Burma will occur only when karmic ideology is given up (467). Compare p. 156, where sociokarmic thinking ("how is it that an entire nation or even . . . the entire world can have the same karma, which produces the same consequence, at exactly the same time?") is dismissed out of hand on the basis of a dogmatic karmic individualism: "Since everyone's karma, and therefore everyone's karmic retribution, is individuated (a consequence of his own unique personal history extending over myriads of rebirths), this is clearly impossible."

34. Frank E. Reynolds, "Rebirth Traditions and the Lineages of Gotama: A Study in Theravāda Buddhology," in Schober, *Sacred Biography,* 22.

35. Ibid., "Rebirth Traditions," 23.

36. John S. Strong, "A Family Quest: The Buddha, Yaśodharā, and Rāhula in the Mūlasarvāstivāda Vinaya," in Schober, *Sacred Biography,* 114.

37. Woodward, "Biographical Imperative," 53–54.

38. Walters, "Stupa, Story and Empire," 170, 175–76. Cites on p. 176 (and p. 191 notes 65, 66, 67, 68) are all specific examples of sociokarmic co-transmigration.

39. One group event that seems to have been particularly charged with soteriologically efficacious karma was attendance at the Buddha's funeral, which I have heard come up in various stories of people remembering past lives.

40. Reynolds and Reynolds, *Three Worlds,* 153.

41. Ibid., 143.

42. I. B. Horner, tr., *The Minor Anthologies of the Pali Canon, Part III: Chronicle of Buddhas (Buddhavaṃsa) and Basket of Conduct (Cariyāpiṭaka)* (London: P.T.S., 1975), 97 (Bv 27:20): "When these kings under Dhamma [all the previous Buddhas] had pointed out the Way for countless crores of others, they waned out with their disciples." Likewise, Gotama Buddha (tr. 95, Bv 26:22): "Living so long I am causing many people to cross over, having established the torch of Dhamma (and) the awakening of the people who come after."

43. Udaya Meddegama, tr., and John Holt, ed., *Anāgatavasa Desanā: The Sermon of the Chronicle-To-Be* (Delhi: Motilal Banarsidass, 1993), 52–54: "Maitreya Buddha . . . will assist those who have gained merit during the lifetime of [Gotama] Buddha to ferry safely across the ocean of *saṃsāra* to attain *nirvāṇa*. . . . During the age of the present [Gotama] Buddha, those who engage in meritorious acts according to their individual capabilities will definitely see Maitreya. . . . Thus all these beings who have performed meritorious work in previous lives will have the fortune of seeing the Buddha. Those incapable of attaining *nirvāṇa* will live happy rebirths in the six heavens and human world. Those who are born as animals will be able to attain *nirvāṇa* in their future rebirths."

44. C. E. Godakumbara, ed., *Visuddhajanavilāsinī nāma Apadānaṭṭhakathā* (London: P.T.S., 1954), 124–25; cf. *Viḍūḍabhavatthu* of the *Dhammapadaṭṭhakathā* (n. 13, above).

45. Cf. n. 26 above on the sociokarma of *anisaṃsa*s in the *suttas*.

46. Godakumbara, *Visuddhajanavilāsinī*, 58, 358, 531, etc.; *Jātaka* i. 54, BvA tr. 395.

47. Thus, for example, King Milinda (demonstrating considerable facility with the *Jātaka* collection!) asks Nāgasena in some detail to explain how it is "that Devadatta was altogether wicked . . . and that the Bodisat was altogether pure, full of pure dispositions . . . and yet Devadatta, through successive existences, was not only quite equal to the Bodisat, but even sometimes superior to him, both in reputation and in the number of his adherents," which of course Nāgasena proceeds to do. Rhys Davids, *Questions of King Milinda,* Part I, 285 (Miln 200).

48. Rhys Davids, *The Questions of King Milinda,* Pt. 1, 291–92; Miln 204.

49. Thus, according to Theravādin versions of the story (e.g., *Mahāvaṃsa* 5:48–61), Emperor Aśoka, Samanera Nigrodha, Devānampiyatissa of Anurādhapura, and Queen Asaṃdhimittā were three brothers and their maid, respectively, during a previous life who jointly (but with varying degrees of willingness) participated in the gift of honey to a Paccekabuddha. Likewise, Nāgasena and Milinda were during the time of Kassapa Buddha a monk and a novice, respectively. The novice belligerently refused a request of the monk to carry away the heap of rubbish swept up in the temple until the latter hit him with the broom. "Then for the whole period between one Buddha and the next these two people wandered from existence to existence among gods and men. And our Buddha saw them too, and just as he did to the son of Moggalī and to Tissa the Elder, so to them also did he foretell their future fate, saying: 'Five hundred

years after I have passed away will these two reappear, and the subtle Law and the Doctrine taught by me will they two explain, unravelling and disentangling its difficulties by questions put and metaphors adduced' " (Rhys Davids, *The Questions of King Milinda,* Pt. 1, 4–6; Miln 2–3). And such co-transmigration continues into the future, too, as in the claim of the *Mahāvaṃsa* that what we might call the "rebirth successors" of Duṭṭhagāmaṇi, his father, his mother, his younger brother and his son will be born together as the Sāriputta, Suddhodana, Mahāmāyā, Moggallāna, and Rāhula, respectively, of Maitreya Buddha (Mhv 32:81–83).

50. Rhys Davids, *The Questions of King Milinda,* Pt. 1, 292; Miln 204.

51. Cowell, *The Jātaka,* Vol. 4, 98ff. (# 466, *Samudda-Vāṇija-jātaka*), explains one strand of the sociokarma that brought them to their ruin together (which was the immediate result of slandering and reviling the Buddha), namely, that in a previous life they were marooned together on an island, which to the disgust of the original inhabitant and the local deities, they befouled with their excrement while eating all the fruits and otherwise spoiling the place. Though they were warned, they grew so fond of this life that they refused to leave even when given the opportunity and were therefore swept off the island to their death by the sea.

52. The story of Bandhula the Mallian, his wife Mallikā, and their thirty-two sons who are slaughtered with him is told in DhA and J (see n. 13). In this instance, the digression is embedded entirely within the story of Viḍūḍabha and his slaughter of the Śākyans (Bandhula is Viḍūḍabha's father's Commander in Chief), which we have seen contains the most explicit evidence of traditional assumptions about "national karma." Thus, context alone would warrant Baptist's assumption that group karma is operative in this part of the cycle too. This could also be argued on the basis of the specific content of the various frame stories that embed it. Thus, having their heads chopped off is clearly a parallel to Bandhula's simultaneous decapitation of 500 Licchavi kings (who try to prevent him from fulfilling Mallikā's pregnancy craving for their private drinking water, after the Buddha himself has foretold her pregnancy, which turns out to be sixteen sets of twins, born in succession), but the "former deeds" of the thirty-two sons, mentioned by Mallikā in consoling her thirty-two widowed daughters-in-law, are not specified. Especially in the context of the Viḍūḍabha story, it does not seem a great stretch to intuit that these former deeds, which produced their remarkable co-birth to be co-decapitated, was in some way a matter of "group karma." Moreover, in the *Jātaka* version the whole cycle is somewhat oddly framed explicitly in terms of sociokarma, as a karmic explanation of why the Buddha is friendly with his kinsmen, to the point of saving them from Viḍūḍabha three times until he finally allows their bad group karma to bear its inevitable fruit. Their this-life deception is a form of false friendliness (they provide Viḍūḍabha's father, Pasenadi king of Kosala, the daughter of a Śākyan nobleman's slavegirl who becomes Viḍūḍabha's mother, rather than the pure Śākyan Pasenadi requests of them, and Viḍūḍabha vows revenge when he learns of it). The request of Pasenadi, ironically enough, is an attempt to get chummy with the Śākyans so that the Buddha and his followers will feel for him the friendship they feel for their Śākyan relatives. So at many levels the concerns

of this particular text clearly do seem to be both society/the group and the shared karmic effects of group deeds, despite McDermott's statements to the contrary (see above, n. 18).

53. The story continues (for first part, see above n. 49) to relate that after being hit with the broom the novice (King Milinda's rebirth precursor), weeping as he carried away the garbage, uttered sociokarmic aspirations that he should be powerful and silver-tongued in future lives. Not to be outdone, the monk (Nāgasena's rebirth precursor) makes a sociokarmic aspiration to be born as the person who in life after life puts that novice in his place.

54. See above, n. 23.

55. These "special" saints who appear in the *Apadāna* are enumerated in an earlier list of foremost *(agga)* disciples, which is found in the *Anguttara Nikāya* (F. L. Woodward, tr., *The Book of the Gradual Sayings [Anguttara Nikāya]* Vol. I [London: P.T.S., 1970 repr. of 1932 original], 16–25). They provide important structure to the *Apadāna* collection as a whole, punctuating the monks' and nuns' sections of the collection, and united according to the pattern of merit/aspiration/prediction/realized statuses described here.

56. For complete text see Jonathan S. Walters, "Gotamī's Story," in Lopez, *Buddhism in Practice,* 113–38. Here this standardized prediction verse, which also appears in the *apadānas* of other "special" members of the early community, is v. 103.

57. King Aśoka's previous life aspiration that the bowl of honey should win him overlordship of all India would be a good example here, and the stories surrounding his unwilling brothers illustrate how literally sociokarma can be taken. Angry that the honey has been given away, the former Nigrodha reviles the Paccekabuddha as an outcaste, and as a result is himself born in low circumstances; the former Devānampiyatissa curses him across the sea and as a result is born in Sri Lanka. But these crimes do not draw them into hell because after their brother promises to share the merit they give their assent to the good deed, which bears its fruit in the positive relationships they enjoy with each other in the present. See Mhv 5:48 ("Well pleased was the king by [Nigrodha's] grave bearing, but kindly feeling arose in him also by reason of a former life lived together"); in the absence of any other explanation, presumably the sociokarmic connection is responsible for the fact that when marvelous treasures appear at Devānampiyatissa's consecration, he immediately wants to give them to Aśoka because "the two monarchs . . . already had been friends a long time, though they had never seen each other" (Mhv 11:7–19).

58. In this same vein, according to the *Mahāvaṃsa* (5:59) the maid who points out the honey store, rebirth precursor of Aśoka's chief queen Asaṃdhimittā, aspires to rebirth as the elder brother's rebirth successor's (Aśoka's) beautiful wife.

59. For a discussion of these co-transmigrating nemeses, portrayals of them in the *Tipiṭaka* and later Theravādin sources, and the Bodhisatta's own role in their enmity for him, see Jonathan S. Walters, "The Buddha's Bad Karma: A Problem in the History of Theravāda Buddhism," *Numen* XXXVII, 1 (1990): 70–95.

60. See above, notes 49 and 53.

61. This way of thinking about social institutions, monuments, and so forth as karmically persistent during the time of four Buddhas seems to have been commonplace, as it is found in sources as widely ranging as Buddhaghosa's commentaries and the travel accounts of the Chinese pilgrims. From the earliest Theravādin work proper, the *Dīpavaṃsa,* it would appear that Mahinda's revelation originally circulated in independent documents, one of which systematized it as "The 13 Subjects and the 4 Names" (Dpv 17:4), that is the institutions with a karmic life of their own and the different names by which they were known during the times of the four Buddhas (Kakusandha, Konāgamana, Kassapa, and Gotama), at least two versions of which have been included in Dpv (15:34–73, 17:1–73). See Hermann Oldenberg, *Dīpavaṃsa: An Ancient Buddhist Historical Record* (New Delhi: Asian Educational Services, 1982), 196 (Dpv 17:4). The institutions are (as named in the time of Gotama Buddha): the Island of Sri Lanka; the Kingdom (of Anurādhapura); the kingship (of Devānampiyatissa); the Island-wide affliction (inhabitation by Yakkhas) which the Buddha came to solve; the first *stūpa* (here the Thūpārāma in Anurādhapura); the main irrigation tank in Anurādhapura (unnamed here); the mountain monastic complex associated with the *pasādaka* (here Mihintale/ Silākūṭa); the garden given over to the *pasādaka* and his disciples (here the Mahāmeghavana=Mahāvihāra); the Bodhi Tree (here the Bodhi Tree of the Mahāvihāra); the nun who brings the Bodhi Tree (Sanghamittā); the monk who brings the *Dhamma* and *Vinaya* (here Mahinda); and the Buddha himself.

62. For specific statements of this truism in terms of Vessantara, the example taken up below, see Forrest McGill, "Painting the Great Life," in Schober, *Sacred Biography,* 207 ("After listening to it [the story of Vessantara], we know what we must do: emulate Vessantara and give"); Richard Gombrich and Margaret Cone, trs., *The Perfect Generosity of Prince Vessantara: A Buddhist Epic* (Oxford: Clarendon Press, 1977), xxi open the possibility that "women could empathize with Maddī. The loss of a child is in poor countries an experience all too familiar," then quickly close it on xxii, dismissing out of hand the possibility of reading from any other subject position ("Maddī and the children may arouse empathy in the audience, but they are not moral agents. The moral problem is that of Vessantara himself: is it right to give away one's family?").

63. John Clifford Holt, *The Religious World of Kīrti Śrī: Buddhism, Art, and Politics in Late Medieval Sri Lanka* (New York: Oxford University Press, 1996), 67–68 and plate 11.

64. See for example Rhys Davids, *The Questions of King Milinda,* Part 2, 47–51, which in addition to answering Milinda's question about why only one Buddha can exist at a time, expands on the peerlessness of Buddhas. That point is explicit several times in the *Mahāparinibbānasutta* (Rhys Davids, tr., *Dialogues of the Buddha,* 152, where the gods declare "Few and far between are the Tathāgatas, the Arahant Buddhas who appear in the world . . ."; cf. 164 on Subhadda).

65. See the "Envoi-verses" of *Cariyāpiṭaka* (102–103, vv. 8–14; translated in Horner, *Minor Anthologies, Pt. III,* 49–50 of Cp), the oldest extant *Jātaka* collection, for an explicit statement of this; these same explicit verses also appear as the conclusion to *Buddhāpadāna,* vv. 69–75 (Mary E. Lilley, ed., *Apadāna* [London: P.T.S., 1925] Vol. I, 5–6).

66. Jones, *Tales and Teachings,* 133–34 finds "disconcerting features" in the story, whose "extravagant scale . . . shows a total disregard for personal feeling and . . . retains a rather distasteful ulterior, contractual character."); cf. Gombrich, *Precept and Practice,* 267 ("Westerners are not favorably impressed by the famous *Jātaka* story of King Vessantara. . . . This strikes us as excessive. It strikes the Sinhalese in the same way. The two monks with whom I brought up the subject both said that Vessantara was *wrong*. Generosity is very well, but even there one must exercise moderation."); Steven Collins, *Nirvana and Other Buddhist Felicities: Utopias of the Pali imaginaire* (Cambridge: Cambridge University Press, 1998), 522ff. for an especially thoughtful treatment of the issues involved in judging Vessantara's moral rectitude; Gombrich and Cone, *Perfect Generosity,* xxi ("Whether any male auditors would identify with Vessantara is doubtful, for he is too apparently superhuman . . ."), xxii–xxiv ("implicit hint that Vessantara is doing something dubious . . ." even in the original text). Whether it is there in the original or not, certainly by the time of the *Milindapañha* it was problematic enough to have a lengthy dilemma conceptualized around Vessantara's excessive generosity (Rhys Davids, *The Questions of King Milinda,* Pt. 2, 114–32).

67. Holt, *The Religious World of Kīrti Śrī,* passim (esp. 89). In his focus on paintings of the *Vessantarajātaka* McGill, "Painting the 'Great Life,'" provides some interesting Thai parallels to Holt's work. Gombrich and Cone, *Perfect Generosity,* provide nicely complementary plates.

68. Holt, *The Religious World of Kīrti Śrī,* 81 (here in reference to the *Khantivādajātaka,* but Holt's plates as well as those in Gombrich and Cone, *Perfect Generosity,* suggest that this was the common practice); for the suggestion that some of this could be direct portraiture cf. ibid., 54 and on Kīrti Śrī as Vessantara above, n. 63.

69. Cited in Dharmasiri, *Fundamentals of Buddhist Ethics,* 58–59.

TWO

TOWARD A THEORY OF BUDDHIST QUEENSHIP

THE LEGEND OF ASANDHIMITTĀ

John S. Strong

> When they had founded settlements in the land, the ministers all came together and spoke thus to the prince: "Sire, consent to be consecrated as king." But, in spite of their demand, the prince refused the consecration, unless a maiden of a noble house were consecrated as queen at the same time.
>
> —*Mahāvaṃsa* 7.46–47

IN BUDDHIST SOURCES, whenever a *cakravartin* (Pāli *cakkavatti*) king goes anywhere, he is always said to take with him his fourfold army, his "*caturanga balakāya*." King Aśoka, for example, equips himself with such an army when he goes to Northwest India to subdue the Takṣaśilā uprising, when he breaks into the Ajātaśatru's stūpa to acquire the Buddha's relics, and even when he goes on pilgrimage with the elder Upagupta.[1] This fourfold army, which may or may not actually be used, is so called because it comprises elephants, cavalry, chariots, and foot soldiers.

It is well known that the makeup of this army is ideologically related to the formation of the game of chess. The *cakravartin* is represented by the king; the foot soldiers by the pawns, the cavalry by the two knights, the chariots by the castles (the rooks), and the elephants, through a curious set of transformations both etymological and cultural, are what Anglo-Americans know as the bishops, what the French know as the court jesters *(fou),* what the Germans know as the couriers *(Läufer),* what the Italians know as the flag-bearers *(alfiere),* and what the Tibetans know as the camels *(ngamo).*[2]

But what of the queen, the most powerful piece on the board? Interestingly, her role, in the history of chess, has been intertwined with that of the minister. In the early Indian game, her position was, in fact, taken by a minister, a counsellor, who stayed close to the king but who had relatively few powers; he could move only one square at a time, and only on the diagonal.[3] Later, in Medieval times, in Europe, this minister became identified with the queen when chess became a metaphor more for the court than for war, and eventually she acquired her present moves and prestige in the new speeded-up game that was called "chess of the mad Lady" ("eschés de la dame enragée").[4] There is some evidence to suggest that this magnification of the powers of the lady—the queen—can be connected to a background of courtly love; indeed, poetic works associating chess with love play were common.[5] There is also the tantalizing suggestion of an etymological confusion between the old French word for counsellor, *fierge* (a man in whom one could confide), with the word for the virgin, "la Vierge," who was seen as the powerful Queen of Heaven.[6]

Some of the same transformations may perhaps be found in the listings of the seven endowments of jewels of the *cakravartin,* in which the perfect queen—that "gem of a woman" *(strīratna)*—figures right up there along with the wheel (i.e., the chariot), the elephant, and the horse, while the minister is relegated to the very bottom of the list.[7] In this mythic set of attributes of the *cakravartin,* however, the queen is described in hackneyed, sexist language. She is "lovely, fair to see, charming, with a lotus-like complexion." She is a sort of living air conditioning unit for the king—cool in summer and warm in winter. She is a model of subservience and obedience; she gets up before her husband and retires after him, is "always willing to do his pleasure," but is never ever unfaithful, in body or in mind.[8]

The queen, whose queenship I wish to examine in this article was not as stereotyped as that. But neither was she an anomalous heroic or saintly female ruler—a Cāmadevī or Empress Wu or Ye-ses-mtsho-rgyal[9]—who never had a husband—a king—nor ever needed one. Reality is both less and more misogynistic than myth. Kings, in ancient India, had several wives. They served different ritual and sexual functions,[10] but some of them at least, by Mauryan times, acted as partners in patronage and power with their husbands. This is clear from a couple of Aśokan inscriptions. In the Seventh Pillar Edict, for instance, there is mention of separate donations made by Aśoka as well as by his queens.[11] More specifically, in the so-called "Queen's Edict," Aśoka's second queen, Kāluvākī, either is given credit for dharmic actions of her own,[12] or takes credit for dharmic actions of the king, in what Bongard-Levin has seen, a little too imaginatively perhaps, as a usurpation of power.[13] In the Sri Lankan chronicles, Aśoka's wife, Vedisa-devī, the mother of Mahinda and Sanghamittā, is left to govern in her hometown when Aśoka acceeds to the throne in the capital.[14] On the basis of this and other evidence, B. M. Barua has speculated that Aśoka may have kept palaces with wives and/or sons in several different key places as part of a network of political alliances that unified and governed his empire.[15] The picture that emerges here is that in ancient India (as elsewhere in Asia) kingship was a family affair, not just because of marital alliances but because of cooperative connubial rule. This meant that the queen was more than just an adornment of the king; she and he were both crucial. Again, the chess metaphor comes to mind: without the queen, the king is as good as dead; without the king, the game is over. What is needed, then, is an understanding of Buddhist queenship that takes this into account and sees her rule and authority as part of a greater symbiosis of power and performance.

In order to move toward such a definition, I want to look at the legend of one of Aśoka's queens, Asandhimittā, whose life story is variously told in a number of different traditions. I first became aware of Asandhimittā when I read about her in the *Three Worlds According to King Ruang,* the fourteenth-century Thai cosmology translated by Frank and Mani Reynolds more than twenty years ago.[16] I distinctly remember Frank's footnote in that work: "In many of the Aśoka legends found in the Buddhist tradition, Asandhimittā is not mentioned at all, whereas in most of the others she plays a different and much less crucial role."[17] Indeed, Asandhimittā is completely unknown in the Sanskrit legend of King Aśoka, and the few references to her in the *Mahāvaṃsa* present, as we shall see, a rather different portrait of her,[18] while the commentaries on the *Dīgha Nikāya,* and on the *Majjhima Nikāya,* recount a completely different episode in her life.[19]

The story of Asandhimittā in the *Three Worlds*—the *Trai Phum*—does appear, however, in two relatively late Pāli sources: the so-called Cambodian or *Extended Mahāvaṃsa,*[20] which G. P. Malalasekera dates to the ninth or tenth century,[21] and the *Dasavaṭṭhuppakaraṇa,*[22] a collection of legends which JacquelineVer Eecke is only willing to say was well known by the fifteenth century.[23] By reading these texts in conjunction with the *Trai Phum* it is possible to form a good idea of the overall legend of Asandhimittā and its particular formulations of a theory of Buddhist queenship. I want to distinguish five separate tales or episodes concerning her which I propose to deal with under the following headings: (1) Asandhimittā's past life; (2) the merit making of a queen; (3) queenship in a piece of cake; (4) Asandhimittā's enlightenment; and (5) Asandhimittā's teaching of the dharma.

PAST LIFE

The fifth chapter of the fifth-century chronicle of Sri Lanka, the *Mahāvaṃsa,* is well known for its story of King Aśoka's past life as a merchant, in which he made a gift of honey to a *pratyekabuddha.* This offering eventually resulted in his kingship and corresponds to the gift of dirt that is featured in Sanskrit texts.[24] Long, long ago, we are told, a certain *pratyekabuddha* was out questing for honey for a sick fellow practitioner. He soon came to a town and stopped at a house where a young woman, upon learning what he wanted, kindly pointed out to him the nearby shop of a honey merchant. The merchant then generously filled the *pratyekabuddha's* bowl up to the rim with honey, and, inspired by the sight of this, he made a vow to one day become lord of Jambudvīpa.[25] The housewife, observing the merchant's gift and hearing his vow, made a wish of her own—that she might become the merchant's queen in the birth that he became king, and that she might be a beautiful woman whose joints (e.g. elbows, knees, etc.) were so smooth and well rounded as to be invisible. Needless to say, as a result of these various deeds and vows, the honey merchant eventually became the emperor Aśoka, and the young housewife became Asandhimittā, whose name, we are told, means "with invisible joints."[26]

This *Mahāvaṃsa* story is noteworthy for the picture it presents of Asandhimittā as being totally secondary to and dependent on her future husband and future king. Granted, it might be argued that she does take the initiative in pointing out the honey shop to the *pratyekabuddha,* but apart from that, her actions and wishes are all appendices to Aśoka's, and her very name is said to reflect her hope for feminine physical beauty. In fact, a more straightforward reading of her name would have been that it means "friend" *(mittā)* of "detachment" *(a-sandhi).*[27]

A rather different picture emerges from the *Extended Mahāvaṃsa,* which summarizes this tale of the gift of honey,[28] but then goes on, a few pages later, to recount a completely different past life story of Asandhimittā in which no mention of Aśoka is made at all and which features her giving a piece of cloth to a *pratyekabuddha.*[29] This, as we shall see, becomes, in this tradition, the standard act of merit that is chiefly responsible for her queenship. The same past life story is found in the *Trai Phum* with, again, no mention of Aśoka.[30] It is as though, in these two texts, she were being given karmic independence.

The *Dasavaṭṭhuppakaraṇa,* on the other hand, combines the two tales, recounting, first, Aśoka's gift of honey and Asandhimittā's desire to become his queen, but adding that she then accompanied her statement of that formal wish with a gift of a piece of cloth—her cloak or shawl *(sā ṭaka)* which she rolled up and presented to the *pratyekabuddha* for use as a *"cumba ṭaka."*[31] This detail is not without significance. A *cumbaṭaka* is a rolled-up circle of cloth whose purpose is to serve as a stand for a round vessel, either when it is put on the ground or carried on the head.[32] Without it, a bowlful of honey or anything else is likely to spill. Thus, we can see that, though made second, after the future king's offering, Asandhimittā's gift here nonethess has primary supportive intent. Her gift is complementary to his, but, without it, his is likely to come to nought.

THE MERIT MAKING OF A QUEEN

In due time, the honey merchant and the housewife are reborn as Aśoka and Asandhimittā, and he becomes king, and she becomes one of his wives. In the *Mahāvaṃsa,* she is said to be his chief queen—his *"agga mahis ī"* (literally, his "number one buffalo cow") with, among other things, authority over all the lesser queens and concubines.[33] In all three of the sources we are dealing with here, we are told how she achieved this position. The version of the tale in the *Extended Mahāvaṃsa* may be translated as follows:

> One day, after assisting in the feeding of 60,000 monks, the queen [Asandhimittā] entered the palace and sat down on a couch. There she noticed a great pile of sugarcane, as big as areca nut trees, which the gods had brought from the Himalayas. Wishing to eat a piece of sugarcane, she had one broken off, about a span in length, and sat there sucking the juice from it. Just then King Aśoka entered the room. Seeing her eating, he teasingly said to her: "O wide-eyed beauty, what is this juice that you are drinking that is smooth and honey-like?"
>
> These words [of feigned ignorance] upset Asandhimittā and she said in irritation to the king: "There is a forest of sugarcane in the Himalayas and the deities have brought this here on account of my merit."
>
> The king . . . replied: "You speak exaggeratingly of your merit, my dear, as though it mounted up to the highest heaven, while you degrade the merit of others as though it were as low as the Avīci Hell. My dear, tomorrow, I need sixty thousand robes in order to give alms to the monks. Please procur them for me. In that way, your merit will be known to all. But if you are unable to get me the robes by tomorrow, you will meet with royal punishment." Thus speaking, he departed.
>
> At this, Asandhimittā thought "the king is angry with me," and, in great distress, she lamented: "Oh, how am I to obtain so much cloth?" Tossing and turning on her bed, she did not sleep the whole night through.
>
> Now the four world guardian gods—Kuvera, Dhataraṭṭha, Virūpakkha, and Virūhaka—protect the world according to dharma. And that day Kuvera saw that the queen was distressed, and approaching her, he said: "Your majesty, do not worry, do not grieve. Long ago, in a past life, you gave a beautiful piece of cloth to a pratyekabuddha; today, you will see the fruit of that deed." And

he showed her then a polished ball made of lacquer which dispensed cloth from within itself by means of its own power. And giving it to her, Kuvera said: "Take this ball and you will be able endlessly to draw precious cloth from it." He then departed.

The next day, the king paid *pūja* to the assembly of monks with flowers and excellent food. He then addressed Asandhimittā: "My dear, give me now the 60,000 sets of cloth which you were to procur by means of your merit so that I could provide robes for the saṃgha."

"As you wish, Lord . . ." she declared, and taking the divine ball given to her by Kuvera, she drew out a pair of robes, priceless like the cloth from the Wish Granting Tree, and she placed them in the king's hand. One by one, she placed garments in the hands of the king, and there was enough cloth to provide three robes for each of the monks there. The king gave the first set to the senior-most monk, and the next to the second one in rank, and so on until he had given enough cloth for all 60,000 monks.

Then, taking leave of the monks, he entered his harem. Wishing to show his delight personally to the queen, he sent for her, and, standing there like Indra in the midst of all his concubines, he said to her: "My dear, I am pleased at your merit. . . . Please forgive my anger. I now give to you my sovereignty, all of it. You will have authority over these 16,000 women."[34]

The *Trai Phum* and the *Dasavaṭṭhappakaraṇa* tell much the same story, but they include a number of interesting additions. First of all, they make it clear that the pile of sugarcane is, in fact, due entirely to Aśoka's merit. It is because of his merit as a *dharmarāja,* a righteous king, that the gods and various animals daily bring him all sorts of supplies and foodstuffs from the Himalayan regions, including special toothsticks made of the best wood, pure water from Lake Anotatta, savory rice hulled by mice, multicolored cloth woven by the gods that never needs washing but can be fire-cleaned, and, of course, the specially succulent sugarcane.[35] In this context, Asandhimittā is clearly in the wrong to be claiming that the sugarcane is due to her merit; it is due to Aśoka's, and he playfully reminds her of that fact by asking her what it is she is eating.[36]

The sugarcane acts, in fact, as a symbol of sovereignty. In the *Trai Phum,* Aśoka himself makes this very clear: "Listen, young Asandhimittā," he asks, "if the *devatā* truly bring sugarcane from the Himavanta forest to offer to you because of your merit, would you say that I have acquired all the royal possessions in the entire Jambu continent because of your merit?"[37] Asandhimittā may have certain rights as queen, or concubine, or whatever status she has at this point (she has yet to be made chief queen), but rights should not be confused with merit, and one of the overall messages of this story is that Asandhimittā cannot truly be a sovereign queen until she has demonstrated her own worthiness.

And herein we can find an assertion of a theory of queenship that confirms what we have already seen in the tale of Asandhimittā's previous life. Buddhist sovereignty, whether that of a queen or of a king, cannot be granted by another, or usurped, or inherited; it must be earned, it must be merited. The same principle may be found in the myth of the *cakravartin* who, each generation, must earn his right to rule (his wheel of dharma) by the demonstration of his merit.[38] Regardless of her rights or relationships, Asandhimittā cannot come to full queenship on the coattails of the king. Thus, the sugarcane, because it ultimately stems from Aśoka's merit, cannot be her vehicle to sovereignty.

Significantly, however, Aśoka is quite willing to give her a chance to prove herself. His asking her to provide, on her own, enough cloth for sixty thousand monastic robes, is not entirely an attempt to put her down. In all of these texts, he indicates that he would be delighted to learn that she is very meritorious, and, in fact, when she successfully meets his test, he expresses that delight by granting her authority over the sixteen thousand women of the harem. In other words, he affirms her as chief queen, as the *agga mahisī*. But if this is to be something more than just another gift of his to her, just another piece of sugarcane, he has to go beyond this. Consequently he is also said to give her all of his sovereignty *(issariya)*. He does the same in the *Dasavaṭṭhuppakaraṇa*.[39] What this means is not spelled out in these two texts, but it is in the *Trai Phum,* where, upon witnessing the proof and power of her merit, Aśoka declares: "Asandhimittā, you are a divine and virtuous woman, and from today on into the future I transfer to you the dwellings, territories, villages, cities, castles, royal houses, elephants, horses, slaves, freemen, all of the soldiers, the silver, the gold, the precious possessions, and all the sixteen thousand concubines. You may be their ruler. Also from today on into the future, if you wish to do anything at all, you may do according to your wish."[40]

This would seem to tip things, pretty clearly, in the direction of Asandhimittā. Aśoka, apparently, is now dependent on her, along with the whole kingdom. But this is a trap that Asandhimittā is wise enough not to fall into. She knows, from Aśoka's own example, that the greatest, most meritorious Buddhist sovereigns are those who are willing to give up their sovereignty.[41] And here we come to a slightly different vision of Buddhist queenship, for not only is Asandhimittā an ideal ruler, she is also an ideal wife. Thus, "even though the splendid King Dhammāsoka had given her permission such as this, [she] could never bring herself to disobey the one who was her husband, even in the slightest way. Whatever she did, no matter how small it was, she consulted with her husband, and then, when he gave the command she did it."[42]

It is interesting to compare and contrast this with the structurally similar refusals of sovereignty by Buddhist kings. When kings give away their kingship—and they do so fairly often—it is usually because of an inclination toward the monastic life, or a desire to express total generosity. In the case of Asandhimittā, however, it is because of an inclination toward spousal virtue. The ideal Buddhist queen must also be an ideal Buddhist wife. The ideal Buddhist king, however, apparently feels no obligation toward being an ideal Buddhist husband.

QUEENSHIP IN A PIECE OF CAKE

Asandhimittā, however, was not always to pull back in this way at the moment of sovereignty. The themes of merit and queenship are continued and developed a bit further in another story which immediately follows in our three texts. Despite Aśoka's affirmation of Asandhimittā as chief queen, or perhaps because of it, the women of the harem are said to be spiteful toward her. They themselves have not seen proof of her merit and grumble at the favor she enjoys with the king. Accordingly, Aśoka arranges for a demonstration of her qualities. Again, the text of the *Extended Mahāvaṃsa* may be translated as follows:

> That very day, Aśoka had sixteen thousand sweet cakes baked and inside one of them, he placed his own priceless signet ring. He put this on top of the pile with the other cakes and then assembled all the women of the harem. "Let each of you, one by one," he declared, "take whatever piece of cake you want." They did so and Asandhimittā, going after all the others, took the only cake that was left. In truth, it was the one with the signet ring! Breaking it open in front of all of them, Aśoka then showed them the ring and declared "Behold, all of you who are angry and of little merit; behold Asandhimittā's glory and great merit!"[43]

This scene, intriguingly reminiscent of the Christian tradition of epiphany cakes, serves, of course, not only to prove Asandhimittā's merit but to offer to her, once again, sovereignty over the realm. Possession of the king's signet ring, with its royal seal, was a mark of power. And this time, Asandhimittā goes a bit further in demonstrating that power. Taking her magical lacquer ball, she proceeds to dispense more offerings of cloth, not as before through the intermediary of her husband, but directly herself to all those assembled. She first gives a thousand pieces of cloth to Aśoka, then five hundred to each of his attendants, and five hundred to the viceroys; then five hundred more to the other queens and to the princes, and fifty to each of the concubines. Then she makes offerings of cloth to every soldier in the army and finally to anyone else who wants some. Declaring that she could cover the whole earth with cloth if she wanted to, she then explains to all, once again, the source of her merit: her gift, long ago, of a single piece of cloth to a *pratyekabuddha*.[44] This whole scenario exhibits two of the proper queenly (and kingly) uses of authority: the provision of goods (in this case cloth) to all in the realm who need it, and the reinforcement of hierarchical structure, in so doing.

It is interesting to contrast this story with the Sanskrit tale of Aśoka's "other" queen, the evil-minded Tiṣyarakṣitā. Tiṣyarakṣitā, as a result of her conniving (and not of her merit), also is granted sovereignty over the realm, for a period of seven days, and also acquires Aśoka's seal. Unlike Asandhimittā, however, she grabs her authority and misuses it for malignant purposes, ordering the blinding of Aśoka's saintly son, Kunāla.[45] The texts we are dealing with here do not know the story of Tiṣyarakṣitā (Pali: Tissarakhā), but the *Mahāvaṃsa* does and it specifically contrasts the two queens. Four years, it tells us, after the death of "that dear consort of the king, Asandhimittā, who was a faithful believer in the Saṃbuddha, . . . the treacherous Tissarakhā was elevated to the rank of queen." It then goes on to tell the story of Tissarakhā's jealousy of the attentions Aśoka was lavishing on the Bodhi tree at Bodhgaya, and her use of black magic to cause that tree to wither and die.[46] This is in clear contradistinction to the tradition preserved in the *Mahābodhivaṃsa* that describes Asandhimittā as extremely devoted to the Bodhi tree, to which she makes all kinds of offerings.[47]

With this story, we have a warning about what might be called "the other side of Buddhist queenship." I have argued elsewhere that Aśoka, throughout his life, exhibits two aspects of kingship: he is both "Righteous Aśoka" (Dharmāśoka), and "Aśoka-the-Fierce" (Caṇḍāśoka). He does both great dharmic deeds, and he occasionally flies off the handle with power-mongering acts of violence.[48] The same dual traits mark queenship, only, since Aśoka's wives are multiple, the ambiguity does not have to fall on a single individual but can be polarized into different persons. Thus, the very meritorious Asandhimittā can be contrasted to the cruel and demeritorious Tiṣyarakṣitā, and neither one is allowed the complexity of contradictory personality traits.[49] And here again, we come to an important factor in considering theories of Buddhist queenship: kings are singular, queens are not. Kings are thus complex individuals; queens tend to be stereotyped.

ASANDHIMITTĀ'S ENLIGHTENMENT

Merit, however, is not the only thing that lies at the basis of dharmic sovereignty; wisdom must enter the picture as well. In this regard, it is important to take an excursus and look at a tale concerning Asandhimittā that is not contained in the three sources we have been looking at. It is found instead in parallel passages in two works attributed to Buddhaghosa: the *Sumangalavilāsinī* (the Commentary on the *Dīgha Nikāya*), and the *Papañcas ūdanī* (the Commentary on the *Majjhima Nikāya*). Both stories are contained within explications of the list of the thirty-two marks of the great man *(mahāpuruṣa),* and they focus specifically on the mark that says that the Buddha's voice was like that of a *karavīka* bird—the so-called Indian cuckoo.[50] The story may be summarized as follows:

> Asandhimittā once asked the monks what the sound of the Buddha's voice was like, and they told her it was like that of a *karavīka* bird.
>
> "And where does this bird live?" she queried.
>
> "In the Himālayas," they answered.
>
> Upon learning this, Asandhimittā then went to Aśoka and told him she would like to see a *karavīka* bird, and he immediately ordered that one be brought. It was put into a golden cage, but, to Asandhimittā's disappointment, it never uttered a sound.
>
> Aśoka went back to the monks and asked them what made the bird sing? They told him it sang when it saw one of its kind. So the king then surrounded the cage with mirrors, and the bird, seeing its reflection, thought there were other birds there. Spreading its wings, it began to sing with an intoxicating voice, as though it were blowing a crystal flute. The whole town was transported with joy, and Asandhimittā herself was so delighted by the realization that this was what the Buddha's voice was like that she attained the first stage of enlightenment, the fruit of stream-winner.[51]

Here, in this dharmic context, we can see some of Asandhimittā's independence return but it is put in a context of interdependence. She attains insight into the dharma as a result of her own efforts and her demand to hear what the Buddha's voice sounds like. But her efforts are also made possible by the support she gets from her husband and the advice they both get from the monks.

DHARMIC LESSONS

Endowed with this wisdom, there is one more thing that Asandhimittā must do in order to make her queenship complete: she must also become a spreader of the doctrine, the dharma. And here, we can return to our three texts to examine the final episode of their accounts of her legend: the story of her "sermon"—not to the women of the harem—but to the king himself. In the *Extended Mahāvaṃsa,* this is given in summary form: "Birth as a human being," Asandhimittā reminds Aśoka, "is a rare thing, and so are faith, and exposure to the Buddha's doctrine, and meeting a preacher of the Dharma."

Furthermore, since he, Aśoka, has come by all these rare things, he should strive with diligence. And she exhorts him as follows: "Great king, give offerings repeatedly, make great merit in support of the Religion of the Buddha. The merit of gifts given to buddhas or pratyekabuddhas or arahants cannot be measured. . . . Guarding morality, discipline your mind, associate with good friends, be diligent, walk in the ways of the Dharma, and be a dharmarāja; protect all beings without exception. Great is the fruit of the seed planted and nurtured."[52]

Much the same sermon is given in the *Trai Phum,* though with greater redundancy, and with the noteworthy addition of the fact that we are told Aśoka's response to this sermon: first, he repeats his commitment to respect Asandhimittā's queenship. "Asandhimittā," he tells her, "from now on into the future I will listen to your words concerning what is wrong and what is right; when you who have merit speak to me, I will listen to everything you say."[53] And then, we are told, he goes on to perform his own greatest royal act of merit: he builds the eighty-four-thousand *stūpas* as well as eighty-four-thousand monasteries throughout the whole of Jambudvīpa.[54]

This dénouement is striking. Here we can see that Aśoka's own final confirmation in the dharma, the act that defines his own identity as a Buddhist king and which truly establishes him as Dharmāśoka, comes as a result of a realization brought on by his queen. Up until now, we have seen Asandhimittā's queenship as more or less being defined by Aśoka, despite the insistence that she have her own merit and realization and that she achieve this independently. Here we find the flipside of that relationship: Aśoka's full kingship is presented as being occasioned by Asandhimittā. The queen is telling the king how to rule, and he is listening.

CONCLUSIONS

What can we say, after all this, about theories of Buddhist queenship? Three things, some of them contradictory, but all of them starting with the sentence "just like a king." First, just like a king, a Buddhist queen is independent; she earns her queenship by virtue of her own merit achieved in her own past life, and by virtue of her own realization of the truth of the dharma. Secondly, just like a king, a Buddhist queen is interdependent; she must enjoy a symbiotic relationship with her husband, whose kingship she supports, just as he supports her queenship. Without him, she is no queen; without her, he is no king. Finally, just like a king, a Buddhist queen is dependent; she must be a good wife, and this implies subservience to her husband. He, on the other hand, is in her debt spiritually; she has the wisdom to know what makes a ruler truly great and is able to tell him that.

NOTES

1. John S. Strong, *The Legend of King Aśoka* (Princeton: Princeton University Press, 1983), 208, 219, 244.

2. Henry A. Davidson, *A Short History of Chess* (New York: David McKay Co., 1949), 36–37.

3. Ibid., 29.

4. Richard Eales, *Chess: The History of the Game* (New York: Facts on File Publications, 1985), 72.

5. Ibid., 62.

6. Davidson, *Short History of Chess,* 28.

7. Maurice Walshe, tr., *Thus Have I Heard: The Long Discourses of the Buddha* (London: Wisdom Publications, 1987), 282 (*D.* 2: 175–76).

8. Ibid.

9. On these figures, see Donald Swearer and Sommai Premchit, *The Legend of Queen Cāma: Bodhiramsi's Cāmadevīvaṃsa* (Albany: State University of New York Press, 1998); R. W. L. Guisso, *Wu Tse-tien and the Politics of Legitimation in Tang China* (Bellingham, WA: Western Washington University Press, 1978); Anne Klein, *Meeting the Great Bliss Queen: Buddhists, Feminists, and the Art of the Self* (Boston: Beacon Press, 1995); Rita Gross, "Yeshe Tsogyel: Enlightened Consort, Great Teacher, Female Role Model," in *Feminine Ground: Essays on Women and Tibet,* ed. Janice D. Willis (Ithaca: Snow Lion Press, 1987), 11–32.

10. See Stephanie Jamison, *Sacrificed Wife, Sacrificer's Wife* (New York: Oxford University Press, 1966), 65ff and 99ff.; I. B. Horner, *Women under Primitive Buddhism* (London: Routledge and Kegan Paul, 1930), 35.

11. Jules Bloch, *Les inscriptions d'Asoka* (Paris: Les Belles Lettres, 1950), 171; see also K. R. Norman, "Notes on the So-called 'Queen's Edict' of Aśoka," in K. R. Norman, *Collected Papers, Volume II* (Oxford: Pali Text Society, 1991), 57.

12. Bloch, *Les inscriptions d'Asoka,* 159; Norman, *Collected Papers, Volume II,* 52–58.

13. G. M. Bongard-Levin, "The Historicity of the Ancient Indian Avadānas: A Legend about Aśoka's Deposition and the Queen's Edict," in *Studies in Ancient India and Central Asia* (Calcutta: Indian Studies Past and Present, 1971), 137–38.

14. Wilhelm Geiger, tr., *The Mahāvaṃsa or the Great Chronicle of Ceylon* (London: Pali Text Society, 1912), 43–44 (Mhv 5: 204–11).

15. B. M. Barua, *Aśoka and his Inscriptions* (Calcutta: New Age Publications, 1968), Volume 1, 52–53.

16. Frank E. Reynolds and Mani B. Reynolds, *Three Worlds According to King Ruang* (Berkeley: Asian Humanities Press, 1982), 172–89. See also Georges Coedès and Charles Archaimbault, *Les Trois Mondes (Traibhūmi Brah R'van)* (Paris: Ecole Française d'Extrême-Orient, 1973), 111–23.

17. Reynolds and Reynolds, *Three Worlds,* 33 n.43.

18. See Mhv 5.49–60, 85; Mhv 20.2 (Geiger, *Mahāvaṃsa,* 30, 33, 136).

19. W. Stede, ed., *Sumangala-Vilāsinī, Buddhaghosa's Commentary on the Dīgha-Nikāya* (London: Pali Text Society, reprint edition 1971), Vol. 2, 253 (*DA* 2: 253); I. B. Horner, ed., *Papañcasūdanī Majjhimanikāyaṭṭkath ā* (London: Pali Text Society, reprint edition 1976), Vol. 3, 382–83 (*MA*. 3: 382–83). In addition, there are passing references to Asandhimittā in the Introduction to the Vinaya Commentary (J. Takakusu and M. Nagai, tr., *Samantapāsādikā: Buddhaghosa's Commentary on the Vinaya Pitaka* [London: Pali Text Society, 1968], Vol. 1, 42; for English translation see N. A. Jayawickrama, tr., *The Inception of Discipline and the Vinaya Nidāna* [London: Luzac and Company, 1962], 37), and the Chronicle of the Bodhi Tree (S. Arthur Strong, ed., *The Mahā-Bodhi-Vaṃsa* [London: Pali Text Society, 1891], 152).

20. G. P. Malalasekera, ed., *The Extended Mahāvaṃsa* (Colombo: The Royal Asiatic Society, 1937), 74–77.

21. Ibid., lii.

22. Jacqueline Ver Eecke, ed. and tr., *Le Dasavatthuppakaraṇa* (Paris: Ecole Française d'Extrême-Orient, 1976), 45–54 (text), 50–59 (Fr. trans.).

23. Ibid., v.

24. See Strong, *Legend of King Aśoka,* 56ff.

25. For an interpretation of the symbolic significance of the overflowing bowl of honey and its relation to kingship, see Paul Mus, *Barabaḍur: Esquisse d'une histoire du Bouddhisme fondée sur la critique archaéologique des textes* (Hanoi: Imprimerie d'Extrême-Orient, 1935), volume 2, 289.

26. Mhv 5.49–60 (Geiger, *Mahāvaṃsa,* 30). On this etymology of Asandhimittā's name, see also G. P. Malalasekera, *Dictionary of Pali Proper Names* (London: Pali Text Society, 1938), vol. 1, 205.

27. See Ver Eecke, *Le Dasavatthuppakaraṇa,* 57 n.2.

28. Malalasekera, *Extended Mahāvaṃsa,* 71–72.

29. Ibid., 75.

30. See, however, Reynolds and Reynolds, *Three Worlds,* 180 n.54, where the suggestion is made that there may be a hint, in the story, at the tale of the gift of honey.

31. Ver Eecke, *Le Dasavatthuppakaraṇa,* 45–46 (text), 51 (Fr. trans.).

32. Robert Caeser Childers, *A Dictionary of the Pali Language* (London: Kegan Paul, Trench, Trübner and Co., 1909), 108.

33. On the mahiṣī's role, see A. L. Basham, *The Wonder that was India* (New York: Grove Press, 1954), 91.

34. Malalasekera, *Extended Mahāvaṃsa,* 74–75. The generation of endless robes as a sign of Asandhimittā's merit and as a way of upholding her honor recalls the similar miraculous production of robes as a sign of Draupadī's merit and honor during her attempted "disrobing" in the *Mahābhārata* (see J. A. B. Van Buitenen, tr., *The Mahābhārata* [Chicago: University of Chicago Press, 1977], 2: 146). The parallelism, which it would be interesting to study, is made even more graphic in stage adaptations of the scene. See Alf Hiltelbeitel, *The Cult of Draupadī,* vol. I (Chicago: University of Chicago Press, 1988), 236ff.

35. Reynolds and Reynolds, *Three Worlds,* 173–76; Ver Eecke, *Le Dasavatthuppakaraṇa,* 48 (text), 52–53 (Fr. trans.).

36. In the *Trai Phum,* Aśoka does not ask what it is that she is eating, but who it is that is eating it, and Asandhimittā gets peeved that he is pretending not to know her (Reynolds and Reynolds, *Three Worlds,* 178).

37. Reynolds and Reynolds, *Three Worlds,* 179. The Reynoldses indicate that the appelation *chao,* here translated as "young," is also a term designating royalty (Reynolds and Reynolds, *Three Worlds,* 179 n.52).

38. See Strong, *Legend of King Aśoka,* 47.

39. See Ver Eecke, *Le Dasavatthuppakaraṇa,* 56.

40. Reynolds and Reynolds, *Three Worlds,* 182.

41. In the Sanskrit tradition, Aśoka gives up his kingship repeatedly, sometimes to the saṇgha, but other times to other relatives.

42. Reynolds and Reynolds, *Three Worlds,* 183; see also Ver Eecke, *Le Dasavatthuppakaraṇa,* 57.

43. Malalasekera, *Extended Mahāvaṃsa,* 76.

44. Ibid., 76; Reynolds and Reynolds, *Three Worlds,* 185; Ver Eecke, *Le Dasavatthuppakaraṇa,* 53 (text), 58 (Fr. trans.).

45. Strong, *Legend of King Aśoka,* 271–79.

46. Mhv 20.3–6 (Geiger, *Mahāvaṃsa,* 136). See also Strong, *Legend of King Aśoka,* 257.

47. Strong, *Mahā-Bodhi-Vaṃsa,* 152.

48. On this, see Strong, *Legend of King Aśoka,* 40ff.

49. On this theme, see John S. Strong, "Aśoka's Wives and the Ambiguities of Kingship," unpublished paper presented to the Evans-Wentz Conference on "Buddhist Priests, Kings, and Marginals," Stanford University, 1999.

50. It should be noted that the *karavīka* bird is featured in the *Trai Phum* as one of the animals that comes from the Himalayas to do homage to Aśoka. There it is described as a bird whose song is so enchanting that it enraptures all the other animals; fish, upon hearing it, stop swimming, other birds stop flying, little children stop running about. See Coedès and Archaimbault, *Les trois mondes,* 114.

51. DA 2: 453; MA 3: 383–84.

52. Malalasekera, *Extended Mahāvaṃsa,* 77; c Ver Eecke, *Le Dasavatthuppakaraṇa,* 59.

53. Reynolds and Reynolds, *Three Worlds,* 188.

54. Ibid.

THREE

Beggars Can Be Choosers

Mahākassapa as a Selective Eater of Offerings

Liz Wilson

IN THIS ESSAY I focus on monastic begging as a means of unburdening others of negative karmic conditions. I showcase the socially conscious begging practices of the saint Mahākassapa as seen through the eyes of redactors working in Pāli and Sanskrit. This Buddhist saint shows a pattern of taking food from impoverished, unfortunate donors so as to vanquish their bad karma and help them to achieve a better rebirth. In the narratives I have selected to discuss here, the former brahmin Mahākassapa goes out of his way to receive highly unpalatable food from a very poor elderly woman donor. He approaches her for alms, knowing that she has very little to give. He receives from her some water in which rice had been cooked (the food was cooked, significantly, in someone else's home: according to several accounts, she had herself obtained the gruel through begging). By taking secondhand cooked food that would be considered by Brahminical authorities to be tainted with impurity for him, Kassapa serves as a field of merit for someone in dire need of the opportunity to gain merit. These stories also have an element of competition, underscoring the intentionality of Mahākassapa's choice of donors. In all the accounts of this incident that I know of, there is also at least one other person on the scene who wishes to seize the opportunity to plant seeds in the fertile field of Kassapa's virtue. Sakka wants to be the donor who feeds the great monk Kassapa. This old Vedic god uses guile to compete with the poor woman. He disguises himself as an old, decrepit weaver and offers divine ambrosia in the guise of a humble meal. But Kassapa—in most accounts—sees through the disguise and spurns Sakka's offering, intent on eating the more unfortunate donor's leftovers so as to benefit the poor woman karmically. In eating her food in preference to what Indra and others offer him, Mahākassapa intentionally favors a disadvantaged donor. In this way he allows those who have little to give to enjoy the fruits of being a *dāna-pati,* a generous donor.

I argue (with help from J. C. Heesterman, McKim Marriott, Jonathan Parry, and others) that in eating the poor woman's food, Kassapa may be said to consume something of the poor woman's bio-moral status. If as Manu suggests, giving *dāna* is a surrogate for the Vedic sacrificial procedure in which sacrificer and victim are identified, the poor woman's rice-gruel (the post-Vedic "victim") contains something of her person (as the post-Vedic "sacrificer"). In one Sanskrit account, this ideology is materially instantiated; her leftovers literally contain something of her person. In the *Mūlasarvāstivāda Vinaya's* account, the woman loses a leprous finger in Kassapa's (Sanskrit: Kaśyapa; for consistency, I will use the Pāli throughout) bowl while fishing a fly out of it. By drinking the liquid remains of her meal, unconcerned about the presence of the fallen finger, Mahākassapa guarantees that the charity of the poor woman will bear karmic fruit in her next life. She plants seeds of merit in feeding Kassapa that she will enjoy at a later time in the form of a divine body by which to consume heavenly ambrosia. Thus, his eating rids her of her lowly status and enables her to take a higher birth with a higher bio-moral status. Thanks to Kassapa's acceptance of her meager secondhand rice-gruel, she will eat much better fare in her next life than she eats in this life. Mahākassapa thus rids her of her bad karma (or at least serves as the material cause for its vanquishing). Put in the food idiom of Vedic texts, one could say that he metabolizes her bad karma. This latter interpretation suggests a Buddhist continuation of the old Vedic pattern of the brahmin guest as consumer of the moral taint *(pāpam)* of the host's sacrificial killing that Heesterman has detected in preclassical texts and that Parry sees in contemporary Varanasi in ritual prestations of *dān.*

In other ways, too, these Buddhist *dāna-dharma* tales show continuity with Vedic practice. Part Three of the essay suggests that these stories about cooking, eating, and the ripening (or natural cooking) of seeds of karma reverse the old Vedic "law of the fishes" alimentary ideology as described by Brian Smith. In the Vedic texts Smith discusses, the big fishes who enjoy superior status and power are said to triumphantly consume their inferiors. In the old dog-eat-dog Vedic world, the top dog is the one with the most status and power. In this Buddhist context, eating is still a mark of superiority, but the top dog is the one with the least status and power. Here, the poor woman triumphs over the king of the gods—the Chihuahua eats the Great Dane.

In addition to considering Kassapa's legendary preference for unpalatable foods, I also discuss in Part Four Kassapa's preference for shabby (and in one interpretation, ritually polluting) robes. Kassapa's mode of dress is a matter of great significance because this saint is said to have exchanged robes with Śākyamuni. Hence, what applies to Kassapa in regard to his legendary filthiness of frock would also apply to the Buddha. In building a case for Kassapa as one who reduces the bio-moral burdens of others, I draw on the Thai text called the *Brapāmsukūlānisamsam* that comes at the end of a collection of Pāli Jātaka tales.[1] This text associates the great Kassapa's robe with a shroud in which a stillborn fetus and afterbirth were wrapped and given to the Buddha as a *pamsakūla* or rag robe, an account that echoes that of the *Lalitavistara*.

PART ONE: MAHĀKASSAPA AS AN AMBULATORY ALTAR

The great Kassapa figures prominently in both Pāli and Sanskrit sources.[2] In some Pāli traditions, he is represented as a monk who loves wilderness, an *araññv āsin* or forest-dweller. In others, he is a *gāmavāsin,* a town-dwelling monk. But whether he is depicted as a forest-dwelling monk or monk of the settled world, he is always shown to be a master of ascetic practices. Mahākassapa exemplifies the meticulous observance of the *dhūtaṇga.* As a practitioner of ascetic ways he is represented as someone with a great capacity to tolerate discomfort; he does not seek pleasure or quality in what he eats, what he wears, or where he dwells. He looks the part, too: Mahākassapa has long hair and a beard that in at least one account of his selective begging practices gets him mistaken for a non-Buddhist renouncer.[3] In fact, all the accounts that I discuss here turn on the fulcrum point of deceptive appearances. Our master of the *dhūtaṇga* is so unkempt that he is taken for a non-Buddhist, and Sakka, when he assumes the appearance of a humble weaver, looks like someone who needs merit badly.

In the *Mūlasarvāstivāda Vinaya's* account of Mahākassapa's taking alms from a leprous woman, he is first turned away by the doorkeeper when he goes to join the sangha as they are dining at the home of Anānthapiṇḍika. His lack of tonsure and beard mislead the doorkeeper into classifying Mahākassapa as a *tīrthya,* a non-Buddhist renouncer. Going unrecognized and being thus turned away from the door of the wealthy merchant serves Mahākassapa's interests, and the story goes on to tell how he set off for the section of Śravastī where poor people dwell. I will return to this narrative presently, but for the moment I will use commentaries on several Pāli accounts that establish a clear profile of selectivity in begging and also highlight the desire of Indra and other divine beings to feed this most abstemious of monks.

Two linked narratives on who gets to feed Mahākassapa are to found in the Pāli *Udāna.* These stories, set in Rājagaha, focus on Mahākassapa's contentment with the bare necessities, praising him for being an austere eater who follows the exacting code of a strictly eremetic wanderer. He avoids flavorful foods in favor of more ordinary fare. He eats to live, eating medicinally for the good of his body, rather than living to eat the next meal. He eats nothing but what he obtains through his own locomotion, begging only what he needs to sustain him for that day. He does not collect extra food beyond his needs to redistribute to others. Dhammapāla's *Udāna* commentary says that Kassapa has no dependents on behalf of whom he begs.[4] He supports no students; he feeds no servants, aged parents, or other dependants through the redistribution of food received as *dāna.* In other words, he does not practice the art of regifting, to use Jerry Seinfeld's term.[5]

There are obviously not many opportunities to feed a highly abstemious monk such as Mahākassapa. His belly can only contain so much food and his legs can only carry him so far. Since he practices the honey-bee vow rather than following the cenobitic monk's practice of eating stored food that's been brought to the *vihāra,* feeding him is a rare opportunity. He is, as John Strong and David White might say, a moveable sacrificial altar of the post-Vedic age, a mouth of Agni who consumes what is offered in the fire pit of his belly.[6] But only a limited number of such oblations can be made.

Moreover, he spends a great deal of time in the forest absorbed in *samādhi* for up to a week at a time, so he will very often go without any sort of material food. For days on end, Mahākassapa feeds on *samādhi* alone. In *samādhi,* as in some forms of illness, the body's metabolic system is suppressed to free up resources for other functions. One who emerges from *samādhi,* like someone recovering from a fever, may have gone without food for a number of days. These analogies between trance and illness are suggested by the two linked narratives in the Pāli *Udāna.* One tells of how Mahākassapa was offered food by divine beings while seeking alms after an extended illness; the other depicts a similar alms-seeking expedition, only this time Mahākassapa goes out to beg after a seven-day *samādhi.*[7]

The first story, briefly recounted in the Bodhi chapter of the Pāli *Udāna* and elaborated in Dhammapāla's commentary on this text, depicts Mahākassapa entering Rājagaha for food after recovering from a serious illness.[8] Dhammapāla's commentary explains that during his illness, the monk had subsisted only on leftover alms collected by other monks. Hence, in Dhammapāla's view, Mahākassapa is not above accepting regifted foods, even if he himself does not regift. In any case, five hundred *apsarās* station themselves along his route and offer him choice foods.[9] The terse *Udāna* account simply says that Mahākassapa dismisses the heavenly nymphs and procedes to seek alms "in the direction of the streets of the poor *(daliddavisakhā),* the streets of those suffering great hardship *(kapaavisakhā),* the streets of the weavers *(pesakāravisakhā).*[10] Dhammapāla enlivens his commentarial narration with a bit of *devatā*-slamming. Kassapa snaps at the nymphs, "Off with you—you've earned merit, you have *mahābhoga* (great enjoyment) because of it. I'm going to act in sympathy with those who are badly off!" And the nymphs respond, "Lord, please don't destroy us; please act in sympathy with us."[11] In other words, "We desperately need to deposit some karmic funds in your high-yield bank account if we are to maintain the lives and the lifestyles to which we've become accustomed due to past meritorious actions."

One can almost see the stern, no-nonsense Kassapa grimacing at this suggestion that *devatās* are truly more needy of merit-making opportunities than the miserable weavers of Rājagaha. His patience at an end, he says, "You don't know your place—go away," and snaps his fingers menacingly. A variant reading suggests that the great Kassapa really loses it at this point and slaps one of the nymphs.[12] Whether he manhandles them or just intimidates them, they flee back to the *devaloka.* The story then quickly comes to a close, with Kassapa going off to the slums for his humble meal and the Buddha, apprehending the choice that the monk has made, speaking this *udāna:* "I call a brahmin the one who doesn't feed others, the one who's well-known, tamed, established in the essence. I call a brahmin the one in whom the *āsava*s have been destroyed and faults purged."[13] What a brahmin indeed! Mahākassapa does exemplify something of the brahmin's legendary discriminative faculties. For example, he does not readily accept food from others. People vie to feed him in the hope of karmic returns; however, he is extremely picky about whom he will permit to feed him. But clearly this is a Buddhist subversion of the *dharmaśastric* profile of the brahmin. This is a man who seeks out food that to another brahmin would be equivalent to poison or toxic waste, requiring elaborate purification procedures. And unlike that brahmin who serves as the butt of folk humor due to his notorious appetite, this brahmin-born monk has a limited need for food. As one who has tamed his senses, who has banked the fires of his appetite, Mahākassapa is a superior field of merit, a higher yielding karma-depository than some portly gentleman with an untamed need to feed—especially one who makes a pretense of accepting little but somehow manages to obtain a great deal more.

There are not many opportunities to feed the great Kassapa because in addition to his abstemiousness, he quite obviously discriminates in favor of those who have the least to give, in material terms. All accounts of Kassapa's begging practices stress the monk's *anukampā,* his compassion for those who are destitute. The Pāli *Vimānavatthu* commentary is most explicit on this point.[14] This narrative is set in Rājagaha, where a poor neighborhood has been struck by an epidemic of some sort. One old woman survives by breaking through a wall, fleeing her infected home, and going to live with others in the city. She survives by begging, eating whatever leftover rice-scum remains in her benefactors' cooking pots after serving their own meals. This secondhand rice-flavored liquid is what Mahākassapa is determined to eat. He knows that the old woman is very near death and that rebirth in hell would be her fate due to a former deed of hers. "When I go to her," Mahākassapa reasons, "she'll give me the rice-scum she's received for herself and by this means she'll arise in the Nimmānarati-devaloka."[15] Continuing his reflections in a vein that Heesterman and Parry would find congenial to their thinking about *dāna* in Vedic-Hindu contexts, Mahākassapa suggests that his eating of her donated food will prevent a bad afterlife and ensure her of a better postmortem fate: "When I have thus released her from arising in hell, come, let me accomplish for her the excellence of arising in heaven!"[16] He sets off to visit the home where the woman is staying. On the way, of course, our old friend Indra appears in disguise and presents Kassapa with divine alms. But the great Kassapa is not fooled. He upbraids the king of the gods: "You've acted well (in the past). Why are you acting this way now? Don't plunder the excellence of those suffering great hardship!"[17]

Mahākassapa continues on to where the old woman is staying and presents himself for alms food, but she is embarrassed by the poor quality of the food she has to offer. Other people in the house offer Kassapa food. But he declines and continues to stand in front of the old woman until she realizes that he had come specifically to beg from her and gives him *dāna.* He eats her rice-scum there in the home and then explains to the old woman that in a former life she was his mother. The woman is overjoyed by this news; that night, she dies and arises as a Nimmānarati deity. "She was," Kassapa explains afterward to Indra, "set free *(vippamuttā)*"—she was released from "this human misfortune through the exercise of the highest compassion."[18]

If it is not *just* the act of offering that changes the woman's fate, if it is Mahākassapa's *consumption* of the food that changes her postmortem destiny—and he is, after all, a superior field of merit, a more productive samsaric garden for the ripening of karmas than others, so his eating matters—then we may be dealing with a ritualized transfer somewhat akin to what Jonathan Parry has observed in contemporary Varanasi. It is not clear from the *Vimānavatthu* account that the woman donor is aware that in feeding Mahākassapa she is unloading a bio-moral burden, but Mahākassapa's language suggests that he sees himself, in his capacity as a field of merit, as a means of atonement for her. In interviews with funeral priests and other ritual specialists, Parry's informants declared themselves anxious about the untoward effects of the *dān* they receive from clients. These foods and other gifts embody "something of the biomoral substance of the donor—and something nasty at that," suggests Parry.[19] In Varanasi, givers of *dān* free themselves of the consequences of their misdeeds by the ritual transfer of gifts. Priests who accept such gifts thereby incorporate into themselves the inferior essence of others. Precedents from Vedic sacrificial practice undergird such ritual transfers, as Parry's citation of Heesterman suggests.

Another precedent—one that may shed light on Indra's persistent attempts at feeding Mahākassapa in our narratives—is the well-known story of Indra's brahminicide. Indra frees himself of the consequences of killing Vṛtra by transfering the sin of brahminicide to others, who are assured that the buck will not stop with them. They will be relieved of the fever of brahminicide by passing it on, in turn, to others. Like the recipients of Indra's sin, Parry's funeral priests have ways to rid themselves of moral burdens assumed from others. Practicing the art of regifting what is taken as *dān,* these ritual specialists toss the moral "hot potato" to someone else. But Mahākassapa, as we know, does not regift. Instead of tossing the potato to someone else, he sits down and eats it. As long as Mahākassapa determines that the donor of said potato is truly in need of karmic relief, the monk takes and consumes it. So in this regard, our stories deviate from Vedic and Hindu patterns.

The perfect donor, in Mahākassapa's eyes, is the donor who has the least to give, in material terms. The most eligible to give, the most deserving of this opportunity, is she who eats recycled remnants, gifted leftovers. She who eats this kind of unappetizing and impure food is worthy to feed this former brahmin. Indra, it would seem, has not got a prayer in his attempt to compete with a woman who truly deserves the merit to be gained from feeding this abstemious monk. But in the Pāli *Udāna,* Indra realizes that Mahākassapa favors the unfortunate and capitalizes on this knowledge. Impersonating a poor weaver, he succeeds in feeding the choosy monk by using deceit. It is really a hilarious account, with Indra and Sūjāta the nymph taking on the appearance of an old and decrepit weaver couple. There is a great deal of what can only be described as wacky physical humor, suggesting the possibility that the text would lend itself to dramatic enactment. For example, the pensioners manqué pretend to be a little hard of hearing, forcing Mahākassapa to make a lot of noise to get their attention. Once they acknowledge the monk's presence, Indra tells his mate to answer the door. His consort replies, rather sassily, "That's YOUR job, mister." Sakka goes to the door and—in the most ludicrous moment of the pretence—slowly and painfully genuflects before Mahākassapa with creaky arthritic limbs, groaning all the while.

All this wonderful geriatric play-acting does not fool Kassapa. But it is not until he detects the smell of the ambrosial offering that the god has in the meantime placed in his bowl that Mahākassapa realizes his error. As in the *Vimānavatthu* account, Mahākassapa sternly upbraids Indra for making off with merit destined for someone else, someone truly in need of it. Sakka counters here with the suggestion that he is truly in need, having had to suffer the dimunition of his previously earned merit to the point where rival gods with greater *tejas* than him are outranking him in radiance. Admitting that he tricked the great monk, Indra asks whether there is merit in his donation even though it was deceitfully done. Mahākassapa admits that it is so, and Sakka and his consort rise into the air singing a pithy verse in praise of *dāna* and of Kassapa as the recipient of the highest *dāna (paramadānaṃ).*

Even though given in deceit, Mahākassapa accepts Sakka's food offering. Receive it Mahākassapa must, in this Pāli *Udāna* account, because he was tricked into taking it. In the *Mūlasarvāstivāda Vinaya,* however, the great Kassapa outsmarts Indra by turning his bowl upside-down so that the food falls on the ground. Here, in contrast to the Pāli accounts, the Buddha is not pleased with Mahākassapa's actions and Mahākassapa is censured for refusing Indra's offering. Kassapa's rejection of the *piṇḍa* on this occasion provides the Buddha with an opportunity to establish a monastic rule that forbids selective begging practices of the very sort that wins Kassapa praise in the Pāli sources. In the *Mūlasarvāstivāda Vinaya,* Kassapa seems to be characterized as the sort who is too choosy in his begging practices. After all, everyone deserves a chance to be a *dāna-pati,* even the dumbest, most ham-fisted of the gods.

Perhaps the insistence on alimentary accessability or openness here has something to do with the fact that this account of Kassapa's spurning Indra's donation is given in the midst of the *Bhaiṣajyavāstu,* a compendium of cases determinative of what foods are permitted as medicine. It is well known that medicinal eating has historically served as the proverbial camel's nose-in-the-tent for liberal monastic eating practices, especially those appropriate for the colder climates associated with the expansionist missionizing milieu of Northwest Indian *Sarvāstivādin* texts.

PART TWO: BUDDHIST SUBVERSION OF VEDIC FOOD HIERARCHIES

My discussion of who by rights ought to reap the rewards of giving by consuming the fruits of generosity suggests that the Vedic pattern Brian Smith has described lives on in the form of karmic accountancy in my texts.[20] In the competition between the old woman and the king of the gods over who will feed Mahākassapa and eat the fruits of generosity later on, our Buddhist tales perpetuate the agonistic aspects of Vedic food theory. Through the mouthpiece of her spokesperson Mahākassapa, the old woman is in effect saying to Indra, the preeminent consumer of the spoils of conflict and offerer of large-scale sacrifices, "Let somebody else eat ambrosia in heaven: you've had your fill!"

But while Buddhist literature continues the contestational aspects of Vedic thinking about food, it also reverses the Vedic pattern. It is not the eater of food but the giver of food, the one who donates what could be consumed as sustenance, who outranks her inferiors. She has the power to plant karmic seeds in a field or *kṣetra* that Indra desires for his own cultivation of merit. She thereby earns merit sufficient to win heaven, perhaps even to attain the position of a deity such as Indra himself in some later life.

And so the Vedic pattern of eating as a show of power remains intact, with the proviso that helping others to eat is itself a kind of eating, a form of deferred consumption in which one skimps now but eats ambrosia in heaven later. But the old Vedic pattern is reversed, quite clearly, in terms of the hierarchy of eaters. Here, the law of the fishes still rules, but it is a different rank order. The little fish eats the big fish, steals the karmic fruit right out of the greedy maw of the king of the gods. A poor woman outranks both a wealthy merchant and the king of the gods.

PART THREE: IMPURE OFFERINGS AND THE TRANSFER OF DEMERIT

I will admit that I am not sure what Mahākassapa's legendary begging practices say about Buddhist renouncers generally. It seems reasonable to conclude from my Pāli materials that the Buddhists who composed and preserved these texts valued monks and nuns who discriminate between worthy and unworthy donors, while those who composed and passed down the *Mūlasarvāstivāda Vinaya* favored indiscriminate eating.

Whether beggars should or should not be choosers is, as I hope my invocation of Heesterman and Parry suggests, a serious issue with consequences for our understanding of Buddhist soteriologies. If I am correct in drawing on Vedic and Hindu notions of food as a mechanism of transfer, then we in Buddhist studies ought to be amending our textbooks to include reference to demerit transfer as well as merit transfer. In other words, just as compassionate people may be said to transfer their merit to those in need of it, so too people such as Kassapa may be said to invite transfers of demerit, to relieve unfortunate beings of their negative bio-moral status by accepting their gifts, especially gifts of food, that ultimate medium of social transaction. For those who may be skeptical of how relevant Vedic and Hindu models of ritual transfer really are to Buddhist studies, I suggest examining how donations of ritually impure cloth operate in various Buddhist economies. This part of the paper explores narratives about donations of cloth to the bodhisattva and to members of the sangha. In some of these legends, the cloth given away is literally soaked with blood from the ritually polluting process of childbirth and in other cases, contains a corpse. In our Thai text, the *Brapaṃsukūlānisaṃsaṃ,* the cloth holds a stillborn child, the afterbirth, and the corpse of the young mother who died giving birth to her first child. From a *dharmaśhastric* point of view, such cloth is clearly infused with the negative bio-moral status of the deceased and the surviving relatives. To make sense of how such gifts operate within Buddhist economies of substance transfer, it seems sensible to draw on the work of scholars such as Heesterman, who says that the preclassical Vedic sacrificer offers donations that "are the sacrificer's dead self, which he disposes of by burdening his guests with it."[21] The Vedic sacrifice is a ritual of transformation, of symbolic rebirth. Sacrificial donations serve as instruments of transformation in this process. By accepting the sacrificer's gifts, guests help the sacrificer to attain a new identity, purified of the sin of sacrificial violence. In carrying off his sacrificial gifts, the sacrificer's guests carry away the sacrificer's old, karmically tainted self. Only by disposing of his old self through gifts that represent his personhood can the sacrificer achieve a new identity.

What is fascinating about these Buddhist accounts of cloth donations, from the standpoint of anthropological theories of the gift, is the insistence of authorities such as Buddhaghosa on the absolute alienation of these gifts from their donors. When you give a cloth to a *dhūtaṇga*-practicing monk, Buddhaghosa says in the *Visuddhimagga,* you are not giving it as a gift but rather throwing it away as refuse. Such a monk can only receive what is abandoned as trash, what is completely alienated from the donor. The "refuse-ragman's practice" is over the moment he accepts a robe given by a layperson. He should refuse such gifted robes and instead practice recycling by washing and re-using cast-off fabrics found in cremation grounds, refuse piles, and other places where old, torn, or filthy cloth is disposed of. The rationale for this recycling can be inferred from Buddhaghosa's comments on the advantages of the refuse-ragman's practice: if a monk takes from no one, he enjoys an "independence of livelihood," an "absence of the lust for enjoyment," and "the fruit of fewness of wishes."[22] If a monk accepts fabric from lay donors, he will presumably more readily succumb to desire for nice fabrics, attractive colors, and so on. His wishes will multiply, thus bringing him more often into relationships of dependence upon donors than is suitable for such a monk.[23]

But what is to prevent a donor from offering his or her finest goods as trash? The offering of expensive cloth disguised as shrouds and other funeral refuse is indeed, if Martini is correct, in her introductory remarks to her translation of the *Brapāṃsukūlānisaṃsaṃ,* the strategy used today for donating rag robes in Thai funerary rites. And disguising expensive cloth as trash is certainly the *modus operandi* of the wealthy donors in the key narrative of the *Brapāṃsukūlānisaṃsaṃ.* Although the cloth such donors give is no longer acceptable to many because sullied by contact with birth and death, it is costly fabric, not something one casually throws away. These fabrics put on the refuse pile or wrapped around a corpse function as status symbols and as vehicles for the transfer of merit. In the *Visuddhimagga,* Buddhaghosa himself cites the example of the mother of the minister Tissa who wrapped the afterbirth of her delivery in an expensive cloth and left it on a trash pile in the hope that a refuse-ragman would pick it up.[24] This valuable cloth not only bespeaks the affluent status of the family but is also emblematic of the newborn son, containing as it does the afterbirth or embryonic housing in which he gestated for nine months. Another example of a cloth given away as waste goods: The *Lalitavistara* tells of how the bodhisattva aquired a rag-robe from a hemp funeral shroud after the death of Rādhā, servant of Sujātā (who, incidentally, is about to become, as this narrative proceeds, one of the first to feed the bodhisattva). When Rādhā died, her corpse was wrapped in a hemp cloth and left in the corner of the cemetery. The bodhisattva saw that dirty, earth-caked rag and took it, to the wonder of the observing deities.[25] In the *Lalitavistara,* it is not clear that anyone intended that the hemp cloth should become the bodhisattva's robe nor that the merit of the donation was dedicated to Rādhā. But this story is invoked in Thai Buddhist funerary rites with the explicit intention of making a meritorious connection between the newly deceased and the monastic wearer of the donated cloth. The *Brapāṃsukūlānisaṃsaṃ* tells a narrative similar to that of the *Lalitavistara,* only here the deceased female is not Rādhā, the servant of Sujātā, but rather the daughter of a wealthy merchant who has died in childbirth.[25] The text explicitly states that she and her stillborn son will receive the merit that accrues from "giving" a *paṃsukūla.*

We can see from these tales about the transfer of merit through the "abandoning" of funeral fabrics that cloth can be as powerful an agent of biomoral transaction as food. Furthermore, if we examine the twenty-three kinds of rags that Buddhaghosa specifies as acceptable to the refuse-ragman, we find some other powerfully transactive examples. We see in Buddhaghosa's list all kinds of fabrics that people would do well to be rid of, like cloth used for purificatory purposes after visiting the cremation ground and cloth that "sick people throw away as inauspicious when, with the advice of exorcists, they have washed their heads and bathed themselves."[27] The cloth that a sick person disposes of to ward off disease-causing forces is a cloth infused with the substance of the giver. It says to the vengeful spirit or deity of disease (in the silent language of sartorial signification, or through sympathetic magic, if you prefer that terminology), "Look, you've got your victim right here, in this cloth; now go away, consume your offering, and leave us alone!" So people would do well to be rid of such cloth. But, consistent with the famous essay on the gift by Marcel Mauss, the cloth by which people get rid of their illness or their status as mourners represents the wearer/donor; it is infused with the spirit of the gift. Hence, it is the perfect medium for improving one's biomoral status through the elimination of demerit. By a kind of postmortem transaction whereby a dead donor can profit from "divesting" him- or herself of cloth that is no longer needed and "investing" in the career and merit-earning potential of a pure *dhūtaṇga*-practicing monk, the dead women and children of our funerary legends can reinvent themselves and reconfigure their fates. Likewise, the poor woman with nothing to give is endowed with a form of agency she never dreamed of, just by giving away that humble rice-gruel for which *her* benefactors had no use.

The unfortunate woman donor of the food-giving accounts is not playing hide and seek with her food tin the way that the wealthy givers of fabric carry on the pretense that their expensive cloth is just rubbish (childbirth and funeral detritus). She does not dispose of her food as if it were trash, although leftover food is pretty much so classified by brahmanic authorities (who admonish Hindus to dispose of their leftover food as if it were contagious). So the parallel between my food stories and my clothing stories is not exact. But in both forms of donation (whether that which is given away is food or cloth) we see that bad karma can be eliminated and bad destinies avoided by donations that relieve the donor of his or her afflicted condition. Just as in the preclassical Vedic sacrifice, where the brahmin recipient of karmically tainted gifts becomes the conduit of purification, so in these Buddhist transactions, the monastic receiver of food or cloth serves as a means of purification and transformation for the donor. By virtue of their abstemiousness, their propensity for recycling waste goods, monastic recipients are in a position to make use of goods that others regard as valueless. In this way, they can bring relief to those who have died or are terminally ill and therefore unable to help themselves through the ongoing performance of meritorious actions. These accounts showcasing the redemptive powers of leftover food and clothing suggest ways in which Buddhists help each other to vanquish bad karma and so constitute communities in which the dispossessed are empowered.

NOTES

1. G. Martini, tr., *Brapāṃsukūlānisaṃsaṃ. L'Ecole Française d'extrême-orient* 60 (1973): 55–78, see esp. 73ff.

2. Sanskrit sources emphasize Mahākassapa's longevity, suggesting that Kassapa still exists today in a state of suspended animation awaiting the arrival of Maitreya, to whom he will give Śākyamuni's robe and bowl. On this, see Etienne Lamotte, *Traité de la Grande Vertu de Sagesse,* 5 vols. (Louvain: Institute Orientalist, 1:1844; 2:1949; 3:1970; 4:1980), 1:191–96; Reginald Ray, *Buddhist Saints In India: A Study In Buddhist Values and Orientations* (New York: Oxford University Press, 1994), 108–109 and 114–15; Bernard Faure,

The Rhetoric of Immediacy: A Cultural Critique of Chan/Zen Buddhism (Princeton: Princeton University Press, 1991), 155–56. On *Sarvāstivādin* links with forest-dwelling monastic traditions, see Thich Minh Chau, *The Chinese Madhyama Āgama and the Pāli Majjhima Nikāya* (Saigon, 1964): 29–30.

3. With no one to ensure that his worn-out robes will be replaced, he wears tattered threads, variously depicted as a rag robe, a coarse robe of hemp, or a robe so faded that it's white.

4. Dhammapāla, *Paramattha-Dīpanī Udānaṭṭhakathā,* ed. F. L. Woodward (London: Pali Text Society, 1926; reprint, 1977), 202.

5. One has only to see the regifting episode of the television show *Seinfeld* to appreciate Americans' resistance to redistributive economies. In this episode, a Seinfeld character contemplates giving away something aquired as a gift, causing great consternation among the friends who learn of this social taboo.

6. On the feeding of Buddhist monastics as structured by relations of giving and receiving in the Vedic sacrificial cult, see John Strong, "Making Merit in the Aśokāvadāna: A Study of Buddhist Acts of Offering in the Post-Parinirvana Age," University of Chicago dissertation, 1977, and David White, "*Dakkhina* and *Agnicayani:* An Extended Application of Paul Mus's Typology." *History of Religions* 26.2 (1986): 188–211.

7. *Paramattha-Dīpanī Udānaṭṭhakathā,* 59–63 and 195–202; Peter Masefield, tr., *The Udāna Commentary: Translated from the Pāli,* 2 vols. (Oxford: Pali Text Society, 1994), 1:95–100 and 1:486–94.

8. *Udāna,* ed. P. Steinthal (London: Oxford University Press, 1948), 4; Peter Masefield, tr., *The Udāna: Tranlated from the Pāli* (Oxford: Pali Text Society, 1994), 5.

9. Dhammapāla specifies them as "dove-footed *apsarās,* attendants of Sakka." *Paramattha-Dīpanī Udānaṭṭhakathā,* 61.

10. Peter Masefield, 98.

11. *Paramattha-Dīpanī Udānaṭṭhakathā,* 62.

12. Ibid.; *accharaṃ pahari* could be read as "he slapped an *accharā.*" This reading would seem, however, to be grammatically inconsistent with the rest of the passage, where the *apsarās* are designated in the plural and speak as a grou

13. *Udāna,* ed. P. Steinthal, 4.

14. Dhammapāla, *Paramattha-dīpanī: Commentary on the Vimāna-vatthu,* ed. E. Hardy (London: Pali Text Society, 1901), 99–105; *Paramatthadīpanī nama Vimānavatthu-aṭṭhakatā (Elucidation of the Intrinsic Meaning: So Named the Commentary on the Vimana Stories),* trans. Peter Masefield and N. A. Jayawickrama (Oxford : Pali Text Society, 1989), 147–54.

15. Hardy, ed., 100; Masefield, trans., 148.

16. Ibid.

17. Ibid.

18. Hardy, ed., 102; Masefield, trans., 150.

19. Jonathan Parry, *Death in Banaras* (New York: Cambridge University Press, 1994), 133.

20. Brian K. Smith, "Eaters, Food, and Hierarchy," *Journal of the American Academy of Religion* 58 (1990): 177–205.

21. J. C. Heesterman, *The Broken World of Sacrifice* (Chicago: University of Chicago Press, 1993), 37.

22. Pe Maung Tin, tr., *The Path of Purity (Vissuddhimagga)* (London: Pali Text Society, 1922–31), 72.

23. Buddhaghosa's insistence that monks practicing austerity should avoid dependence on donors is consistent with internal developments within brahminical culture with regard to the giving and receiving of gifts. As Heesterman has suggested, the reciprocity encoded in the highly charged relations between sacrificial givers and brahmin recipients in the preclassical period gave way to a renunciatory model in which brahmins stand aloof from the social world, opting out of reciprocal relations with donors in favor of individualistic self-sufficiency. Not accepting gifts becomes the mark of the highest class of brahmin. In this way, Heesterman argues, this renunciatory ideology "opens a way for the brahmin to enter into relation with the world without losing his purity. Having emancipated himself from the world, the renouncer can from his sphere of independence reenter into relation with the world, where he now enjoys unequalled prestige." J. C. Heesterman, *The Inner Conflict of Tradition: Essays in Indian Ritual, Kingship, and Society* (Chicago: University of Chicago Press, 1985), 43.

24. Malalasekera identifies Tissa as a minister of Dutthagāmaṇi; Malalasekera, *Dictionary of Pali Proper Names,* 2 vols., vol. I (London: Pali Text Society, 1974), 1024.

25. Gwendolyn Bays, tr., *The Voice of the Buddha (Lalitavistara),* 2 vols., vol. 2 (Oakland: Dharma Publishing, 1983), 405–406.

26. *Brapāṃsukūlānisaṃsaṃ,* trans. G. Martini, 71ff.

27. *Vissuddhimagga,* trans. Pe Maung Tin, 70.

FOUR

THE INSIGHT GUIDE TO HELL

MAHĀMOGGALLĀNA AND THERAVĀDA BUDDHIST COSMOLOGY

Julie Gifford

INTRODUCTION.

ONLY TO A SELECT FEW are given both the gift of insight and the ability to use it to guide an entire community. In his introduction to *Three Worlds According to King Ruang,*[1] Frank Reynolds—building on the work of Joachim Wach—claims that the history of Theravāda cosmology develops from a fundamental insight which the Buddha gained on the night of his Enlightenment. During the second watch of the night, the Buddha acquired the Divine Eye, which allowed him to see the various karmic circumstances of all beings caught in the web of samsara.[2] Reynolds adds that the "visionary experience" from which Theravāda cosmology developed was not limited to the Buddha, but was also the "special forte of the Buddha's great disciple Mahāmoggallāna."[3] This last remark is what we might call an "anticipatory contribution" to what has now emerged in the field as a discourse on the character and social role of Buddhist saints. My concern here will be to draw out a few of the theoretical implications of Reynolds's remark by examining the particular nature of Mahāmoggallāna's legacy, and exploring its implications for the theoretical discussion of Buddhist sainthood.

Perhaps the most sustained recent comparative study on Buddhist saints is Reginald Ray's *Buddhist Saints in India.*[4] Not only does Ray offer a wealth of descriptive material, he also provides two theoretical models. First, he lists thirty-five characteristics which constitute a paradigm that distinguishes forest-dwelling saints from monks living in settled monastic communities. He then argues that the usual two-tier model of Buddhism, which contrasts the practices and goals of the monastic community with those of the laity, is inadequate because it does not acknowledge the distinctive practices and goals of forest saints. He therefore proposes a threefold model of Buddhism that includes a separate category for forest saints and describes the ways in which they interact with the monastic community on the one hand, and with the laity on the other.

The picture of Mahāmoggallāna that emerges from legends found in the Pāli canon and in the commentarial literature fits Ray's paradigm of the forest saint quite well. But as I will show, Mahāmoggallāna's legacy affects the larger Theravāda community—particularly the lay community—in ways for which Ray's threefold model does not fully account. Mahāmoggallāna's meditative practice, though it may be pursued in solitude, is directed toward establishing a public teaching: his storied insights are not so much aimed at his own liberation as they are intended to guide others by providing a cosmological and karmic map of samsara. To do justice to his legacy, it is necessary to account theoretically not only for the charismatic presence of this forest saint, but also for his activity as a teacher whose efforts shape the larger Buddhist community.

MAHĀMOGGALLĀNA, MEDITATION, AND THE COSMOLOGICAL MAP OF KARMIC FATES

Since there is likely to be little controversy about the matter, I will not demonstrate in detail that Mahāmoggallāna's hagiography features most of the characteristics listed in Ray's paradigm of forest sainthood. Instead, I will focus on the two characteristics listed by Ray that are most closely associated with Mahāmoggallāna: the possession of supernatural powers, and the intensive practice of meditation.

According to the *Aṅguttaranikāya,* Mahāmoggallāna is foremost among those who possess the *abhiññās*, or supernormal powers.[5] These include: 1) *iddhi* powers, such as the ability to walk on water, fly through the air, multiply oneself, pass through solid objects, and the like; 2) the ability to hear conversations and other sounds at ordinarily impossible distances; 3) the ability to read minds; 4) the ability to recollect one's previous lives; 5) the ability to know the rebirths of others; and 6) the certain knowledge of one's own final liberation.[6]

The possession of supernatural powers is not unique to Mahāmoggallāna, but as Ray states, is one of the standard elements of forest sainthood.[7] But the legends suggest not only that Mahāmoggallāna characteristically uses these powers more often than the Buddha's other disciples, but also that he possesses them to a greater degree. For example, before the Buddha performs his famous Miracle of the Doubles, several members of his entourage offer to display their own supernormal powers. The miracles they offer to perform become progressively grander and more complex, until Mahāmoggallāna makes the most astonishing offer of all: he vows to crunch Mount Meru between his teeth like a kidney bean, to roll up the earth like a mat and thrust it between his fingers, to cause the earth to revolve like a potter's wheel, and so forth, and finally, to use Mount Meru as an umbrella-stick, put the earth on it and walk around in the air using it as a parasol.[8] The fact that Mahāmoggallāna's offer is the last suggests that his miraculous powers are second only to the Buddha's own, and the story makes it clear that he is able to transform the entire cosmos at will.

Although the legends describe cases in which people attain the *abhiññās* almost instantly in a face-to-face encounter with the Buddha, these powers are usually acquired through the intensive practice of meditation. So it is not surprising that some sources state that Mahāmoggallāna is particularly adept at meditation.[9] This, perhaps more than any other element of his profile, identifies Mahāmoggallāna as a forest saint, because as Ray argues, "the intensive practice of meditation . . . makes up the substance of the spiritual quest" in the lives of the saints.[10]

But it is important to note that according to the legends, Mahāmoggallāna's meditative practice exhibits features that do not figure in Ray's discussion. Quite rightly, Ray says that the practice of meditation is primarily a quest for enlightenment. In general, acquisition of the *abhiññās* is not the goal of meditation, but merely a byproduct of intensive practice aimed at enlightenment.[11] When people continue to meditate after enlightenment, Ray explains that this is either because it makes them happy to do so, or because the practice has become so internalized that it simply is what the saint does.[12] Mahāmoggallāna, by contrast, continues to meditate after his own enlightenment in part to facilitate the deployment of his supernormal powers. For example, when the obstreperous *nāga* Ahicchatta spits smoke and fire at Mahāmoggallāna, the saint enters into a "meditation on the element of fire" and while in that trance, bursts into flames that reach all the way up to the world of Brahma, yet do not burn the saint.[13] Mahāmoggallāna fights the *nāga*'s fire with his own meditationally produced fire and wins—in the end, the *nāga* spreads his cobra-like hood to shelter the saint.[14] This pyrotechnic one-upmanship is not without a higher purpose. When a group of local sages learns that Mahāmoggallāna has tamed the *nāga,* the sages become receptive to the Buddha's teaching as the thought occurs to them: "If such is the supernatural power of a mere disciple, what must the supernatural power of this man [the Buddha] be like?"[15] Here, Mahāmoggallāna's meditation facilitates the deployment of his supernatural powers in the service of a religious conversion.

Mahāmoggallāna also meditates in order to deploy his physics-defying power to travel through the air. For example, at the end of his life, Mahāmoggallāna is lying on the ground after thieves have beaten his bones literally to a powder when he decides that it would not be proper to die before paying his respects to his guru, the Buddha. He then "swathes himself with meditation as with a cloth" and "makes himself rigid" before flying through the air and into the Buddha's presence.[16] In this case, Mahāmoggallāna meditates in part literally to pull himself together, and in part to access the particular *abhiññā* that will allow him to make the journey.

Meditation also facilitates Mahāmoggallāna's travels to cosmological realms ordinarily inaccessible to human beings, and it is this aspect of the saint's activity with which I am primarily concerned. According to the commentary on the *Vimānavatthu,* Mahāmoggallāna meditates prior to his extended "*deva* tours" through heaven. At the beginning of a tour, he "enters upon the fourth *jhāna* which provides the basis for the *abhiññā*s and, emerging therefrom, goes at that very instant through the power of *iddhi* to the Heaven of the Thirty-three . . ." in order to meet a series of deities and ask them to recount the meritorious deeds by which they achieved rebirth in heaven.[17] Each karma conversation begins when a particular heavenly being notices the saint and approaches in order to worship him. Mahāmoggallāna assesses his or her karmic condition first by conducting a detailed visual inspection of the deity's physical beauty, the richness of his or her raiment, and the shape, size, and adornments of his or her heavenly palace.[18] Although the *Vimānavatthu* commentary suggests that Mahāmoggallāna experiences these visions after he has already concluded his meditation, the care with which he observes each visual detail suggests some relationship to visualization-inspection meditation, a practice that is fully developed in the Mahāyāna and later Pure Land traditions.[19] In any case, as Reynolds observes, Mahāmoggallāna's contribution to the development of Theravāda cosmology is rooted in experiences that are vividly visual.

These visual experiences, facilitated by meditation, are not for Mahāmoggallāna's own benefit, but rather for the benefit of gods and human beings. When the saint has seen a particular deity, he asks for an account of the meritorious deeds that led to his or her rebirth in heaven, and the deity obliges. But as the *Vimānavatthu* makes completely clear, Mahāmoggallāna already *knows* what each deity has done, because he possesses the fifth *abhiññā*—

knowledge of the rebirths of others. Regarding his first visit with a goddess, the text says:

> Even though the Elder, by means of the diversity of the power of his wisdom, saw clearly for himself as though beholding a myrobalan fruit placed upon the palm of his hand the good and bad deeds that had been accumulated by her as well as by other beings, on account of the potency of his knowledge of correspondent results of deeds, nevertheless . . . wanting to make clear the fruit of the deed to the world with the devas, [he] made this devī tell about the deed she had done. . . .[20]

In the first instance, then, the deity's story benefits other heavenly residents who may be listening because, although they clearly figured out how to get to heaven once, they will eventually be reborn elsewhere and will need to accumulate more good karma in order to return.

But Mahāmoggallāna undertakes his cosmic journeys and collects these stories about the workings of karma primarily for the benefit of human beings. When he has completed a particular "*deva* tour," he returns to this world, goes to see the Buddha, and tells the stories to him so that he in turn will "take them as a matter arising and set forth a great teaching on Dhamma. . . ."[21] As a result, those present hear the Buddha teach about the workings of karma, which he does *by telling Mahāmoggallāna's stories.* We might say, then, that Mahāmoggallāna teaches by proxy.

Not only does Mahāmoggallāna provide the occasion for the Buddha to teach, he also performs a service for those present by asking for clarification—which he, of course, does not need—of difficult or surprising points. For example, on one particular *deva*-tour, Mahāmoggallāna sees a vast, incredibly beautiful, fabulously adorned heavenly palace which, though fully staffed with nymphs, has no resident "master of the house." When the saint inquires, he is told that the palace belongs to a man named Nandiya, who has accumulated so much good karma by giving regular and lavish *dāna* that his heavenly palace has come into being even though he has not yet died. When Mahāmoggallāna returns to this world, he asks the Buddha if it is really true that one's heavenly rewards could begin to appear while one is still alive. Thus, he provides an opportunity for the Buddha to clarify the point for others. To make it clear that his answer is not for Mahāmoggallāna's benefit (and perhaps also to let the saint know that he has presented enough teaching opportunities lately) the Buddha replies: "Moggallāna, you have seen with your own eyes the heavenly glory which Nandiya has attained in the World of the Gods; why do you ask me such a question?"[22]

Of course, Mahāmoggallāna's visionary experiences are not by any means limited to the splendors of the heavens, but also include the wretchedness of ghostly states and hellish realms. The legends include several stories that describe Mahāmoggallāna's visions of suffering ghosts, or *peta*s, which he sees as he accompanies the disciple Lakkhaṇa on a descent from Vulture's Peak. For example, in one story, Mahāmoggallāna sees a *peta* with the head of a man and the body of a giant snake entirely engulfed in flames.[23] Like his visions of the heavens, Mahāmoggallāna's visions of ghostly states provide the occasion for teachings on the nature of karma. When Mahāmoggallāna sees each *peta,* he smiles, and because the *peta*s are invisible to others, his companion Lakkhaṇa asks why. Later, in the presence of the Buddha, Mahāmoggallāna explains his smiles by recounting his visions of the *peta*s. The Buddha confirms that these beings exist, and explains what each *peta* did in a previous life to deserve his suffering in the present. The burning snake-man, for example, had once been a farmer who, in order to prevent his crops from being trampled by hoards of devotees, burned the residence of a pratyekabuddha.[24]

Mahāmoggallāna's travels to the hellish realms are systematically described in the first chapter of the *Mahāvastu,* which lists eight levels of hell and gives vivid descriptions of the saint's visions of six of these.[25] But the accounts of Mahāmoggallāna's cosmic travels to the hells become even more detailed, gruesome, and oddly fascinating in the later vernacular stories of Theravāda Southeast Asia. In addition to the stories from Thailand and Laos that discuss Mahāmoggallāna himself, there are also several tales devoted to the cosmic travels of Phra Malai, who is explicitly said to be "like Moggallāna."[26] Though it might be possible to trace the narrative genealogy of the Phra Malai stories back to the Pāli or Sanskrit tales of Mahāmoggallāna, such a project is beyond the scope of this essay.[27] Here, I claim only that Phra Malai is modeled on Mahāmoggallāna and that the stories about him are therefore a part of Mahāmoggallāna's legacy. Phra Malai's visits to the hells are rendered particularly vividly in the *Phra Malai Klon Suat,* which describes the tortures undergone by various types of hell beings and recounts the misdeeds that led each one to be reborn in his or her particular condition.[28]

Taken together, Mahāmoggallāna's insights and the tales of karmic reward and retribution that they generate constitute a kind of cosmological travel guide—an "*Insight Guide*" to heaven and hell. They describe a world of exotic places, explain how to get to each one, and give reviews of the accommodations and amenities to be had on arrival. And like the books in the *Insight Guide* series, the tradition surrounding Mahāmoggallāna also includes a wealth of visual detail intended to help one anticipate the joys (or torments) of one's destination. This aspect of Mahāmoggallāna's legacy, inherent already in the descriptive passages of the texts, is realized fully in the rich Southeast Asian visual culture devoted to Phra Malai. One finds vivid illustrations of his visits to heavens and hells on the walls of temple compounds, on temple interiors, in posters and comic books, and in three-dimensional sculptures. These images, found usually in very public places, are an important part of the way in which the legacy of the forest saint is currently disseminated in the wider monastic and lay Buddhist communities.

But unlike most travel guides, this one is ultimately more about the place one is leaving than it is about the place to which one is going. Each future journey is launched by deeds that affect the community within which one acts. Clearly, the consequences of *dāna* on the one hand, or of murdering one's parents on the other, are inherently *social.* Karma is, among other things, a way of explaining how it is that each of us has a personal stake in the quality of our community. Ultimately, then, Mahāmoggallāna's "*Insight Guide*" is intended to help each of us plan a trip that will make home better.

CHARISMA AND BUDDHIST SAINTHOOD

According to Ray, lay Buddhists may expect to receive three things from forest saints: 1) merit stemming from *dāna;* 2) teachings, possibly including meditation instruction; and 3) the opportunity to "participate in the intensity of his or her enlightened charisma."[29] However, the first two of these benefits may also be obtained from monks living in a settled community; the only benefit obtained exclusively from contact with a forest saint is that of participation in his enlightened charisma. Drawing on Max Weber, Ray argues that the charisma of the forest saint, which derives not only from his personality, but also from his ascetic and meditative practices, is perceived as a kind of religious power that may be partially transferred to others in face-to-face interactions.[30] Writing a decade earlier, Stanley Tambiah makes a similar point: contemporary Thais seek out charismatic forest monks, he says, because merely being in their presence is thought to confer powerful religious benefits.[31]

If one could not participate in a saint's charisma except by meeting him face to face, then one could obtain this distinctive benefit only while the saint was still alive. And this is clearly not the case. Although a face-to-face meeting with a living saint is the primary way in which one may participate in his charisma, one may also derive benefits by coming into contact with a place or thing ritually imbued with his power. Ray asserts that the body of the Buddha, and by extension the bodies of the saints are "even after death, imbued with enlightened charisma."[32] One may still derive benefits, then, from worshipping reliquary *stūpas* and other sacred objects/places infused with a saint's postmortem charisma. And as Tambiah explains, the charisma of a saint—living or dead—may also be objectified in small portable items such as amulets.[33]

Certainly, there is ample evidence to show that after Mahāmoggallāna's death, cult practices arose that allowed both monks and laity to derive at least some of the benefits that would have accrued from a face-to-face meeting with the saint. According to Faxian, there were in the early fifth century various *stūpa*s at Mathurā that memorialized several of the Buddha's disciples, including Mahāmoggallāna. He reports that there was a yearly ceremony in which various groups of people each made offerings to the *stūpa* of their special disciple, presumably to obtain some facsimile of the powerful qualities that disciple had embodied.[34] Although Faxian does not tell us which group worshipped the *stūpa* of Mahāmoggallāna, Xuanzang's seventh-century account of similar ceremonies at the Mathurā *stūpa*s explains that Mudgalaputra (i.e., Moggallāna) was worshipped by "the Samādhists."[35] One presumes that these devotees—who, incidentally, were monks rather than laypeople—hoped to increase their facility at meditation, and perhaps thereby to acquire supernormal powers. Analogously, in contemporary Rangoon, there is a pagoda with a number of shrines to various disciples, each of which has a sign that "announces," as John Strong puts it, "what each saint is good for." Not unexpectedly, Shin Moggallāna turns out to be good for getting magical powers.[36] From ancient to modern times, then, people have worshipped *stūpa*s and other powerful objects/places associated with Mahāmoggallāna in order to participate in the saint's objectified charisma.

But this does not account for a significant portion of Mahāmoggallāna's legacy—that is, his substantial contribution to the vividly rendered cosmological map of karmic fates. There are at least two ways in which one might try to extend the Weberian analysis of personal charisma to explain this aspect of the saint's continuing influence in modern Southeast Asia, but neither of them is entirely satisfactory.

The first is to attempt to account for the visual culture surrounding Mahāmoggallāna by extending the (already extended) rubric of objectified charisma so that it applies not only to ritually charged objects such as *stūpa*s and amulets, but also to objects more usually described as "art." In this case, one would begin with the hypothesis that images of Phra Malai are infused with the saint's charismatic power, and that viewing them allows one to participate in it. This approach might work for three-dimensional images if ethnographic materials were to show that Southeast Asian Buddhists see Phra Malai in his statues in a manner that parallels the way in which South and Southeast Asian Hindus see (and are seen by) the gods in their images.[37]

However, the vast majority of visual representations of Phra Malai are not three-dimensional images but two-dimensional paintings. Could these, too, be infused with the saint's charismatic power? Something akin to this has already been suggested in relation to medieval Christian art by David Freedberg,[38] who argues that images may be suffused with power by virtue of the fact that they *resemble* their subjects so thoroughly as to create a cognitive slide between image and subject, signifier and signified. In other words, seeing a realistically rendered image is so much like seeing the original person that it has a similar effect. Tambiah explains the efficacy of amulets partially in this way.[39]

But to make this line of argument convincing in relation to temple paintings of Phra Malai, it would be necessary to show that indigenous artists and viewers are deeply concerned that paintings of the saint realistically depict him. While it is not impossible that at least one case of this might exist, and further research is needed, the flat and highly stylized appearance of many of these paintings suggests that this avenue of inquiry will prove less than fully satisfying. And even in the odd case in which resemblance may turn out to be crucial, this would explain only the images of Phra Malai himself, not the elaborate depictions of heavens and hells that figure so prominently in these paintings.

The other way in which one might try to extend Weber's analysis of personal charisma to explain Mahāmoggallāna's continuing influence is to claim that the communal uses of the cosmological schema constitute an institutional routinization of the saint's charisma. Although the theoretical construct of the routinization of charisma is more fully developed in the post-Weberian work of Edward Shils and others, Weber himself makes it clear that personal charisma must be transmuted into institutions in order to survive the death of the charismatic individual. He gives a brief account of the way in which this process—here conceived as a continuous decline—occurred in the history of Buddhism. Early on, "Buddhism's influence beyond the circle of the educated was due to the tremendous prestige traditionally enjoyed by the *śrāmana,* i.e. ascetics, who possessed magical traits of anthropolatry."[40] Certainly, Mahāmoggallāna's propensity for effecting conversions by performing miracles qualifies him as the type of person Weber has in mind. But then Weber goes on to explain how this sort of personal charisma eventually gives way to an institutionalized "popular" religion that substitutes—very imperfectly—for the personal presence of ascetic practitioners. "As soon as Buddhism became a missionizing popular religion, it duly transformed itself into a savior religion based on *karma* compensation, with hopes for the world beyond guaranteed by devotional techniques, cultic and sacramental grace, and deeds of mercy."[41] According to Weber, the "popular" tradition, including the teachings on karma and, by implication, almost the entire Theravāda cosmology, is a kind of lesser substitute for the powerful presence of individuals whose personal charisma derived in part from ascetic, and one might add meditative, practices.

But this clearly cannot work as an explanation of Mahāmoggallāna's legacy, because the evidence does not support Weber's distinction between an early, elite, and pure Buddhism and a later, popular, and degraded Buddhism. Even in the canonical literature, Mahāmoggallāna's extraordinary powers, which are integral to his charismatic presence, are deployed in the service of concretizing what Weber posits as their inferior substitute—that is, a system of ethical norms based on the operations of karma and mapped onto a cosmological scale. In Mahāmoggallāna's case, the vivid portrayal of karmic deeds and their consequences is not a later and lesser substitute for his charismatic presence; it is one of the central reasons that he is charismatic in the first place.

TEACHING AND BUDDHIST SAINTHOOD

If Mahāmoggallāna's legacy cannot be satisfactorily explained by these extensions of the Weberian concept of personal charisma, then what sort of account might one give of it? Recall that Ray lists three things that laypeople may expect to receive from forest saints: in addition to benefits that stem from participating in the personal charisma of the saint, a layperson may also expect to accrue merit from the act of giving *dāna,* and to receive teachings. Initially, I set these latter two items aside because merit and teachings are benefits that can also be obtained from monks who are not saints; to explore these categories of interaction would therefore seem to do little to advance a theoretical discussion of Buddhist sainthood as such. But "teachings" is a very broad category, and it may be possible to arrive at something distinctively saintly by narrowing it a bit.

Ray argues that teachings of saints can be distinguished from the teachings of monastics in the following ways. "The saints teach others, including both human beings and the gods," but they do so without regard for the "scholarly considerations" that attend "textual study."[42] Rather, the saints teach in the context of "oral interchanges between master and followers, both renunciate and lay."[43] Not only do the saints instruct others orally, they also tailor each lesson to a particular audience. "[D]octrine appears less as an abstract and free-standing phenomenon with its own internal logic and more as a clarification of immediate life situations and experience."[44]

Clearly, oral teaching that addresses the particular character and circumstances of the student requires that teacher and student meet face to face. This is also precisely the situation in which it is possible to experience and to participate in the saint's charisma. Ray explicitly states that for a layperson, the face-to-face activity of giving alms provides both the opportunity to participate in the saint's charisma and the opportunity to receive teachings. "[T]he situation of the laity's donation, a source of the forest renunciants' indebtedness, also provides the occasion for their discharging of it through the transmission of their charisma to the laity and through teaching and counseling them at the time of receiving alms."[45] For Ray, it would seem that a saintly teaching is one that is necessarily accompanied by a surge of the saint's personal charisma. With this, we return to the original set of difficulties.

But it is possible to make headway by drawing out the implications of points that Ray makes elsewhere. If, as Ray argues, the intensive practice of meditation is the sine qua non of Buddhist sainthood, then it stands to reason that one criterion of a distinctively saintly teaching is that it be a product of the saint's meditative practice. Obviously, the Buddha's own meditative practice is both the source of and the ultimate warrant of authority for his teachings, and one might expect that the teachings of the saints would be similarly grounded. With minor qualifications, it can be said that the cosmological visions of Mahāmoggallāna are grounded in this way. While the visions themselves are not clearly meditative, the saint's supernormal powers, which make his cosmological travels possible, are derived from and deployed by meditation. The saint's meditative practice is therefore the ultimate, if not the proximate, source of his teachings on karma. As I have shown, the ultimate warrant of authority for these teachings usually derives not from the saint's own meditative experience, but rather from the fact that the lessons are actually delivered by the Buddha himself. But there are also cases in which the Buddha's own visions of karmic states are subsequently validated by Mahāmoggallāna's similar visions. For example, when Mahāmoggallāna sees a *peta* with the body of a man and the head of a pig, the Buddha says: "I also saw this creature as I sat on the Throne of Enlightenment. But I thought to myself, 'Should men not believe me, it would be to their woe.' Therefore, out of compassion for others, I said nothing about it. But now that I have Moggallāna for my witness, I speak the truth boldly."[46]

The second criterion of a distinctively saintly teaching, I would argue, is that it be motivated by compassion. Although Ray identifies compassion as "a central component in the saint's enlightened personality,"[47] he does not explicitly link this component to the teaching activity of the saint. But one of the primary expressions of the Buddha's own compassion is that he agrees to teach, and this creates the expectation that the saints will be similarly inspired. The evidence shows that Mahāmoggallāna's teachings on karma are motivated by compassion: he undertakes his cosmic journeys in order to help make manifest for others what he himself already knows about actions and their karmic consequences. The compassion inherent in this is underscored, I believe, by the saint's own unusually poignant karmic situation. As a disciple of the Buddha, Mahāmoggallāna experiences the fruits of eons of positive actions. But he is also acutely aware of the fact that, despite the nearly innumerable rebirths he has already spent in hell, there remains a heavy, unexpiated karmic residue resulting from a single truly hideous act committed in a life he lived long, long ago. In that life, he killed his mother and father by beating them to death; in this, his final life, he will be beaten to death by robbers before he enters nirvana.[48] It is not unreasonable to suppose that Mahāmoggallāna's particular preoccupation with teaching about the workings of karma might be aimed at least in part at compassionately helping to prevent others from making such a costly mistake.

Although it is certainly an important component of the saintly profile, personal charisma alone cannot account for the variety of ways in which a Theravāda saint may influence his or her community. In order to explain the social relevance of Theravāda saints more fully, it is necessary to explore their role as teachers who compassionately shape their social worlds by making the insights gained in the practice of meditation available to the wider Buddhist community.

NOTES

1. Frank E. Reynolds and Mani B. Reynolds, *Three Worlds According to King Ruang: A Thai Buddhist Cosmology* (Berkeley: Asian Humanities Press/Motilal Banarsidass, 1982).

2. Ibid., 11–13.

3. Ibid., 15.

4. Reginald A. Ray, *Buddhist Saints in India: A Study in Buddhist Values and Orientations* (New York: Oxford University Press, 1994).

5. F. L. Woodward and E. M. Hare, tr., *The Book of Gradual Sayings (Anguttara Nikaya) or More Numbered Suttas*, vol. 1 (London: Pali Text Society, 1932–36), 16–25.

6. Ray, *Buddhist Saints in India,* 90.

7. T. W. Rhys Davids and William Stede, eds., *The Pali Text Society's Pali-English Dictionary* (London: Pali Text Society, 1986), 64.

8. Eugene Watson Burlingame, tr., *Buddhist Legends,* vol. 3 (London, 1921; reprint, Luzac & Company, Ltd., 1969), 44–45.

9. André Migot, "Un grand disciple du Buddha: Śāriputra," *Bulletin de l'École Française d'Extrême-Orient* 46, 2 (1954): 447, 503ff., 509. Cited in Ray, *Buddhist Saints in India,* 133.

10. Ray, *Buddhist Saints in India,* 87.

11. Ibid., 90.

12. Ibid., 87.

13. Burlingame, *Buddhist Legends,* vol. 3, 65.

14. Ibid.

15. Ibid., 65–66.

16. Burlingame, *Buddhist Legends,* vol. 2, 305.

17. Peter Masefield, tr., *Elucidation of the Intrinsic Meaning: so named The Commentary on the Vimāna Stories* (Oxford: Pali Text Society, 1989), 6.

18. I. B. Horner, trs., "*Vimānavatthu*: Stories of the Mansions" in *The Minor Anthologies of the Pali Canon,* part IV, Sacred Books of the Buddhists, vol. XXX (London: Pali Text Society, 1974), 2–4.

19. For a description of the means and ends of visualization-inspection meditation, see Julian F. Pas, *Visions of Sukhāvatī: Shan-tao's Commentary on the Kuan Wu-Liang-Shou-Fo Ching* (Albany: State University of New York Press, 1995), 163–78.

20. Horner, "Vimānavatthu," 3.

21. Masefield, *Elucidation of the Intrinsic Meaning,* 5.

22. Burlingame, *Buddhist Legends,* vol. 3, 93.

23. Burlingame, *Buddhist Legends,* vol. 2, 139–40.

24. Ibid.

25. J. J. Jones, trans., *The Mahāvastu* (London: Luzac and Co., 1949), 6–21.

26. Bonnie Pacala Brereton, *Thai Tellings of Phra Malai: Texts and Rituals Concerning a Popular Buddhist Saint* (Tempe: Arizona State University Press, 1995), 123–24, 189.

27. It should be mentioned, however, that to provide a complete genealogy, it would be necessary to examine Chinese sources as well as those in Pali and Sanskrit.

28. Brereton, *Thai Tellings of Phra Malai,* 110.

29. Ray, *Buddhist Saints in India,* 436.

30. Ibid., 23–24, 44, 437.

31. Stanley Jeyaraja Tambiah, *The Buddhist Saints of the Forest and the Cult of Amulets: A Study in Charisma, Hagiography, Sectarianism, and Millenial Buddhism.* Cambridge Studies in Social Anthropology, no. 49 (Cambridge: Cambridge University Press, 1984), 76.

32. Ray, *Buddhist Saints in India,* 58.

33. Tambiah, *The Buddhist Saints of the Forest and the Cult of Amulets,* 335–36.

34. James Legge, *A Record of the Buddhistic Kingdoms: being an account by the Chinese Monk Fa-Hien of his travels in India and Ceylon (A.D. 399–414) in search of the Buddhist Books of Discipline* (Oxford: Clarendon Press, 1886; reprint, New York: Dover Publications, 1965), 44–46.

35. Thomas Waters, *On Yuan Chwang's Travels in India,* vol. 1, ed. T. W. Rhys Davids and S. W. Bushell (London, 1904; reprint, Delhi, 1961), 302.

36. John S. Strong, *The Legend and Cult of Upagupta: Sanskrit Buddhism in North India and Southeast Asia* (Princeton: Princeton University Press, 1992), 144.

37. See Diana L. Eck, *Darśan: Seeing the Divine in India* (Chambersburg, PA: Anima Books, 1981).

38. David Freedberg, *The Power of Images: Studies in the History and Theory of Response* (Chicago: University of Chicago Press, 1989).

39. Tambiah, *The Buddhist Saints of the Forest and the Cult of Amulets,* 230–42.

40. Max Weber, *The Sociology of Religion,* tr. Ephraim Fischoff (Boston: Beacon Press, 1963), 268.

41. Ibid.

42. Ray, *Buddhist Saints in India,* 91–92.

43. Ibid., 92.

44. Ibid.

45. Ibid., 437.

46. Burlingame, *Buddhist Legends,* vol. 3, 153.

47. Ray, *Buddhist Saints in India,* 90.

48. Burlingame, *Buddhist Legends,* vol. 2, 304–308.

FIVE

WHEN THE BUDDHA SUED VIṢṆU

Jacob N. Kinnard

SETTING THE STAGE

CONTEMPORARY BODHGAYĀ presents a decidedly polyvalent scene, with all sorts of variations and permutations of tourism and religious praxis on display: around the Mahābodhi temple and its environs co-mingle American and European tourists, Tibetan, Japanese, and Burmese Buddhists, Śaiva *sannyāsins,* Vaiṣṇava pilgrims, each responding to and interacting with the same images in sometimes very different ways. Only one hundred years ago, however, Bodhgayā would have been a very different place, and although there may well have been crowds, the crowds would have been distinctly more homogenous than they are today. Indeed, of the various groups and individuals that gather at the temple complex today, probably only the Śaivas and the Vaiṣṇavas would have been present a century ago. This paper examines how this transformation in the make-up of Bodhgayā's religious and cultural community has come about, and in particular, the ways in which the various individuals and groups who make up that community have altered and redefined both their relationships with one another as well as their self-identities as part of the process of community formation. I begin with what is at least in appearance the most significant moment in the process.

On May 28, 1953, a ceremony was held at Bodhgayā marking the formal transfer of control of the Mahābodhi Temple, the site of Śākyamuni's enlightenment, from the Śaiva Mahant, Harihar Giri—whose lineage of *sannyāsins* had overseen the temple complex for nearly four hundred years—to the Mahābodhi Temple Management Committee. Assembled together on that day were Buddhist monks from Sri Lanka, Burma, Cambodia, Tibet, and India; Śaiva *sannyāsins* from Bodhgayā's *math;* the nine members of the Committee itself (four Buddhists, five Hindus); various government officials, foreign dignitaries, and influential Hindu and Buddhist lay people; and a sizable crowd of local Hindus and Muslims.[1] During the ceremony, Sanskrit verses were recited by one of the *math*'s brahmin priests; a *bhikkhu* from the Mahābodhi society recited the *tiratana* in Pāli; a popular Indian singer performed two *bhajans* (in Hindi) in praise of Viṣṇu; felicitations from Jawaharlal Nehru, the Sri Lankan prime minister, the Mahārāja of Sikkhim, and others, were read aloud; and, finally, an employee of the Bihar Education Department read passages from Edwin Arnold's epic poem, *The Light of Asia*.

On the surface, this was a stunningly ecumenical moment, bringing together not only individuals and groups with different and heretofore competing interests and conceptions of Bodhgayā—Śaivas, Buddhists, Vaiṣṇavas, government officials—but also very different factions within the Buddhist world. The obvious question, then, is how did this apparent moment of *communitas* come about after what had been many years of acrimony at Bodhgayā? And, perhaps more importantly, what did this coming together signify? Was this indeed the realization of Arnold's vision of Bodhgayā as the place where, as he put it, "a million oriental congregations" would come together?[2]

The answer to such questions are, predictably, complex, but one thing that can be said at the outset is that this apparent moment of unity seems to bear little resemblance to the *communitas* described by Victor Turner, the "spontaneously generated relationship between leveled and equal total and individuated human beings, stripped of structural attributes. . . ."[3] Certainly, the group gathered to mark the transfer of control of Bodhgayā could be said to represent a single community, a pan-Asian religious community with its roots in India: in this they would appear to be both "leveled" and "equal," and the very fact that they were gathered together seems to indicate a certain "stripping" of their individual identities, and the formation of what Turner describes as a "comity of comrades and not a structure of hierarchically arrayed positions."[4] However, there was virtually nothing spontaneous about the relationships between the individuals who seemed to constitute the single community represented that day at Bodhgayā. Rather, this was a highly orchestrated and tensely negotiated single moment, and must be seen not so much as a conclusion but as simply one act in an ongoing drama being played out at Bodhgayā, a long process of intentionally constructed definitions and redefinitions of the different communities that had a stake in the place.

Furthermore, when we look beyond the single moment, at the actual process of communal definition that led up to it, one thing that becomes clear is that the definition of a religious community is not merely a matter of how that particular community constitutes itself, internally—as I think is implicit in Turner's discussions of liminality and *communitas* in the context of pilgrimage—but also of how it is conceived of and constituted by those who do not belong to it. What we see played out at Bodhgayā over the last one hundred years conforms to what Vasudha Dalmia and Heinrich von Stietencron have called, describing specifically the construction of Hindu identity in India, "a growing tendency towards ingroup-outgroup polarization," which "has resulted in most communities in a negative projection of the 'Other' against which the self is set off and defined."[5] Thus, although there was in the last quarter of the nineteenth century the construction of a new understanding of the Buddhist community centered on Bodhgayā, one that was both international and nonsectarian, this new communal vision was not a wholly internal matter, but was in part constituted by various orientalist conceptions of Buddhism, and, in part, constituted by this very community's sometimes vitriolic rejection of Hinduism.[6] Likewise, we see the Hindu community at Bodhgayā redefining itself, in part influenced by how it was portrayed by the Buddhists and colonial administrators during the protracted legal wrangling over control of the temple, during which the courts on a number of occasions defined, delineated, and divided Hinduism. Finally, we see these two separate communities, the Buddhist and the Hindu, redefining themselves again, not as two but as one, and this in response to both the introduction of a (largely foreign) "brotherhood of religions" motif into the Bodhgayā discourse, and also to the growing political discourse of "Indianness" that gains momentum at around the time of Independence.

ACT ONE: BUDDHISM REDISCOVERS ITS CENTER (AND RECONSTRUCTS ITS OTHER)

In the early years of the nineteenth century, the British East India Company began to show a new interest in the people and culture of the regions of North Eastern India, and in 1807 the Court of Directors of the Company commissioned Francis Buchanan to "inquire" into the habits and conditions of the people (and, while he was at it, to survey the resources of the country as well).[7] Part of this massive project, which took seven years to complete,[8] was a survey of what is now Bihar, which Buchanan visited in 1811–12. Although this was the birthplace of Buddhism, Buchanan records that in the entire region he had encountered only one indigenous Buddhist,[9] and this a former Śaiva *sannyāsin* who had been converted by two Burmese Buddhists on pilgrimage to Bodhgayā.[10] On its face, there is nothing particularly surprising about this absence of Buddhists; Bodhgayā had been essentially abandoned by Buddhists since the twelfth century, except for sporadic visits by foreign monks on pilgrimage,[11] and those of various groups of Sri Lankan and Burmese monks working to restore and maintain the temple.[12] What is surprising, however, is that only seventy-five years later, Edwin Arnold would, in a series of articles about his 1886 pilgrimage to India published in the *London Daily Telegraph,* describe what seemed to be hordes of Buddhist pilgrims, "wending their way to the immeasurably holy place towards which we also are bound."[13] If both accounts are correct, then the number of Buddhists *in situ* had increased from one to a multitude in only seventy years. Thus, given that this purported growth in the Buddhist population of Bihar seems nothing short of miraculous, a closer examination of the context of Arnold's account is in order.

It was these articles, and not his more famous *Light of Asia,* that were the impetus of what became a kind of Buddhist revival centered at Bodhgayā, for as Anagarika Dharmapala, the most prominent of the Buddhists acting at Bodhgayā, would later write: "The idea of restoring the Buddhist Jerusalem into Buddhist hands originated with Sir Edwin Arnold after having visited the shrine, and since 1891 I have done all I could to make the Buddhists of all lands interested in the scheme of restoration."[14] The attempts to restore Buddhism to Bodhgayā, and the conflict that ensued between 1886 and the eventual handover of control of the temple in 1953, have been well documented,[15] but two intertwined aspects of Dharmapala's statement warrant further thought here: the idea that Bodhgayā needed to be returned *from* the Hindus, and that it then would become the domain of *"Buddhists of all lands."* I will discuss the first of these in this section, and the second in the third part of this essay, "Hinduism, Buddhism, and *Sanātana Dharma.*"

At the time of Arnold's visit, Bodhgayā had been occupied by a lineage of Śaiva ascetics, the Giris, who traced their inhabitancy of the temple to the late sixteenth century, when Gosain Ghamandi Giri, according to Śaiva histories,[16] arrived at the abandoned temple complex. He was then succeeded by Caitanya Giri (1615–42), who was succeeded by Mahādeva Giri, who is said to have set up the *math* that is still in existence after having received a grant from Shah Alum.[17] According to Rajendralala Mitra, there were between fifty and one hundred *sannyāsins* at the *math* at the end of the nineteenth century,[18] although Buchanan records that there were thousands,[19] an almost certain inflation and a significant negative mirror image to his report that there was only one Buddhist to be found.[20] At any rate, it is certain that there were virtually no Buddhists in residence, and this greatly upset Arnold: "I was grieved to see Mahratta peasants performing 'Shraddh' in such a place and thousands of precious ancient relics of carved stone inscribed with Sanskrit lying in piles around. . . . Buddha-Gaya is the most dear and sacred to Asiatic Buddhists.

Why, then, is it to-day in the hands of Brahman priests, who do not care about the temple, except for the credit of owning it, and for the fees which they draw?"[21] Arnold proposed that Bodhgayā be returned to the Buddhists, so that it could once again become "what it should be, the living and learned centre of purified Buddhism. . . ."[22]

If, then, Arnold's *Daily Telegraph* piece is taken to be the beginning of an attempt to restore not only Bodhgayā, but Buddhism itself, it becomes apparent that at the center of this discourse is not, in fact, the *axis mundi* of Bodhgayā, but rather a vilified Hindu Other. This anti-Hindu/pro-Buddhist dichotomy was not new to either colonial or orientalist discourse, and to a degree Arnold was merely replicating a general characterization of Hinduism, in contrast to Buddhism, that had been in the air for at least a century.[23] Buchanan, for instance, although he could not exactly be characterized as a champion of Buddhism,[24] portrayed Buddhism as possessing an ethical system that was "perhaps as good as that put forth by any of the religious doctrines prevailing among mankind";[25] Hinduism, by contrast, he describes as "the most abominable, and degrading system of oppression, ever invented by the craft of designing men."[26] Similarly, other influential Westerners who wrote about Bodhgayā in the early nineteenth century had little positive to say about Hinduism. Alexander Cunningham wrote of "the menaces of the most powerful and arrogant priesthood in the world."[27] In the same vein, Rajendralala Mitra described the Śaivas this way: "The monks lead an easy, comfortable life; feasting on rich cakes *(malpulya)* and puddings *(mohanbhog),* and freely indulging in the exhilarating beverage of *bhanga*. Few attempt to learn the sacred books of their religion, and most of them are grossly ignorant."[28]

In comparison to these administrators and scholars, Arnold himself was relatively moderate in his views of Hinduism, and seemed to be at least tentatively respectful of the Mahant and his Śaiva followers, writing that, "I think the Mahunt a good man. I had never wished any but friendly and satisfactory arrangements with him."[29] However, Arnold also felt that the only reason that the Hindus were at Bodhgayā at all was to collect fees from Vaiṣṇavas who came as part of their *śraddhā* rituals centered at nearby Gayā—a fairly typical view of the "wily Brahmin." Thus, in his view, they were outsiders who did not belong, and in a letter to Sir Arthur Gordon, Governor of Ceylon, appealing for assistance in the restoration of Bodhgayā, Arnold complains that "Buddha-Gaya is occupied by a college of Saivite priests, who worship Mahadeva there, and deface the shrine with emblems and rituals foreign to its nature."[30] This last phrase is extremely important, for it raises what would become perhaps the most central question in the growing storm over control of Bodhgayā, the question of origins, a discourse that resonated with what had become an incredibly powerful and persuasive argument in the late nineteenth- and early twentieth-century British intellectual milieu, the basic belief that if one could uncover the origins of a given phenomenon, then one would also uncover the essence of the thing itself (witness Max Müller's influence on the study of religion).[31]

This is also, of course, an issue that is intimately related to the nineteenth-century construction of an original, purified Buddhism. The Buddha was viewed, as Gregory Schopen has put it, as a "kind of sweetly reasonable Victorian Gentleman,"[32] and Buddhism was seen as rational, ethical, devoid of superstition and ritual—the exact opposite of the simultaneous Western construction of Hinduism.[33] Furthermore, because Bodhgayā represented the font of Buddhism, what Aśvaghoṣa referred to in the second century as "the navel of the world,"[34] and what Arnold celebrated as the Buddhist Mecca and Jerusalem,[35] the presence of the Hindu Other was all the more offensive. In sum, then, what we see in discussions about Bodhgayā in the latter part of the nineteenth century is not only a discursive polarization of Hinduism and Buddhism that had been developing since orientalists in the early eighteenth century had first realized that they were different traditions, but the construction of a Hindu Other who had usurped the Buddhists' rightful place of origins. Thus, the Śaivas who effectively owned the temple, and the Vaiṣṇavas who came there to worship, were portrayed by the non-Indians who opined on the matter as outsiders, *mlecchas* in their own country, polluting the birthplace of Buddhism. What is more, we see evidence of this not only in the derisive comments of the orientalist experts whose work informed Dharmapala and the others who championed the Buddhist position, but also in Western visual representations of the site. Thus, the Indians who would have been present at Bodhgayā (in other words, the Hindus) were all but absent from the drawings and paintings of the temple and its environs that were created by Western artists for a Western audience eager for images of the mystical Orient; as Janice Leoshko has noted, "For the Indians included in such views, their presence is at best cursory, decorating the magnificent monuments which were so admired by those of the picturesque persuasion."[36] This can be seen in virtually all of the popular drawings produced by Charles D'Oyly in the 1820s and 1830s, and in another set of illustrations, *Oriental Annual, or Scenes from India,* by William Danell, the accompanying text describes the temple as "entirely deserted so that a scene of gloomy desolation is at the forsaken sanctuary."[37] But as much as the Western champions of Bodhgayā tried to exclude them from the site, the Hindu Other proved rather more difficult to avoid on the ground, and when attempts were made to remove them, they proved to be far more active and far more vocal than the indolent natives in Mitra's writings and D'Oyly's drawings.

Act Two: Taking It to the Courts

From the time of the publication of Arnold's *Light of Asia* in 1871, various attempts were made by Arnold, Dharmapala, and other Buddhists to gain control of Bodhgayā, all to no avail. Dharmapala, in particular, became increasingly impatient with the status quo, and after trying to persuade the Mahanth to sell the Mahābodhi temple, he resolved to take matters into his own hands, and in the process brought things to a dramatic boiling point on the morning of February 25, 1895, when he attempted to install a bronze Buddha image in the Mahābodhi temple.[38] The image that Dharmapala set up in the Mahābodhi temple did not stay there for very long, however; shortly after it was placed on the altar it was removed by a group of the Mahant's followers and rather unceremoniously dumped on the temple lawn.

Dharmapala, outraged at the way he and the Buddha image had been treated, pressed criminal charges against the Mahant and his followers, charges that included defiling the Buddhist religion, disturbing a religious gathering, and using criminal force—all of which rested upon the assumption that the Buddhists held some basic rights of worship at Bodhgayā.[39] Although Dharmapala's lawyer, Nanda Kishan Lall, opened the case for the prosecution by stating that the "question of who is the proprietor of the Temple . . . is quite irrelevant to this case,"[40] it was precisely this issue that was, in fact, at stake.

The legal wrangling over the proprietorship of Bodhgayā largely revolved around two issues: whether it was the Buddhists or the Śaiva Mahant who could rightfully claim control of the temple complex, and what sorts of worship were appropriately directed toward the Buddha image. The latter issue, one might think, would also intimately involve the Vaiṣṇava community, since it was they who had for centuries been making the short trip from nearby Gayā as part of their extended *śraddhā* rites, and it was they who venerated Bodhgayā's Buddha images as part of the long-standing tradition in Vaiṣṇava circles of responding to Buddha images as Viṣṇu's ninth avatāra. In fact, however, the issue of the Vaiṣṇavas' right to venerate the Buddha image was rather quickly dealt with in the initial court proceedings, and, as we shall see below, it would not be until the 1930s that the Vaiṣṇavas would begin to have a substantive voice in Bodhgayā's religious community.

The Buddhist prosecution offered what was essentially a twofold argument. First, since the government of India had neutral guardianship over the temple as an ancient monument,[41] the Buddhists, as a legitimate religious group under government protection, had the right to worship at the temple, a right clearly denied by the Mahant's aggressive removal of Dharmapala's Buddha image. As Lall, the lead prosecutor, put it, it was "the long-standing right of every Buddhist to worship and perform any ceremony in accordance with the tenets of his religion in the Temple, and neither Government nor the Mahanth is entitled to prevent the full exercise of that right."[42] Second, Lall argued that the Giris could not contend—as they continuously had in the period leading up to the trial, and as they would repeatedly during the trial itself—that they had removed the Buddha image in order to protect their own religious worship because, according to Lall, no Hindus had ever worshiped there.[43] Indeed, argued Lall, it was agreed upon by any number of the authorities that Bodhgayā was a Buddhist site in both origin and in contemporary practice, and he brought forth several witnesses to testify that they did not worship there because it was not a Hindu temple and to do so would be to defile themselves. Furthermore, he called the custodian of the temple, Bepin Behari, to testify, who said that not only did Hindus not worship there, but that he had actually heard brahmin priests on several occasions forbid Hindus from even entering the temple.

The Śaiva defense, for its part, put forth a number of counterarguments, some of which attempted to establish the Giri's long-standing legal ownership at the temple, and they offered as evidence the fact that government officials had felt it necessary to consult with the Mahanth before allowing the Burmese to begin renovations of the temple in 1877. Furthermore, they asserted that Dharmapala himself had recognized this ownership when he and the Mahābodhi society attempted to purchase the Mahābodhi temple from the Mahant; if he had not thought that the Mahant owned the temple, then why had Dharmapala made such an offer? As additional proof, the Mahant's lawyers put forth a significant amount of textual evidence to prove that the Buddha was in fact an *avatāra* of Viṣṇu, in an attempt to establish that the Buddha image did not really belong to the Buddhists at all.[44]

This last argument may seem self-defeating, given that the trial centered on the Hindus' *removal* of the Buddha image (which was, according to such logic, not a Buddha image at all, but a Viṣṇu *mūrti*). However, the Mahant and his legal team were attempting to legitimize their own religious—as opposed to proprietary—rights in order to establish that Dharmapala, as a Buddhist, himself had no rights to worship in a Hindu temple. Most of the defense's evidence was, as one would expect, based on the Vaiṣṇava textual tradition—notably, the *Bhagavata, Agni,* and *Vāyu purāṇas*—as well as scholarly studies by orientalists such as Alexander Cunningham, J. D. Beglar, and Rajendralala Mitra, which attested to the very old Hindu presence at the temple.[45] The defense also cross-examined the prosecution's witness, the temple manager Behari, and got him to admit that Hindus did, in fact, bow down before the Bodhi tree and the Buddha image in the main part of the temple (although he did stipulate that the latter practice had begun only recently).

As might be expected, the argument over the essential nature of the figure of the Buddha proved to be a slippery legal slope, for although it is true that from a Hindu point of view the Buddha *avatāra* had defeated the enemies of Hinduism and restored *dharma,* for the Buddhists the *avatāra* discourse was nothing but a bold-faced polemical attack on Buddhism;[46] in other words, from the perspective of the Buddhists and their orientalist sympathizers, this was incontrovertible evidence of Brahmanical hegemony at its worst. Thus, in raising the Buddha as *avatāra* issue, the Mahant's legal representatives opened themselves up to a blistering rebuttal from not only Dharmapala's lawyers, but also from the judge himself, who was already predisposed against the Hindus, and viewed this claim as nothing more than an obfuscating ploy, a smokescreen intended to hide their duplicity and greed. Indeed, in a stunningly partisan and dismissive remark, George Macpherson, the local magistrate who heard the case, pronounced that the purported Hindu bowing down before the Buddha image was, "I dare say, of no more significance than my taking off my hat, as I do, when I enter the sanctum."[47]

But the slope proved to be even more treacherous than merely raising doubts as to the credibility and objectivity of the evidence. When the defense argued that the existing Buddha image in the first floor of the Mahābodhi temple was indeed venerated as Viṣṇu (Dharmapala, it is worth noting, had attempted to install the Japanese image in the empty sanctuary on the second floor of the temple), the prosecution countered by denouncing this as nothing more than an attempt to influence the court's decision based on a recent innovation instituted by the scheming Mahant—and here Behari's testimony under cross-examination proved to be a nasty double-edged sword—in order to create the appearance of Hindu worship in the Mahābodhi, and therefore the precedent of normal and customary worship, which gave them certain legal rights, when in fact no such worship had ever been performed until the Buddhists began to claim a right to the temple. Furthermore, the prosecution argued that even if the Buddha image in the Mahābodhi were venerated as a Viṣṇu *mūrti,* as a Śaiva the Mahant had no business regulating such a temple, since it was only Vaiṣṇava theology that recognized the Buddha. Edwin Arnold himself had already raised this issue years earlier, when the Buddhists had unsuccessfully attempted to purchase the Mahābodhi temple from the Mahant, arguing that the Mahant could sell the temple to the Buddhists without offending the sentiments of any Hindus, because, Arnold explained, "by strict truth, the Mahunt, as a Brahman and follower of Sankaracharya [in other words, a Śaiva], goes against his shastras" by keeping control of what might be regarded as a Viṣṇu temple.[48]

Magistrate Macpherson for his part accepted none of the defense's argument, and he echoed Arnold's logic almost exactly when he pronounced:

"If in any case, it was felt expedient to endeavor to establish Vaisnavite worship of Buddha Bhagavan at Mahabodhi, it was an anomaly for the Mahanth, a Śaivite, to set himself up as its founder."[49] This pronouncement became a crucial moment in the establishment of Bodhgayā's community, because, in effect, the judge was asserting that if Hindus had any legitimate religious interest in the temple, only a particular kind of Hindu could claim such interest: namely, the Vaiṣṇavas. And since the Vaiṣṇavas themselves were not, in fact, staking any claim to the temple, Buddhist rights to the temple were, by default, *prima facie* valid. It is important here to stress that Macpherson was explicitly avoiding the issue of legal ownership of the temple; his opinions were, ironically enough, limited to the religious status of Bodhgayā, and to him it was clear that nothing put forth by the defense altered the essentially Buddhistic nature of the temple. However, in his final remarks on the case, Macpherson went so far as to denounce the "semblance of Hindu worship" performed by a priest who "passes a light in front of the image, sounds bells and laves the image and altar,"[50] and he castigated the Mahant for the ploy, which he saw as a mere "strategem for giving him a pretext for interfering with the dealings of the Buddhists in the Temple and strengthening whatever prescriptive rights he may possess to the usufruct of the offering made at the Temple."[51] Not surprisingly, Macpherson found the Mahant's followers guilty of interfering with Dharmapala's lawfully assembled religious congregation; he sentenced them to one month each in jail and fined each one hundred rupees.

In this first trial, there can be no doubt that Macpherson was highly biased; indeed, on the day that Dharmapala placed the Amitābha image in the Mahābodhi temple, Macpherson himself had been summoned (by the Mahant, ironically enough), and upon arriving on the scene was said to have remarked that "a great desecration has been committed," in the Mahant's followers' removal of the image.[52] By contrast, when the Viceroy, Lord Elgin, came to Bodhgayā shortly after Dharmapala's image had been removed—a testimony to the potential volatility that the Government of India saw in the situation—he had expressed the hope that an amicable solution could be found, although he himself felt that the Buddhists' rights to worship in the temple must be protected. He stressed, however, the need for a solution that would also protect the Mahant's rights, and noted that a certain amount of tact would be required, since, as he put it, "on some of the minor points of religious controversy a wrong word might be very unfortunate." The Lieutenant-Governor of Bengal, Gilbert Elgin, who seemed to be acquainted with magistrate Macpherson's opinions on Indian religions, was not convinced that he would be capable of such tact: "I am afraid that Macpherson does not take quite the same view of his [the Mahant's] rights as I do."[53]

When the new Mahant, Hem Narayan Giri, appealed the case in June 1895, it was not heard at the local level, but in the Sessions Court at Gayā, and the judge in that venue, Herbert Holmwood, was quick to castigate Macpherson for his impartial meddling, which he perhaps too charitably described as "a good deal of unnecessary animadversion on Mr. Macpherson's assumed unconscious bias in the matter."[54] Holmwood, however, was also not impressed with the Mahant's defense, and in particular took issue with the defense's insistence that their legitimate and long-standing religious rights had been threatened by Dharmapala's action. On appeal, the defense explained that in removing the Buddha image, the Śaivas were only protecting their own right of worship. Holmwood, however, agreed with the prosecution that Dharmapala's right to worship had been blocked by the removal of the Amitābha image, and thus disregarded the Śaiva's claims.

In particular, Holmwood singled out the current Mahant's offer to place Dharmapala's image back in the Mahābodhi, but only if it first underwent the *prāṇapratiṣṭhā* ritual, an offer that was rejected by the Buddhists outright.[55] This was a remarkable gesture on the Mahant's part, and it is difficult to discern Hem Narayan Giri's precise motives in making it. Was he suggesting that the image could at once represent the Buddha and at the same time embody Viṣṇu? If so, this would have been a striking recognition on his part of the inherently polyvalent identity of sculptural images in India, and, in particular, at Bodhgayā.[56] This was not, at any rate, how Holmwood interpreted the offer; he said that when the Mahant expressed his willingness to enshrine the image, "whatever his theories may be as to Buddha being an avatar of Vishnu, he must thereby have intended to prevent Buddhists from ever offering impure articles of food, candles, scent, etc.," this because the Hindus found the kinds of things offered by the Buddhists to the Buddha image (as part of the ritual installation performed by Dharmapala and company)—Huntley and Palmer's biscuits, candles of lard, cheap English eau-de-cologne—to be utterly impure, and therefore unacceptable in a Hindu temple.[57] In other words, the Mahant was, according to the judge, trying to prevent Buddhist worship of the Buddha image on the grounds that any such worship would be offensive and polluting to the Hindu community. Notice, however, that in contrast to Macpherson and his "assumed unconscious bias," Holmwood went to considerable lengths to avoid any judgment of the validity or appropriateness of a particular form of worship.

In the end, the conviction was upheld, although Holmwood suspended the jail terms (but let the fines stand). The defendants again appealed, this time in the Calcutta High Court, and the case was heard before Goroo Das Banerjee and Justice William Macpherson (no relation to the magistrate George). The latter specifically addressed the question of whether the Mahant, as a

Hindu, had any right to interfere with Buddhist worship at Bodhgayā; but like Holmwood, this new Justice Macpherson made a point to avoid any pronouncements on the religious aspects of the matter, and held that because the case at hand was a criminal one, "No such broad questions arise."[58] Instead, he focused on the issue of proprietorship, and found that it was clear that the Mahant "held 'possession' of the Temple and had control and superintendence over it, subject to the right of Buddhists to worship there."[59] He raised the real possibility that Dharmapala's veneration of the image, just after he had installed it, might not, in fact, have been genuine—and might have simply been intended, as the defense alleged, to incite the Mahant's followers—but he refused further speculation on the matter. However, according to the High Court, Dharmapala's actions had to be seen in the larger context of his motives and attitudes toward the Mahant and his community, which were clearly the eventual removal of the Śaivas (and here Dharmapala's own writings, including his diaries, were brought into the discussion).[60] In this context, his veneration of the recently installed (and soon to be removed) image of Amitābha did not, contra his lawyers' claims, constitute normal or customary worship at Bodhgayā. Instead, Macpherson focused on the fact that the legal proprietor of the temple, the Mahant, had explicitly refused Dharmapala permission to install the image (although he had never refused him admission to the temple, nor the right to worship there). Thus, Macpherson concluded: "They went to enshrine an image in a place where they had no right to enshrine it."[61] As such, the removal of the image on the part of the Hindus was justified. He then set aside the original conviction, although this would prove to be merely a brief intermission.

ACT THREE: HINDUISM, BUDDHISM, AND *SANĀTANA DHARMA*

It had taken three years to resolve the case between Dharmapala and the Mahant, far longer than anyone had foreseen; however, given the years that the issue would continue to simmer and occasionally boil over, with what seemed to be an unending succession of suits and countersuits being filed every few years, this was in hindsight a speedily resolved dispute. Indeed, it took another fifty years to settle the issue, to get to the ecumenical moment with which I began this essay, and even then, as I have earlier suggested, it would be hard to see the handover of control of the temple to the Bodhgayā Temple Management Committee as anything like closure.[62] Nonetheless, it is perhaps surprising, given the discomposed and acrimonious state of things in 1896, that such a sharing of the stage could ever be affected at all: the Buddhist and Śaiva communities were openly hostile toward each other, the Vaiṣṇavas were without a voice, and the government had managed to alienate and offend virtually everyone involved with its open disdain for the Mahant and its ruling against the Buddhists.[63]

During the period after the ruling against the Buddhists, Dharmapala's authority in the matter was greatly diminished, and although he continued to be involved in Bodhgayā until his death in 1933, with his removal to the wings the tenor of the discourse over the constitution of Bodhgayā's community changed dramatically. Trevithick has suggested that a pivotal figure in this change was Kakuzo Okakura, a Japanese intellectual who brought his hybridized Buddhist vision—as much influenced by Vivekananda's neo-Vedanta and Tagore's humanism as by anything contained in the Pāli canon—to Bodhgayā in 1903.[64] Although I am somewhat skeptical as to the particular influence that Okakura had on the debate, simply because it is impossible to tell exactly what he said to whom,[65] he does stand, at the very least, as an important figure symbolically, because his rhetoric seems to bring together the hitherto hostile factions at Bodhgayā into a single Asian brotherhood with a mutual understanding and commitment to the true *dharma,* a discourse that was, as Trevithick rightly notes, strikingly similar to the theosophical vision put forth by Dharmapala himself, prior to his break with Olcott.[66] The different Asian religions, sects, and subsects were, in Okakura's opinion, just so many offspring of a single mother: "The great Vedantic revival of Sankaracharyya is the assimilation of Buddhism, and its emergence in a new dynamic form. And now, in spite of the separation of ages, Japan is drawn closer than ever to the motherland of thought."[67] The question, however, was whether or not the mother would recognize, let alone embrace, this particular child.

Okakura had come to Bodhgayā specifically to ask the Mahant for a small plot of land and permission to build a resthouse for Japanese pilgrims; although the Mahant was at the time engaged in another legal fight with the Mahābodhi Society (he wanted to evict the Sri Lankans from the Burmese resthouse), he was happy to grant Okakura's request.[68] The government of Bengal, however, was not so willing, and refused to grant the Japanese a building permit, professing that there was no need for another resthouse at Bodhgayā, and that the further "multiplication of interest there is undesirable."[69] Although on its face this was a relatively small matter, it represents an important development in the formation of Bodhgayā's religious community. On the one hand, it marks a growing reluctance on the part of the government to meddle in matters of religion at Bodhgayā, perhaps because the colonial administrators had learned from the earlier trial what a tangled mess the issue of proper religious practice could become. From this point on, in fact, the government would officially maintain this policy of neutrality in religious questions. On the other hand, however, the refusal of the permit to the Japanese is indicative of the government's desire to avoid sectarian disputes and to promote a certain ecumenical spirit amongst the religious communities of India. However, rather than Okakura's very broad pan-Asianism, it was vested in a nonsectarian pan-Indianism, and thus the community that was envisioned at Bodhgayā quite explicitly excluded the Chinese, Japanese, and Tibetan Buddhists, since they did not fall within the political control of the British Empire.[70] The Burmese, who had been an active presence at Bodhgayā, would also eventually be excluded from this community when Burma ceased to fall under the administration of British India in 1935.

Thus, what we see developing at Bodhgayā in the early part of the twentieth century is a new sort of community, a single community that is not now defined primarily by its individual components of Hinduism and Buddhism, but by Indianness, and we see both Hindus and Buddhists expressing the same commitment to this new Indian Brotherhood.[71] As early as 1911, Nanda Kishan Lall—who, recall, had in his represention of Dharmapala in his suit against the Mahant shown little restraint in his anti-Hindu rhetoric—describes the mutual admiration for Bodhgayā: "Nor does the Hindu of the day look upon it with any less reverence than the Buddhists."[72] And one of the most prominent Indian intellectuals of the period, Rabindranath Tagore, expressed great sympathy with the Buddhist cause: "I am sure it will be admitted by all Hindus who are true to their own ideals that it is an intolerable wrong to allow the temple raised on the site where Lord Buddha attained His enlightenment to remain under the control of a rival sect. . . . I consider it to be a sacred duty for all individuals believing in freedom and justice to help to restore this historical site to the community of people who will reverently carry on that particular current of history in their own living faith."[73] Even Dharmapala himself got in on the Indian brotherhood act, however grudgingly: "To the Buddhists the Lord Buddha is the Supreme One. The Hindus have many devatas to receive their worship. The Buddhists do not worship Vishnu; neither do they worship Siva. But Ceylon Buddhists hold Vishnu as the patron God of Ceylon."[74] Thus, the Buddhist representatives at the Indian National Congress, although still requesting Buddhist priority at the temple, appealed to their Hindu kin: "[W]ill not our Hindu Brothers join hands with us and give us our shrine, at which all are free to worship."[75] And finally, in a 1935 article in the *Journal of the Mahābodhi Society*, the Hindu-Buddhist cooperation in the matter of control of Bodhgayā was praised, and an appeal to their shared conception of true *dharma* was made: "The session also demonstrated that Buddhists and Hindus are culturally one and that there should be complete harmony between them, if the true spirit of the Arya Dharma is understood."[76]

This certainly seems to be moving toward something very close to Turner's *communitas,* affected in large part by the cultivation of a kind of cultural liminality in which the substantial differences between and amongst the actors are now being downplayed. As such, it can be seen in the larger context of both the development of a monolithic conception of Hinduism (which, in very many cases, encompassed Buddhism as well) and the emergence of a single Indian identity and a united India that grew particularly powerful in the 1930s and '40s leading up to Independence in 1948. At the center of this discourse was a shared religious heritage, essentialized as *sanātana dharma*. Dalmia and von Stietencron note that "there was no place in this scheme of things for overlapping identities which had once been possible when the concept of a monolithic 'Hinduism' had not yet come into existence. Its emergence . . . led to a disregard for, if not suppression of, all the differentiations within 'Hinduism'. The smaller local community which had been accustomed in everyday situations to tolerate and live with differences, was now inflated to much larger, 'national' proportions. These demanded a display of unity and uniformity."[77] In this sense, the individuals gathered at Bodhgayā for the handover ceremony in 1953 can be seen as representing this new community of Indians, a seemingly liminal state in which hitherto divisive differences of culture, belief, and practice were negated to give way to the bond of dharmic brotherhood.

If this all sounds a bit too good to be true, it should, because it is essential to recognize that this spirit of inclusion is predicated on exclusion: the necessary condition for membership in the community was not just Indian roots or a common understanding of *dharma* (as the Buddhists of China, Tibet, Japan, and Burma all could legitimately claim), and not just Indian residence (as the Muslims could certainly claim, if they had so chosen), but the combination of the two. Furthermore, these necessary conditions for membership were not unambiguous. For instance, in 1925 the Burmese delegates to the Indian National Congress put forth a proposal for the formation of a committee that would look into the Bodhgayā situation and attempt to find an equable solution to it. The future president of India, Rajendra Prasad, a lawyer from Bihar and a close associate of Gandhi, was chosen to head this committee. In 1926, Prasad presented a proposal for the joint management—by a committee of Hindus and Buddhists—of the Mahābodhi temple, but stipulated that "we should not have Buddhists from outside the British Empire, e.g. from Japan or China or Tibet."[78] Ironically, as I have noted, this would eventually exclude the Burmese themselves. Questions were also raised as to whether the Sinhala Buddhists should be included. Indeed, Sanjit Roy, a Bengali Buddhist and one of the cofounders of the "Buddha Gaya Defense League," a group that pressed both the Indian National Congress and the Hindu Mahasabha to resolve the Bodhgayā matter, eventually became so disenchanted with the Sri Lankans and Burmese because of their treatment of the Indian Buddhists that he wrote to Prasad, complaining that "Indian Buddhists who come here on pilgrimage are not given even as much attention [as] what common courtesy demands. . . . We the Indian Buddhists want some concessions to do our 'pujas' in our own way."[79]

So, in the end, we see that the formation of Bodhgayā's religious community, or at least the community on display in May 1953, has been a tension-filled process, one that has involved both the formation of some unlikely alliances as well as the exclusion of a number of would-be members. As I have noted, this is a process that is still very much, in process, as many of India's Dalit Buddhists lobby (and protest) for a greater representation in the running of the Mahābodhi temple. There is also evidence that various members of the extant community wish to exclude other members, and I want to end with a particularly clear, if not also a quite familiar and, in the end, outrageous example, one that ironically harkens back to the old orientalist distinction between proper and improper religious behavior. Here, a Western scholar remarks on the various visitors to Bodhgayā, and implies that it is not the Westerners who are flocking to Bodhgayā for the wrong reason, but the Indians: "[T]he Hindus, curiously enough, behave more or less as tourists. They are the ones who look bright and worldly, carrying cameras, and exhibiting only a minimum of ritual behaviour."[80]

NOTES

1. According to the report in the *Times of India* (May 29, 1953: 7), there were some 100,000 people in the crowd; Michael Trevithick, rather more conservatively, has suggested (without corroboration) that there were more like five thousand people in attendence; see his, "A Jerusalem of the Buddhists in British India: 1874–1949" (Harvard University, 1988), 247.

2. Sir Edwin Arnold, *East and West: Being Papers Reprinted from the 'Daily Telegraph" and other Sources* (London: Longman's, Green, and Co., 1896), 311.

3. Victor Turner, *Dramas, Fields, and Metaphors: Symbolic Action in Human Society* (Ithaca: Cornell University Press, 1974), 202.

4. Victor Turner, *The Forest of Symbols: Aspects of Ndembu Ritual* (Ithaca: Cornell University Press, 1967), 100.

5. From the Introduction of *Representing Hinduism: The Construction of Religious Traditions and National Identity*, ed. Vasudha Dalmia and Heinrich von Stietencron (New Delhi: Sage Publications, 1995), 28.

6. For the fullest treatment of this topic to date, see Philip Almond, *The British Discovery of Buddhism* (Cambridge: Cambridge University Press, 1988).

7. For the history of the East Indian Company, Stanley Wolpert, *A New History of India* (New York: Oxford University Press); for more on Buchanan and other similar early

orientalists, see also John Keay, *India Discovered* (London: Collins, 1988), as well as Abu Imam, *Sir Alexander Cunningham and the Beginnings of Indian Archaeology* (Dacca: Asiatic Society of Pakistan, 1966).

8. Buchanan's complete manuscript is located in the Indian Office Library and Records; his account of Bihar is published as *An Account of the Districts of Bihar and Patna in 1811–1812* (Patna: Bihar and Orissa Research Society, 1986; first published in 1934); a partial account, with illustrations, was published in 1838 as *The History, Antiquities, Topography, and Statistics of Eastern India*, ed. Montgomery Martin (Delhi: Cosmo Publications, 1976).

9. Buchanan, *An Account of the Districts of Bihar and Patna,* 100.

10. Ibid., 140.

11. Most notable among these is the Tibetan Dharmasvāmin, who left a detailed account of his travels in Bihar; see George Roerich, tr., *Biography of Dharmasvāmin: A Tibetan Monk Pilgrim* (Patna: K.P. Jayaswal Research Institute, 1959).

12. For details of the Burmese mission in particular, see W. S. Desai, "History of the Burmese Mission to India, October 1830–July 1833," *Journal of the Burma Research Society* 26 (1936): 71–109; for more general treatments of the various missions to Bodhgayā, see Rajendralala Mitra, *Buddha Gaya: The Great Buddhist Temple, Hermitage of Sakya Muni* (Calcutta: Bengal Secretariat Press, 1878); Alexander Cunningham, *Mahabodhi or the Great Buddhist Temple Under the Bodhi Tree at Buddha-Gaya* (London: 1892); and Benimadhab Barua, *Gayā and Buddha-Gayā (Early History of the Holy Land),* 2 vols. (Calcutta: Indian Research Institute, 1934); for more specific discussions of the activities of these missions, particularly as they effected the Mahābodhi temple itself, see Geri H. Malandra, "The Mahabodhi Temple," in *Bodhgayā: The Site of Enlightenment,* ed. Janice Leoshko (Bombay: Marg, 1988): 10–28; and Jeremiah P. Losty, "The Mahabodhi Temple Before its Restoration," in *Aksyayanivi: Essays Presented to Dr. Debala Mitra in Admiration of Her Scholarly Contributions* (New Delhi: Sri Satguru, 1991), 335–57.

13. Arnold, *East and West,* 307.

14. In Ananda Guruge, *Return to Righteousness: A Collection of Speeches, Essays, and Letters of Anagarika Dharmapala* (Colombo: Government Printing Press, 1965), 336.

15. Two excellent Ph.D. dissertations have recently focused on the issue: Trevithick's, "A Jerusalem of the Buddhists in British India: 1874–1949" (see note 1 above), and Tara Doyle, "Bodh Gayā: Journeys to the Diamond Throne and the Feet of Gayāsur" (Harvard University, 1997); see also Jacob N. Kinnard, "When Is the Buddha not the Buddha? The Hindu/Buddhist Battle over Bodhgaya and the Buddha Image," *Journal of the American Academy of Religion* 66, 4 (1999): 817–39.

16. For details on the Giris, and the larger Dasanāmi orders of which they are generally considered to be a part, see Bahadur Singh and Rai Ram Anugrhraha Narain, *A Brief History of Bodh Gayā Math, District Gayā* (Calcutta: Bengal Secretariat Press, 1893), and also Wade Dazey, "Tradition and Modernization in the Organization of the Dasanāmi

Samnyāsins," in *Monastic Life in the Christian and Hindu Traditions*, ed. Austin Creel and Vasudha Narayanan (Lewiston: Edwin Mellen Press, 1992), 281–321.

17. See Rajendralala Mitra, *Buddha Gaya,* 5.

18. Ibid., 6.

19. Buchanan, *An Account of the Districts of Bihar and Patna,* 90.

20. Significant in that in at once so radically overestimating the number of Śaivas and at the same time reporting a single Buddhist, Buchanan was implicitly drawing attention to the fact that the Buddhists had been forced out of their sacred center by the Hindus.

21. Arnold, *East and West,* 310 and 311.

22. Ibid., 314.

23. See Almond, *The British Discovery of Buddhism,* especially 29–32.

24. There were, however, abundant nineteenth-century characterizations of the Buddha as one of the Great Men of history; ibid., 69–77.

25. Francis Buchanan, "On the Religion and Literature of the Burmese," *Asiatick Researches* 6 (1799): 163–308, p. 255.

26. Ibid., 166.

27. Alexander Cunningham, *The Bhilsa Topes, or Buddhist Monuments of Central India: Comprising a Brief Historical Sketch of the Rise, Progress, and Decline of Buddhism* (Varanasi: Indological Book House, 1966), 33.

28. Mitra, *Buddha Gaya,* 6.

29. Arnold, *East and West,* 313.

30. Ibid., 312.

31. For a very insightful discussion of this topic, see Tomoko Masuzawa, *In Search of Dreamtime: The Quest of the Origin of Religion* (Chicago: University of Chicago Press, 1993). Ironically, though, it is precisely this claim of origins that appears, inverted, in subsequent polemical efforts to create a space—both a physical and a rhetorical space—for Viṣṇu and the Vaiṣṇava community at Bodhgayā, and the focus of many of these efforts has not been on the Buddha images at all, but rather on the footprints *in situ* at Bodhgayā and their relationship to the famous *viṣṇupāda* at Gayā, both of which Vaiṣṇavas claim significantly predate the arrival of Buddhism; see Jacob N. Kinnard, "The Polyvalent *Pādas* of Viṣṇu and the Buddha," *History of Religions* 40, 1 (2000):32–57.

32. Gregory Schopen, "The Buddha as an Owner of Property and Permanent Resident in Medieval Indian Monasteries," *Journal of Indian Philosophy* 18 (1990): 181–217, p. 181; for more on the character of the Buddha as viewed by nineteenth-century West-

erners, see also Almond, *The British Discovery of Buddhism,* and Étienne Lamotte, "La légende du Buddha," *Revue de l'histoire des religions* 134 (1948): 37–71.

33. See Peter Marshall, ed., *The British Discovery of Hinduism in the Eighteenth Century* (Cambridge: Cambridge University Press, 1970), and also Partha Mitter, *Much Maligned Monsters: A History of European Reactions to Indian Art* (Chicago: University of Chicago Press, 1992).

34. In Cowell, *The Buddhacarita of Asvaghosa,* in *Buddhist Mahayana Texts,* Sacred Books of the East, vol. XLIX (New Delhi: Cosmo Publications, 1977), p. 115 of the Sanskrit portion of the text.

35. Arnold, *East and West,* 311.

36. Janice Leoshko, "On the Construction of a Buddhist Pilgrimage Site," *Art History* 19, 4 (1996): 573–97, p. 580. This exclusion was not, however, limited to the Hindus. Indeed, only a particular sort of Buddhism—the Theravāda—was included in the Western imagination of Bodhgayā, a perception that persists to this day. For as Leoshko notes, "Many scholars have tried to construct a singular truth about a site a the expense of a more complicated picture offered by the evidence of subsequent developments," 573.

37. For more on this topic, see Jeremiah P. Losty, "The Mahābodhi Temple before Its Restoration," in *Aksyayanivi: Essays Presented to Dr. Debala Mitra in Admiration of Her Scholarly Contributions,* ed. G. Bhattacharya (Delhi: Sri Satguru, 1991), 235–57.

38. There is a notable irony embedded in this act, because the image Dharmapala carried was in fact a very old image of Amitābha that he had been given in Japan, an image that *prima facie* was as "foreign" to Bodhgayā as were any of the Śaiva or Vaiṣṇava images and rituals that so offended him; see Kinnard. "When Is the Buddha not the Buddha," for more on this.

39. It is worth noting that Dharmapala was acting against the advice of his mentor, Henry Steele Olcott, who urged further negotiations instead of legal actions, and also against the advice the Sri Lankan monk that he frequently turned to for authority in religious matters, Hikkaḍuve Sumangala. Indeed, Olcott and Dharmapala were growing increasingly estranged during this period, in large part due to Dharmapala's escalating anti-Hindu polemics. From Olcott's theosophical perspective, Bodhgayā should be a shared religious site, bringing together the various religions of the Orient; this was a perspective that Dharmapala essentially abandoned for an exclusively Buddhist ideology. Interestingly, though, as we shall see below, it was Olcott's basic vision that would win the day at Bodhgayā.

40. *Journal of the Mahabodhi Society* 4, 6 (1895): 44.

41. When Lord Elgin visited Gayā and Bodhgayā in the Spring of 1895, he explicitly stated the government's policy of neutrality in matters regarding religion, and although the specific context was the contemporary "cow controversy," his words, delivered as they were on the very day that he visited the Mahābodhi temple, were

clearly meant to pertain to the conflict there as well: "Government, as you are aware, must preserve a strict, perhaps even stern impartiality of which you have indicated your appreciation, but it has seemed to me that when we approach spots or deal with institutions which others hold in veneration and affection, our first object should be to do our best to appreciate the feelings inspired by them, and our second to see that we do nothing by word or deed to injure those feelings," quoted in Trevithick, "A Jerusalem of the Buddhists," 121.

42. *Journal of the Mahabodhi Society* 4, 6 (1895): 45.

43. Ibid. Lall did note, however, that it was possible that some Hindus had begun worshiping in the temple in the months leading up to the image incident, but that this was merely a recent innovation intended to establish a precedent for precisely such a legal claim; more on this point below.

44. For a list of texts cited by both the prosecution and the defense, see *Journal of the Mahabodhi Society* 4, 10 (1896): 80.

45. It is of course ironic that the defense would choose Cunningham and Mitra, since as we have already seen, both professed highly unfavorable views of Hinduism, and Mitra, in particular, was unrelenting in his castigation of the Mahant and the Giri *sannyāsin:* recall his remarks about their laziness and ignorance cited above.

46. Indeed, in the *Viṣṇupurāṇa* itself, there is no question as to the derisive position regarding Buddhism: according to this text, Buddhists are unclean and impure, and the Hindu who so much as dines with a Buddhist goes to hell. See K. Klostermaier, "Hindu Views of Buddhism," in *Canadian Contributions to Buddhist Studies,* ed. R. Amore (Waterloo: Wilfred Laurie University Press, 1979), 60–82, pp. 65–66.

47. *Mahabodhi Journal* 4, 7–8 (1895): 56.

48. "Daily Telegraph," 321. Notice that this implicitly damages the Buddhists' case, for it implied that the Mahant's ownership was at least recognized by the Buddhists themselves.

49. *Journal of the Mahabodhi Society* 4, 11 (1896): 93.

50. Ibid., 79.

51. Ibid., 80.

52. See Trevithick, "A Jerusalem of the Buddhists," 118.

53. Ibid., 122–23.

54. Quoted in Trevithick, "A Jerusalem of the Buddhists," 137, from the *Buddhist* 45, 7 (1895), no page given.

55. This is an offer that had first been made when Dharmapala initially approached the Mahant about installing the Amitābha image; see *Journal of the Mahabodhi Society* 4, 7–8 (1896): 56.

56. See J. Kinnard, "When Is the Buddha not the Buddha," and "The Polyvalent *Pādas* of Viṣṇu and the Buddha."

57. Quoted in Trevithick, "A Jerusalem of the Buddhists," 140, from the *Buddhist* 45, 7 (1895), no page number given.

58. Quoted in Trevithick, "A Jerusalem of the Buddhists," 142, from the *Indian Law Reports* (Calcutta Series) 23 (1896), 62.

59. Quoted in Trevithick, "A Jerusalem of the Buddhists," 143, from the *Indian Law Reports* (Calcutta Series) 23 (1896), no page given. Note that this right to worship was a legal right, not a religious one.

60. It is interesting that Macpherson would explicitly consider what he saw as Dharmapala's ulterior motives, since in the first trial, Macpherson noted: "I do not think there is any ground for believing that Dharmapala was animated by any other motive than a genuine one to discharge the trust he had undertaken in Japan to enshrine a suitable image of Buddha in the sanctum sanctorum, where one was need . . . ," *Journal of the Mahabodhi Society* 4, 7–8 (1896): 56.

61. Quoted in Trevithick, "A Jerusalem of the Buddhists," 147, from the *Indian Law Reports* (Calcutta Series) 23 (1896), 72.

62. Most recently, Dalit Buddhists, who were left out of the discourse during the original negotiations, have agitated for greater representation; see Doyle, "Bodh Gayā: Journeys to the Diamond Throne," 387–422.

63. See Trevithick, "A Jerusalem of the Buddhists," 154–56, and also Doyle, "Bodh Gayā: Journeys to the Diamond Throne," 170–72.

64. Okakura, who served as curator of the Department of Japanese and Chinese Art at the Museum of Fine Arts, Boston, from 1903 to until his death in 1913, was a complex figure, at once a staunch defender of the traditional arts and culture of Japan, and at the same time a key interlocutor in the early East-West dialogue. See in particular his works in English, *The Ideals of the East, with Special Reference to the Art of Japan* (New York: Dutton, 1903), *The Awakening of Japan* (New York: The Century Co., 1904), and *The Book of Tea* (New York : Duffield, 1906). For a useful study of his interactions with various American intellectuals, see Tachiki, Satoko, "Okakura Kakuzo (1862–1913) and Boston Brahmins," Ph.D. Dissertation, The University of Michigan, 1986.

65. Dharmapala mentions his visit to Bodhgayā in his diaries, and states elsewhere that Okakura "with the help of the Bengalees belonging to a neo-Hindu school opened negotiations with the Saivite Mahant stating that Japanese Buddhism is similar to Hinduism, and that they have no relationship with the Buddhist of Ceylon," Anagarika Dharmapala, *Buddhism in its Relationship to Hinduism* (Calcutta: Mahabodhi Society, 1918), 205.

66. See Trevithick, "A Jerusalem of the Buddhists," 187.

67. Kakuzo Okakura, *The Ideals of the East,* 81.

68. It is not clear what the Mahant's motives were here, but certainly he did not wish to continue to alienate the entire Buddhist world, and this minor gesture afforded him the opportunity to appease those who had been angered by his legal fights with the Mahābodhi temple. Furthermore, he must have known that the Japanese and Sri Lankan Buddhists were hardly allies, and thus siding with the former—and bringing them into the Bodhgayā community—might lessen the latter's influence.

69. Quoted in Trevithick, "A Jerusalem of the Buddhists," 190.

70. There was an important political dimension to both the government's refusal of Okakura's request, and also their view of non-Indian Buddhist groups, because the government was increasingly concerned about the issue of foreign influence in India, and it had no desire to allow the Japanese or any other foreigners even this minor outpost.

71. It is important to note, however, that the Mahant and his followers continued to assert their own rights, and did not cease their polemical attacks on Buddhism; see, for instance, the volume, *Buddha-mimamsa, or the Buddha and his relation to the religion of the Vedas* (London: W. Thacker and Co., 1922), for a good sampling of the sort of attacks in which the Śaivas were engaged.

72. Quoted in Trevithick, "A Jerusalem of the Buddhists," 196.

73. From the *Journal of the Mahabodhi Society*, 1922, reprinted in *Journal of the Mahābodhi Society: Diamond Jubilee Souvenir, 1891–1951* (Calcutta: Mahābodhi Society Press, 1952), 95.

74. *Journal of the Mahabodhi Society* 33, 4 (1925): 203.

75. Quoted in Trevithick, "A Jerusalem of the Buddhists," 202.

76. Ibid., 210.

77. Vasudha Dalmia and Heinrich von Stietencron, eds. *Representing Hinduism,* 20.

78. Quoted in Trevithick, "A Jerusalem of the Buddhists," 204–205.

79. Ibid., 214–25.

80. Albertina Nugteren, "Ritual Around the Bodhi-Tree in Bodhgaya," in *Pluralism and Identity: Studies in Ritual Behaviour,* ed. J. Platvoet and K.van der Toorn (Leiden: E.J. Brill 1995), 145–65, p. 156.

SIX

MINISTER OF DEFENSE?

THE VIṢṆU CONTROVERSY IN CONTEMPORARY SRI LANKA

John Clifford Holt

INTRODUCTION

WHEN WILHELM GEIGER published his German and then English translations of the Pāli *Mahāvaṃsa* in 1912,[1] his accomplishment was a major and lasting contribution for the study of Buddhism in the West. It also produced, unwittingly so, profound affects on how many Theravāda Buddhists in twentieth-century Sri Lanka came to understand significant aspects of the nature and legacy of their own religious culture. With Geiger's translation published for the Pali Text Society in London, the *Mahāvaṃsa* was not only more readily available to scholars and interested readers in the West, but it also enjoyed an increasing popularity and enhanced authority among the English-reading Sinhala elite in colonial Ceylon. (Indeed, a Sinhala translation of the *Mahāvaṃsa* was not available to read in Ceylon for many years after the appearance of Geiger's.) Subsequent to Geiger's translation, Western and Western-educated Sinhalese scholars have analyzed its mythic values;[2] Ceylonese and Sri Lankan scholars have mined it for its historical revelations;[3] in turn, public school educators in Sri Lanka have used its accounts continuously as bases for English and Sinhala textbooks on Sri Lanka's history; on Buddhist holidays such as *Poson poya* (full moon day), Sri Lankan newspapers print critically "innocent" articles that report *Mahāvaṃsa* episodes as if they are historical givens; and post-Independence politicians have not hesitated to legitimate Sinhala nationalistic ideologies or government initiatives, often for politically hegemonic purposes, by appealing to the text's seemingly unquestionable authority.[4] While the *Mahāvaṃsa*'s general scope of influence upon historical, cultural, and political understandings in modern Sri Lanka has been as broad as it has been thorough, at times producing what has been labeled a "*Mahāvaṃsa* mentality," Geiger's specific translations of crucial passages have also contributed to definitive perspectives on particular issues that remain, upon closer scrutiny, matters of perhaps irresolvable ambiguity. In this essay, I will begin by examining implications of Geiger's seemingly innocuous translation of *Mahāvaṃsa* 7.5 (I: 55), wherein he rendered Pāli *devass' uppalavaṇṇassa* into English as "the god who is in colour like the lotus" and then added an an enormously influential explanatory footnote that says simply: "that is, Viṣṇu." I will then proceed to a presentation and analysis of an ongoing and contemporary controversy in Buddhist Sri Lanka about the place of deities, especially Viṣṇu, in Sinhala religious culture.

BACKGROUND

The *Mahāvaṃsa* passage I have cited is part of a seminal myth that has assumed great importance to the Sinhalese, especially in the twentieth century when hotly contested ethnic claims to "home lands" or separate states have been advanced by rival communal constituencies. It forms part of the well-known mythic story of how Vijaya, son of the lion-man king Sinhabāhu, the progenitor of the Sinhala race, was banished from India for his ignoble conduct and together with seven hundred men and their families, put on to a ship and sent forth to sea in exile. Vijaya and his retinue landed in Lanka "on the day that the Tathagata lay down between two twinlike sala-trees to pass into nibbana" (*Mahāvaṃsa* VI. 47; I: 54).

> When the Guide of the World, having accomplished the salvation of the whole world and having reached the utmost state of blissful rest, was lying on the bed of his nibbana, in the midst of the great assembly of the gods, he, the great sage, the greatest of those who have speech, spoke to Sakka [Indra] who stood near him: "Vijaya, son of king Sihabahu, is come to Lanka from the country of Lala, together with seven hundred followers. In Lanka, O lord of the gods, will my religion be established, therefore carefully protect him with his followers and Lanka."
>
> When the lord of the gods heard the words of the Tathagata he from respect handed over the guardianship of Lanka to the god who is in colour like the lotus.
>
> And no sooner had the god received the charge from Sakka than he came speedily to Lanka and sat down at the foot of a tree in the guise of a wander-

> ing ascetic. And all the followers of Vijaya came to him and asked him: "What island is this sir?" "The island of Lanka," he answered. "There are no men here, and here no dangers will arise." And when he had spoken so and sprinkled water on them from his water-vessel, and had wound a thread about their hands he vanished through the air. (*Mahāvaṃsa* VII. 1-8; I: 55)[5]

This specific passage, together with the narrative in the very first chapter of the *Mahāvaṃsa* in which the Buddha proclaims that Lanka will be a place where his *dharma* will bear fruition (*Mahāvaṃsa* I.20; I: 3), are frequently cited *Mahāvaṃsa* episodes by those Sinhalas who make national primoridal claims on Sri Lanka's custody and assert the island's special place in the history of the Buddha's dispensation.[6] The Vijaya myth is thus taken very seriously, even literally, by many Sinhalas in modern Sri Lanka as veritable political and social history and as an ancient warrant for its continued undivided political integrity. Within this framework of understanding, Viṣṇu is understood to play an ancient and hallowed role as the island's and the religion's "minister of defense." As such, he is understood popularly, indeed it is his primary claim to importance in contemporary Sinhala religious culture, to have prevailed over the well-being of Buddhism and Sri Lanka since its "historical" inception.

In several tracts of late medieval Sinhala poetry dating from the seventeenth through the nineteenth centuries C.E.,[7] and in the contemporary liturgical petitions *(yātikā)* chanted by *kapurālas* (shrine priests) recorded recently at important Viṣṇu *devālayas*,[8] Viṣṇu is uniformly praised for his prowess in protecting the Buddha *sāsana* ("dispensation") for a period of five thousand years following the enlightenment of the Buddha and for defending and supervising the general well-being of the island. That Viṣṇu's profile as defender of Buddhism and Sri Lanka is more important than what might seem a mere folkloric accommodation can be indicated in several ways. Just one example from among many in history can suffice: in the mid-nineteenth century, a rebel named Gangalagoda Banda from Matale, leader of one of the two most serious insurrections faced by the British during their political administration of colonial Ceylon, swore an oath in front of the Viṣṇu image at Dambulla claiming that he was, indeed, a descendent of the last Kandyan king and that he was determined to wrest power back from the foreign usurpers with the blessings of the god.[9] No doubt Geiger was very aware of Viṣṇu's acquired popular and by then "historical" reputation as defender of Buddhism and the country, and this awareness led him to make what is now seen, in hindsight, a controversial identification, an identification that inadvertently further cemented Viṣṇu's place for virtually all sections of the modern Buddhist community.

Although, historically, Viṣṇu's Buddhistic identity as "minister of defense" cannot possibly antedate the sixteenth century C.E. (if even by then), it is now difficult to find any general appraisal of Sinhala religion, or of Sinhala deity propitiation more specifically, in either English or Sinhala, that does not assume that Viṣṇu is one of the four guardian deities of the island, and that he has been, since ancient times, specifically in charge of protecting the Buddha *sāsana*. Moreover, Viṣṇu *devālaya*s are now ubiquitous throughout all Sinhala cultural areas in Sri Lanka, especially in village contexts. His integration into popular conceptions and transactions of Buddhist ritual cult has been as thorough as any other deity in the country, probably even more so than the very popular Kataragama Deviyo (a.k.a. Murugan, Skanda). Very recently, a small and inconspicous Viṣṇu *devālaya* has been opened within the confines of the Daḷadā Māligawa ("Temple of the Tooth-Relic") in Kandy, the only *devālaya* that has ever been allowed within its premises during the Māligawa's long history. It is clear that Viṣṇu has been and continues to remain, an important, politically significant deity in Sri Lanka, one whose veneration is now at the center of partisan political bickering.

Given Viṣṇu's immense popularity among Sinhala Buddhists, it is surprising to find a comparative dearth of Sinhala literature that takes Viṣṇu directly as a protagonist or as primary subject matter. When he is mentioned, and he is mentioned often, it is usually within ritual invocations that simply recall his function as a defender of the faith and the well-being of the island. Because of this, writers such as Gombrich have understood Viṣṇu to be a rather "colorless" character.[10] However, this is really not a fair appraisal if the full scope of relevant late medieval Sinhala literature is studied more closely. Here, Viṣṇu figures in many supportive roles in any number of episodes, often reminscent of his beguiling and powerful presence in the Sanskrit *brāhmaṇ*ical *purāṇa*s. While his best known trait recalled in ritual procedings has become his *bodhisattva* destiny to become a future buddha in view of his exhalted profile and performance as "minister of defense," and while he is rarely a protagonist in Sinhala myth, Viṣṇu has been thoroughly interwoven into numerous mythic stories about how various other gods have come to Sri Lanka and received warrants *(varam)* to establish their powers by means of Viṣṇu's permission.[11] However, his own "mythic biography" is very difficult to reconstruct, owing to the foci of the available sources at hand.

Viṣṇu's conflation in identity with Uppalavanna (Sinhala: Upulvan), confirmed so influentially by Geiger in his *Mahāvaṃsa* translation, and to a certain extent, his overlapping profile and relations with Aluthnuwara Deviyo (a.k.a "Dädimunda" and "Devata Bandāra") have been the subject of much scholarly inquiry.[12] In brief, what this scholarship indicates is that Viṣṇu per se is a latecomer on the Sinhala religio-cultural scene, and that Upulvan's earlier identity is rather obscure. It would seem that Geiger's "clarification" of Uppalavaṇṇa as Viṣṇu glossed over a confusing and complicated late medieval transformation which finally occured perhaps in the early-eighteenth-century reign of King Narendra Sinha of Kandy,[13] or even later in the mid-eighteenth century when the *nayakkar* king, Kīrti Śrī Rājasinha, definitively reorganized royal and civic ritual life in the capital,[14] in a manner in which it generally is retained today.[15] It may very well be the case that *brāhmaṇ*ical priests in Devinuwara, on the southernmost tip of the island where Upulvan's major temple was located from perhaps as early as the eighth century C.E., began the process of identifying Upulvan with Viṣṇu before the destruction of the temple by the Portuguese in 1588 C.E.,[16] but until more evidence is discovered, this cannot be proved with any degree of certainty.

THE PROBLEM

Be that as it may, it is now a cultural fact that Viṣṇu has been thoroughly assimilated into Sinhala religious culture as a Buddhist, rather than a Hindu deity. Indeed, many Sinhalas living in rural areas of the country would be surprised to learn that Viṣṇu is a deity of vedic and *purāṇ* ic origins. A study of Viṣṇu's assimilation into the Sinhala Buddhist religious culture of Sri Lanka makes an excellent case study of how people in one religio-cultural orientation transform the identity and function of a deity whose origins lie within another. Such a study would pose the questions: What do other people do with other people's gods? And why do they do it as they do? This is not a new problem in the history of religions: Jesus becomes a prophet rather than a messiah for Muslims, and the Buddha is regarded by some Hindus as an avatar of Viṣṇu.[17] However, this is not the specific problem I wish to probe in the remainder of this essay. Instead, I shall be concerned with a process that sometimes occurs subsequent to the types of assimilation I have just noted. That is, *how* and *why* do people of a religious culture that has assimilated or domesticated gods of a "foreign" origin go about attempting to divest them? Who decides? And why? This is a very important and currently topical issue that has arisen in contemporary Sri Lanka. In what follows, I will attempt to illustrate that current attempts by some sections of the Sinhala community to eliminate deity propitiation, specifically veneration of Viṣṇu, attempts that are couched in doctrinal terms in order to "purify" Buddhism, are a byproduct of: 1) current ethnic tensions reflecting the deteriorating state of intercommunity relations in Sri Lanka; and 2), the assertion of a class-bound religious consciousness on the part of the urbanized, professional, and middle-class populace which is aimed at transforming the religious consciousness of rural villagers, or those who have inherited and continue to preserve the legacy of a more inclusive religious ethos that formerly dominated Sinhala religious life in previous eras. In the most abstract general sense, I am arguing that social, economic, and political conditions are often refracted in the substance and dynamic of movements for religious reform, even though the ostensible rationale for these reforms is often presented within a doctrinal frame.

The nature and function of the divine in Buddhism is one of the issues least understood by the general reading public in the West. Almost all books on the spirituality of Buddhism sold in European and American bookstores scarcely mention deity veneration at all. If deities are mentioned, it is usually negatively or even derisively so. For Buddhism is often championed in popular Western circles as a religion without gods, a type of spiritual self-effort totally dependent upon the will of a determined practitioner. In that sense, it is presented as a religion of personal self-attainment, one in which mental, ethical, and emotional proclivities causing existential unsatisfactoriness can be overcome by disciplined intentional assertions generated out of contemplative serenity. Logical rationality, the pride of the post-Enlightenment era, is often emphasized in these presentations too. Most introductory academic textbooks in use at American colleges and universities still present the teachings of the Buddha and the historical development of doctrine in this manner. Moreover, Buddhism is understood in many circles as a philosophy, not a religion, and to others as atheistic, proudly proclaimed insofar as it is not seen as a religious discipline dependent on the power of savior figures or omnipotent gods. On the Sri Lankan side, learned monographs by Buddhist studies academics, while noting the ubiquitous presence of the gods even within the oldest layers of classical literary tradition, assert that divinity is beside the concerns of the basic Buddhist soteriological quest.[18] My critique of these characterizations of Buddhism, the Western and Sri Lankan, is that they are basically presented without the benefit of social, cultural, and historical analyses and assume often a normative posture exclusively. Historians and anthropologists who have studied aspects of the religious cultures of South and Southeast Asia have labored, for the past forty or fifty years, to point out that while the gods may not be soteriologically significant in Buddhism, they function as genuine expressions of religious consciousness for many people and that they implicate or signify important cognitive and emotive experiences.

This persistent problem of ignoring or banishing the gods into insignificance has been compounded for two fundamental reasons. In the first instance, there is a venerable tradition, a kind of "Hindu deity-bashing," within the textual and historical traditions of Sri Lanka's monastic Theravāda Buddhism itself. There are, indeed, a number of references in the Pāli canonical corpus of the Theravādins that verge on ridiculing the perceived efficacy of *brāhmaṇical* gods, either within the context of ritual implorations,[19] or as impediments to maximizing the cultivation of the ethical life.[20] Moreover, there are clear instances in the history of Theravāda Buddhism in Sri Lanka, particularly in the thirteenth, fifteenth, and nineteenth centuries C.E., when learned monks chastised their followers for worshiping the gods.[21] It is an old problem. It has sometimes divided the Buddhist community. But it must be kept in mind that monastic hardliners on this issue do not exhaust the totality of Buddhist culture.[22] The second reason for the persistence of this problem is that popular cultural flows from the West are frequently exported to Asia and thoroughly embraced uncritically, and not the least of these has been, ironically, popular Westernized understandings of Buddhism available to the English-reading public.[23] How the West understands Buddhism has had an indelible effect on how some Sri Lankans have come to understand their own tradition. Geiger's translation of the *Mahāvaṃsa* is but one small episode in this general process. A combination of these two reasons, one internal to the culture and the other an influence from without, is part of what is driving the contemporary incarnation of this controversey today, but here I will also identify other contemporary forces that have led to the rekindling and renewal of the debate.

The controversy about Viṣṇu, which now is about to be detailed, can almost be seen as running parallel to the public fortunes of Sinhala-Tamil relations in medieval and modern Sri Lankan history. That is, it seems to be the case that monastic reactions against deity veneration, especially to the gods of Hindu origins, occurs in conjunction with the significant establishment and assimilation of South Indian religious cultural traditions among the Sinhalese. While these assimilations belie a Sinhala historical genius for inclusivity, they have been, periodically, perceived by some as threats to the indigenous culture, or possibly as an advance signal of potential political domination. For example, sculpted gods of Hindu origins were first placed inside of image houses of the Buddha at Gadaladeniya and Lankatilaka, two historically important temples built and patronized by the kings and courtiers of the fourteenth-century Gampola period in the upcountry region of the island. The Gampola period witnessed unprecedented migrations of peoples of South Indian origins into this upcountry region of Sri Lanka. A tremendous amount of folklore, including epic migration sagas, myths about the goddess, and the introduction of several minor deities, are still extant in upcountry villages as derivations from this migratory experience. It is not surprising that we would find concurrently in the Gampola era, one of Theravāda's most outstanding critics of deity veneration, Dharmakīrti Thera, the chief monastic incumbent of Gadaladeniya itself, articulating his perspective forcefully at this time.[24] The same pattern might be seen in the fifteenth-century Kotte era, when Sanskrit, devotional Hinduism, and caste became pronounced features in Sinhala literary, religious, and social structures, but not without strident voices of dissent.[25] In the eighteenth century, during the Kandyan period of *nayakkar* rule, the *sangharāja* Saraṇāṃkara, with royal support from Kīrti Śrī Rājasinha, led a conservative monastic movement to purify the sangha of what he perceived to be decadent practice, including the worship of the gods. What I am suggesting is this: it should not be surprising that during this recent period of ethnic strife, especially since 1983, that the old issue of Buddhists worshipping "Hindu" gods would arise once more. As the civil war has unfolded, Sinhala public fears of potential Tamil political domination, founded or not, are surfacing in reactionary sections of the Sinhala community and being expressed sometimes in a xenophobic fashion.[26] There is a fear of being taken over.

THE CONTEMPORARY EXAMPLE OF THE PROBLEM

The issue of worshiping gods and the practice of Buddhism has been rather dramatically brought to the general public's attention by the monastic and charismatic television personality, Venerable Gangodawila Soma Thera. During the past three years, Ven. Soma has become one of the most popular and highly visible monks in Sri Lanka, frequently making the rounds of Colombo-based television talk shows, hosting his own air times on various TV channels, and consequently becoming an eagerly sought-after source for publishable quotes, including comments critical of the government and the religious establishment, by Colombo newspaper columnists. Ven. Soma's style of argument and presentation is widely acclaimed and appreciated by his Sinhala Sri Lankan audiences, even more so than the way that Ralph Buultjens appealed to the country on the radio in the mid-to-late 1980s. Ven. Soma is quietly frank, delightfully so to many. His criticisms of government policies, and the political dynamics occuring between the government and the opposition party, are often witty and pointed. He is a highly recruited public speaker and has toured the country broadly preaching at many town and village temple venues throughout. The rise in his stock has been meteoric.

Soma has made many controversial public statements on various issues. He has been continuously outspoken about how Muslims and Tamils do not practice birth control and, as an eventual result, how population demographics will lead to the inevitable domination of these communities over the Sinhalese in Sri Lanka.[27] He has campaigned for the return of temple lands distributed by the colonial British to Muslims around the sacred site of Dīghavāpī in the extreme southeast quadrant of the island, an area that has been for many centuries and remains predominantly Muslim.[28] He has chided both the government and the opposition for being bankrupt in relation to the *pañcas īla* (the five cardinal moral principles of Buddhism), especially the policies of taxing alcohol and cigarettes which, he argues, gives the government an interest in promoting these vices.[29] He is now extremely well known, respected in many quarters while somewhat feared in others, owing to the nature of his biting criticisms. The government seems to regard him warily, as he no longer has easy access to Rupavahini, the government-controlled television channel. Newspaper columnists generally critical of recent Sri Lankan governments' economic and political policies, which have brought about rapid social and cultural change, applaud Ven. Soma's reactionary positions. Here is how one columnist hailed the recent impact of Soma's now widely disseminated views and rising popularity among Colombo's youthful elite:

> Young people whose heroes are Madonna, Michael Jackson, Maduri Dixit and Sachin Tendulkar started listening to Ven. Soma Thero on TV. Devotees flocked in thousands to the temples to listen to his bana [sermons].
>
> While the [g]ods were displaced in homes, the nation and the religion were energized anew in importance. Every kind of question was asked, 'is there a creator god? [h]ow does science look at these problems? [a]re the Sinhalese becoming extinct because of population control? [c]an the Buddhists eliminate terrorism?[30]

The widely read author of this column, Kumbakarana (an alias) cites the fact that Ven. Soma appeals to modern, educated, professional, and urban people and goes on to suggest that these people should consider uniting behind Ven. Soma in a new political initiative independent of the established Sinhala political parties. As a columnist, Kumbakarana is known for his strident defense of Sinhala interests and he sees in Ven. Soma a leader with the potential to galvanize them. Kumbakarana's slightly less communal, but sympathetic columnist colleague at the *Sunday Times*, Rajpal Abeyanayake, also has acclaimed the rising popularity of Ven. Soma.

> Ven. Soma striking at the core weakness of Lankan mentality [worship of the gods] has placed him[self] in a unique position. The man is on the tube. From that vantage point, once he has captured the imagination of the audience, he becomes a superstar and like Michael Jackson he becomes a god.[31]

Ven. Soma's political ambitions and potential clout are also seen in a number of statements he has issued directly to the press. Here, for example, is what he said in an interview to the oppositional newspaper, *The Sunday Leader,*[32] about the developing political situation in the spring of 2000; that is, after government forces had lost the *Vanni* (the far north central region of the island in November 1999) to the Liberation Tigers of Tamil Eelam, Chandrika Kumaratunga had been reelected President in December 1999, the Sri Lankan Army was retreating on the northern Jaffna peninsula, and the government and opposition were in the midst of talks regarding a constitutional package that would devolve more power to the provincial level in the hope that it would meet the political aspirations of the moderate segment of the Tamil minority:

> The choice between the UNP [the chief oppositional United National Party] and PA [the People's Alliance coalition of parties led by Chandrika Kumaratunga and the Sri Lanka Freedom Party, the coalition holding government power] is like choosing between an insecticide and pesticide to commit suicide with. One party won and the other collected more votes than usual. In this sense the people approve of both so they have to put up with both.

Here, Ven. Soma seems disappointed that the electorate had not followed his call to spoil ballots in the December 19, 1999, presidential election contested chiefly between the People's Alliance candidate, Chandrika Kumaratunga,[33] and the United National Party candidate, Ranil Wickremesinghe.[34] Soma sees both leaders and their parties as being too interested in caving in to the demands of militant Tamils.

> Now the two have got together to discuss how to give Eelam [a separate wholly autonomous Tamil state]. Prabhakaran [the military-political leader of the Liberation Tigers of Tamil Eelam, or LTTE] will not settle for anything less. How can you hold talks with someone who is not willing to negotiate? The only option is war under the circumstances.

On this issue, the Sinhala polity has been divided between a negotiated or a military strategy for ending the almost twenty years of civil war. In point of fact, the two approaches are not exclusive, but Ven. Soma is among those hardline Sinhala voices who sees no hope in negotiation, arguing that the only realistic solution to the problem of ethnic strife in Sri Lanka is a total military victory over Prabhakaran and his LTTE forces. The phrase "give Eelam" would be especially galling to both the PA and the UNP, given how much has been sacrificed and lost by all sides in the conflict since 1983. With specific regard to current initiatives aimed at renewing discussions through third party mediation as suggested by Norway, Soma says:

> I do not think we need foreign intervention to solve a national problem. Besides, Norway has always supported the LTTE. In the first place they don't treat the minority group in their own country properly so I can't see how they could help us solve our problem. This is all a ploy to spread their religion here.

In the spring of 2000, the Norwegian government generously offered to mediate talks between the LTTE and the Sri Lankan government. But Ven. Soma's comment is a good example of the kind of cynicism Norway's initiative generated in Colombo among Sinhala hardliners who see a conspiracy rather than diplomacy in Norway's initiative. A series of venomous articles appeared in various newspapers attacking the sincerity of the Norwegian initiative. One even went so far as to ridicule Norway's constitutional monarchy as medieval. Ven. Soma's suspicions about the Norwegians wanting to spread their religion also reflects his characteristic antipathy for any religion other than Buddhism. It plays to a Sinhala penchant for conspiracy theories. The conclusion to Soma's interview in the *Sunday Observer* contains a rather chilling suggestion that the military might be called upon to run to the affairs of the country.

> The war is now a game on which the kings dine. Everyone is just interested in clinging on to power and are *[sic]* willing to do whatever it takes to stay there at the cost of the community and country. It should be handled by those who know how to fight and not by ministers or members of parliament who do not know the art of winning a war.

This last parting shot is aimed not directly at President Chandrika Kumaratunga, though it is she who holds the government defense ministry portfolio. Rather, the more pointed target is her uncle, Gen. Anuruddha Ratwatte, an outspoken deputy minister of defense whose advocacy of a military solution and celebration of past temporary successes has looked increasingly problematic following the massive military setbacks of late 1999 and the spring of 2000. Indeed, there are other reasons, including specifically the issue of venerating deities, for why Ven. Soma would want to target Gen. Ratwatte. Members of the Ratwatte family (i.e., President Chandrika Kumaratunga's mother's side), are ardent supporters and patrons of the cult of Viṣṇu,[35] the very contested issue which brought Soma to contemporary public fame.

Soma's position in relation to deity veneration is usually couched first in doctrinal terms in an attempt to establish its veracity among his Buddhist listeners. Then he appeals to ethnic sentiments. Until recently, his fundamental position has been "that the idea of the gods is totally unacceptable to Buddhism."[36] However, in late October 1999, he published a column in *The Sunday Times* that indicates a distinction he now draws between Christian, Hindu, and Muslim conceptions of the gods on the one hand, and Buddhist conceptions on the other. Here is what he said with my own commentary on Soma's statement interspersed:

> Every other religion in the world is founded upon the belief that God created the world, that the world is composed of *nithya* [permanence], *sukha* [happiness] and *athma* [self] and that belief in God will help you.

Soma seems to have confused the tenets of "every other religion in the world" with those of Hinduism alone. In analyzing many of his public statements about "other religions," it becomes clear that either he has never systematically studied the major religions of the world and is therefore intellectually innocent of his mistakes, or he wittingly distorts doctrinal positions for an intended political affect. It would seem that many of his statements with regard to "other religions" are simply stereotypes that play to the emotionally charged xenophobic views of Sinhala hardliners.

> According to Buddhism, if the gods possess power, that too was gained through *kamma* and can be changed by no being and therefore there was *[sic]* no powerful being.
>
> The concept of gods in Buddhism teaches that there is no all powerful being. Gods are just another group of beings whose bodies are more beautiful, sensitive and radiant than human beings.

Here Ven. Soma asserts the ontological primacy of karmic retribution. This is his major appeal to Buddhist doctrine and it should be noted that he is, in general, correct in this assertion that the Sinhala Buddhist conception of deities is dependent upon the assumption of cosmic karmic retribution. Since his style of public speaking is *bana* (preaching), his references are often made to particular scriptural passages to warrant his assertions. That is, the "Buddhism" he refers to is a de-contextualized or "textual reality" and usually is not based on appeals to history, society, or culture. It is a kind of abstract understanding only. It is clear that by "Buddhism," Soma does not have in mind Sinhala Buddhist culture as it has developed over the past two millenia. Indeed, he frequently laments that "pure Theravāda Buddhism" (apparently his "Buddhism") is not practiced by most people in Sri Lanka. Rather, "what the Buddhists in Sri Lanka practice is a mixture, a concoction of Buddhism, Hinduism and Christianity."[38] To return to his desiderata: Humans are not governed by gods. However, good comes to people who receive the blessings of the gods. Not everyone can receive the blessings of the gods.

> To receive blessings a person must have an inherent fear and shame of committing sin. Thus gods love people who refrain from sin and are humane. There is a scientific basis to this too. Those who avoid committing sin, and follow the five precepts and other forms of righteousness and possess compassion and loving kindness *[sic]*, have serene and contented minds. When the mind is happy, the hormones will be activated and the power of hormones which are linked to the blood cells will cause a special power and purity in the blood.
>
> The aura generated by a good person's body possesses magnetism. The gods who see this virtuous person's behavioral patterns are drawn to bless this person.

> Then as the blessings of the gods encircle him he becomes a person liked by others, a charismatic person even non-human.[38]

Ven. Soma often appeals to science in his presentations. References of this nature help him in his appeal to his supportive urbanized and educated professional constituency of Colombo who are quite understandably unable to identify very much with the residual traditional religious life of the village. For them, Soma has styled himself appealingly as the "modern monk" who has emerged from a tradition that has allowed itself to become immersed in superstition. These references to science are often regularly coupled with his appeals to the fundamental five ethical precepts *(pañcas īla),* rationality, and logic. But in making a closer reading of his statement above, it is quite clear that Soma has interjected, quite unwittingly, basic Christian understandings of guilt and original sin into his analysis of the gods' relations to human beings. It would be easy to label what he preaches as a kind of concoction of its own. Moreover, what passes for his scientific view regarding hormones, blood, an aura, magnetism, and charisma reflects, unfortunately, the narrow scope of his own monastic education with its absence of basic science as a field of study.

While Ven. Soma seems to be somewhat anti-Christian and has clashed in a publicly televised debate with a leading Muslim MP and member of the government's cabinet, he and his fellow columnists at the *Sunday Times* save their most virulent attacks and outlandish claims for Hindus and Hinduism. In the following piece,[39] Ven. Soma is quoted at length by Rajpal Abeyanayake on how he understands the concept of the divine in Hindu tradition. Here, Soma is trying to distance Hindu from Buddhist understandings and chastises Buddhists for venerating deities of Hindu origin. The degree of Soma's understanding of the Hindu world view is self-evident in what follows. And so are his motives as well.

> Whenever a great son is born to humankind in India, it's a practice of the Hindus to call him a reincarnation *[sic]* of Vishnu—it's a tradition. For example, they say Sai Baba is a reincarnation *[sic]* of Vishnu. Now we know that Sai Baba is not an *avatharaya* [apparition] *[sic!]* and that he is a good man. . . . The Hindus say that the Buddha is a reincarnation *[sic]* of Vishnu. Are we prepared to accept Buddha as a reincarnation *[sic]* of Vishnu? Not me! I know that the Buddha descended from a clan of Indian kings, he is no apparition or incarnation. Even Sai Baba, if you touch him nicely, would not feel to the touch as an apparition because he is a good man.
>
> The Hindus know their religion is the polar opposite of Buddhist philosophy. The Buddha says the world is the result of causal phenomena, but the Hindus say Brahma created the world. So they don't try to match their religion with ours. In which case, why do Buddhists try to match Buddhism with theirs?

> When a Buddhist worships various imaginary gods [Viṣṇu and Skandha] and other [Buddhistic] gods, he must be suffering from some mental condition!

The political significance of this final sentence should not be lost when it is recalled that both the leader of the opposition and the current deputy minister of defense have both engaged in high-profile activities in which they have indicated that Sri Lanka could benefit from the assistance of the gods Viṣṇu and Skanda in order to find its way out of the current morass. Perhaps smarting from Ven. Soma's recent criticisms of the deputy defense minister (which are detailed below), the political columnist Lucien Rajakarunanayake of the government newspaper, *The Sunday Observer,* actually co-opted Ven. Soma's increasingly popular perspective to the advantage of the government when he wrote in response to the fact that opposition leader Ranil Wickremesinghe had undertaken a highly publicized pilgrimage with many UNP followers to the town of Kataragama to invoke the blessings of Kataragama Deviyo (a.k.a. Murugan, Skanda) in the hopes of enlisting the blessings of the god to help find an end to the ethnic conflict. Again, my comments are interspersed.

> It seems time for all those individuals, secular and religious organizations, members of the Maha Sangha, sections of the media, political parties, and all others who were opposed to the Indo-Lanka Accord, the arrival and stay of the IPKF here, and the 13th amendment, to make a collective apology to India for the manner in which our closest neighbour who came to assist us on the last occasion was treated.

This is a sarcastic reference to the fact that Sri Lanka had recently asked for India's military assistance as the situation on the Jaffna peninsula worsened while at the same time keeping in mind how Sri Lankans reacted so negatively to the previous Indian military presence on the northeast of the island between 1987 and 1993, which ended when then President Premadasa (UNP) actually colluded with the LTTE before finally asking the Indians to leave.

> One does not know what Ven. Gangodawila Soma Thera will have to say about the UNP leader making a special political pilgrimage to Kataragama, to plead with the deity there and all other deities to save the country at this hour of crisis.
>
> With all his opposition to the worship of deities, we have not heard a word from him about the UNP's pleadings at Kataragama. Whatever Ven. Gangodawila Soma Thera, who is on BBC record saying "We must fight!" has to say about the UNP seeking the aid of Kataragama to fight Prabhakaran, it would appear that the first apology for the previous ugly treatment of India should come from the UNP and Mr. Ranil Wickremesinghe.

> Breaking all the coconuts possible at Kataragama, and offering the richest "pooja vattiya" cannot make up for his silence at the time Premadasa ordered the IPKF out, and his continued silence about that shamed act even today.
>
> It is difficult to see the UNP genuinely seeking the blessings of the Kataragama deity for the success of Sri Lanka in the current war, because such success would mean even further defeat for the UNP. However, to give the devil its due let's believe that's what they have done.
>
> But do they really think that Skanda, whose shrine Kataragama is, would listen much to the pleadings of the UNP that carried out so many attacks on Tamil Hindus in Sri Lanka during its 17 years in power?
>
> Would not Skanda lend at least a little more ear if the pleas for assistance come from Velupillai Prabhakaran, not because Skanda likes terror, but because the Tiger leader at least comes from the people who were barbecued alive, and had their homes and shops torched by the thugs of the UNP.[40]

The Sunday Observer is a veritable mouthpiece for the government and this article is grist for much discussion, but here I would simply note how Ven. Soma, a noted critic of the government, is here co-opted by the very government he criticizes. Note also that the author uses Sanskrit "Skanda," rather than the more familiar Sinhala reference to "Kataragama Deviyo" to indicate the Indian origins of the god, though Tamil "Murugan" would have been more appropriate for the point that the columnist is making. That is, just as Soma would say, Rajakarunanayake is pointing out that this god is of Hindu origins and, as such, is more likely to show favor for the Tamil community in their times of suffering. The columnist is more generally asking: Why is the UNP falling over itself, particularly in light of its sorry history of relations with India after the ethnic conflict that broke out so seriously during its regime? The barbed reference to Soma's silence is because the popular monk has been so vocally critical of how PA government ministers have participated in and supported the cult of the gods, particularly Viṣṇu.

In early June 1999, *The Sunday Times* (the independent newspaper that Soma frequently writes for and the one containing the columns written by Abeyanayake and Kumbhakarana), in one of its "special assignments," published a highly polemical expose on plans to build a multireligious complex,[41] including a Viṣṇu temple, just north of Colombo in Muthurajawela. Adversarial in strategy, style, and substance, the expose identified the deputy minister of defense, the minister of Buddha *sāsana,* and the president, among others, as backing the project, which would require Rs. 600,000,000 ($8,000,000) to complete.

> Grasping at straws and blaming external factors for the war that is raging in Sri Lanka, the two ministers have made the extraordinary request for funds on the

> advice of some South Indian priests who say that a Vishnu temple in Tiruchchirapalli has malefic effects on Sri Lanka.
>
> But religious elders and businessmen who have been approached for funds feel the scheme is based on some religious belief or some attempt to blame the whole ethnic crisis on supernatural forces instead of facing reality and taking responsibility. . . .
>
> This temple, according to these priests, is facing Sri Lanka, thus casting evil effects. They believe it is largely responsible for the turmoil in the country.

The article goes on to state that a large Viṣṇu image will be sea-freighted to Sri Lanka from South India at great expense and that the entire project is "shrouded in secrecy." Much space is then given to the solicited reactions from the likes of the Roman Catholic bishop of Mannar, well-known Buddhist prelates and laymen in Colombo, the president of the Hindu Cultural Council, etc., all of whom express their "shock and amazement" at how two cabinet ministers could be heading a project based on "mere superstition." "From the sublime to the ridiculous," "waste of brick and mortar," "total fabrication" are but a few of the phrases attributed to the reactions of these well-known religious leaders. Two weeks later, *The Sunday Times* columnist Rajpal Abeyanayake added Ven. Soma's reaction: "It is imbecilic to construct a Hindu Kovil to deflect a curse on this island bestowed on it by Lord Vishnu."[42]

In the wake of this publication, I held conversations with Mr. Dennis Ratwatte, the *basnayake nilame* of the Maha (Viṣṇu) Devālaya in Kandy, in which we discussed extensively the contents of this particular story. I engaged Mr. Ratwatte frequently during the course of intensive field work at this venue in February and March 2000, and he was kind enough to assist me in answering whatever inquiries I had to make about Viṣṇu, the ritual and devotional life at this *devālaya*, and so on. Mr. Ratwatte is also a trustee on the committee formed to oversee the funding and building of the multireligious complex in question. He is also the brother of the current deputy minister of defense and the uncle of President Chandrika Kumaratunga. Mr. Ratwatte had been quoted in the the *Sunday Times* expose as saying, "[I]t was not Lord Vishnu who was looking upon Sri Lanka unfavorably, but his benevolent view was being blocked by a building 35' above sea level." He complained that even though he had tried to explain that the matter was a problem of *darsan* and not sorcery, the writer of the article kept referring to curses and malefics instead, and that this is how the rationale for the project had been presented in a distorted fashion to the religious and lay officials who had reacted so negatively to the idea, as quoted in the expose. Mr. Ratwatte explained that M. G. Ramachandran, a Tamil movie star turned politician whose native home is Kandy, a key early supporter in arming the LTTE, and at the time the chief minister of Tamilnadu in 1983, had built a *gopuram* at Sri Rangam temple in Tiruchipalli in front of Viṣṇu's gaze. The obstruction of this gaze corresponded with the terrible riots of July 1983, and Sri Rangam priests had expressed the view to his brother, the deputy defense minister, that the loss of Viṣṇu's benevolent gaze may be why Sri Lanka's experience since 1983 had been so problematic.[43] Mr. Ratwatte explained that the Viṣṇu temple was part of a larger plan to build a church, a mosque, Buddhist and Hindu temples in a complex that could come to symbolize the multireligious character of Sri Lanka and that "the story had blown the Viṣṇu aspect way out of proportion."[44] Finally, the cost of the project was estimated at Rs, 60,000,000 ($800,000) and not Rs. 600,000,000 ($8,000,000) as sensationally reported by the *Sunday Times*.

Perhaps the most vituperative attack upon worshiping the gods, and Viṣṇu in particular, occurred two months later, again in the *Sunday Times,* in a column by Soma's ardent well-wisher and colleague, Kumbakarana. The column was entitled: "Sanctioned by Religion, Killing Goes On."[45] The core paragraph recorded below speaks for itself and requires little commentary for the reader to understand its political purport:

> According to a dialogue between Krishna (Vishnu) and Arjuna, the taking of one's life and that of another is endorsed by religious belief. Under the Hindu concept of an unchanging soul transmigrating from life to life, death does not end life, and life does not end with death. Krishna tells Arjuna that there is no sin in taking one's own life. So suicide and killing others is justified by religion. Sections of the Defense authorities who are falling over each other to build Hindu kovils would do well to realize the newest sustenance of the Tiger killers is the Hindu atman concept. With great foresight, the LTTE is publicizing a video which shows Black Tigers performing Vishnu pujas before their departure to kill their targets and themselves. The Christian missionaries supporting the LTTE and propagating their religion will soon meet the reincarnation of Vishnu, in the Wanni and the East.

CONCLUSION

The contemporary Sri Lankan controversy about worshipping the gods, Viṣṇu in particular, is but the most recent manifestation of an enduring issue within the history of Buddhist religion. In the abstract, the problem would appear to be a classic doctrinal debate between those claiming purity in adherence to the Buddha's "original" teachings, and those who have assimilated popular aspects of South Asian religious culture. But as I have tried to demonstrate, abstract analyses, without benefit of historical analysis, can be incomplete if one is trying to ascertain what is driving the issue at hand. This contemporary manifestation is driven by an ethos of exclusivity among some sections of the Sinhala Buddhist community, which have been made to believe their veritable future is under siege. They are less concerned about doctrine than with political and economic survival. That is, the catalyst for the current controversy is based on fears, real or not, experienced by a largely urban, educated, middle-class, and "modern" segment of the Sinhala Buddhist community: precisely those who are the ardent supporters and share the religio-political views of Ven. Soma.

This ethos of exclusivity embraced by this section of the Sinhala Buddhist community may not be, however, indicative of the community's views in general. Over several months of field work at Viṣṇu *devālaya*s in Sri Lanka, I directly asked scores of *kapurāla*s and lay devotees for their reactions to Ven. Soma's views regarding the worship of gods, especially Viṣṇu, in Buddhism. At the time, I realized that what I was doing might be compared to asking church-going Catholics whether or not they believed in the authority of the Pope. But I asked anyway just to get a sense of what might be a Buddhist cultural response to Soma's Buddhist doctrinal critique, or to see if my interviewees were aware of the class and ethnic factors driving this particular aspect of Soma's critique. Not a single respondent mentioned class and ethnic issues. Instead, responses to Ven. Soma were uniformly very personal in character and varied from the polite to the agitated. While most said that worshiping the gods was a matter of personal religious discretion, part of the heritage of Sinhala religious culture, or that gods such as Viṣṇu protected the Buddhist *sāsana,* the more extreme responses included charges that Ven. Soma was a liar, really a Catholic sent to destroy Buddhism, and was not aware of the damage he was doing to Buddhism. These were among the more visceral reactions. But perhaps the most thoughtful response was given by a *kapurāla* at the Viṣṇu *devālaya* in Kandy who said: "Ven. Soma doesn't have a wife. He doesn't have children. So he doesn't have family. He doesn't have property to look after, doesn't need to worry about his food and seems to be in good health. If Ven. Soma had any of these problems, like the people who come to this *devālaya,* he would also come to worship Viṣṇu Deviyo and to seek his help."

While I have tried to make the case that the recent attack on the practice of Buddhists worshiping the gods has been driven by an ethos of exclusivity bred by ethnic and class consciousness, the *kapurāla*'s response gives an existential indication as to why Sinhala Buddhists worship the gods. They don't seem to do it for ethnic or political-economic reasons, yet these are the real reasons that they are being asked to stop worshiping the gods by Ven. Soma and his followers. Rather, most of them do it to express some hope that the current existential problems they encounter might be recognized by someone, and that some compassionate force in the cosmos will respond to their entreaties for help. Ven. Soma persuasively argues that people ought to solve their own problems rather laying them at the altar of the gods. What he may have overlooked, and perhaps his monastic ancestors overlooked this too, is that some people may not be in a position to solve their problems by themselves in rational, disciplined, and "scientific" ways. They recognize that they need some extraordinary kind of help and so they appeal to the gods for their assistance. Here are three examples of these appeals for divine protection and assistance which indicate why the gods continue to have appeal among Sinhala Buddhists.

It is not uncommon to see young families, especially mothers with infants, ask the *kapurāla* at *devālaya*s for the deity's *santiya* ("general well-being," "blessing," "peace") for their children. Young children, especially infants, are not yet equipped to handle whatever life might be ready to serve them. Moreover, it is customary in Sinhala Buddhist culture to bring a newborn infant to receive the blessings of the gods at the age of three months. Worshiping the gods on these occasions, then, is a recognition that life is full of unpredictable occasions, that in some circumstances, at least until children become adults, all can use some help and protection in finding their ways. Asking for the god's protection does not imply that parents will cease to look after their children's well-being. Rather, worshiping provides parents with a psychological reassurance, or a feeling that as parents they have done whatever they can for their children, including asking for divine protection.

The second example is more to the point. Many people making *pūja*s in *devālaya*s are seeking justice of one sort or another. It may be that neighbors are stealing coconuts, someone is practicing sorcery against them, or that a more powerful land owner has filed a court case against them. Anyone living in Sri Lanka today knows that the police, the politicians, the courts, and businessmen can often act in absolutely capricious ways. Justice is often elusive and no amount of self-effort or ethical diligence is going to change that. Viṣṇu is particularly relevant in this context. Unlike other deities who exist on the lower rungs of the pantheon's hierarchy, Viṣṇu is never invoked to undertake any actions that might be regarded as unethical. His *bodhisattva* status is not congruent with such behavior. He can only be petitioned to perform actions that are intrinsically good and ethically just. What he represents to those who call for his intervention is a hope for the existence of responsive justice in this world. Without this hope, or without gods who embody these hopes, existence can become a matter of dejection.

Finally, the third example is a direct answer to Ven. Soma's campaign. Over months of field work at Viṣṇu *devālaya*s in upcountry Sri Lanka, many devotees have made *pūja*s to the gods because their sons, brothers, and husbands are currently serving in the government's security forces fighting the civil war with the LTTE. They are frightened and concerned for the safety of their loved ones and they have come for the obvious reason that they are seeking the protection of the gods, expecially Viṣṇu, the "minister of defense." Most of these devotees are not urban, educated, and professionals, because almost all the young men serving in Sri Lanka's armed forces are from the rural areas of the country. The matter is put bluntly by some who say that "village boys are fighting Colombo's war." In this context, it can then be seen that not only do Ven. Soma and his supporters want villagers to fight their war, but Soma also wants to relieve them of one sure source of their family's hopes that they will survive the carnage: that is, *santiya,* the protective blessings of the gods.

NOTES

1. Geiger's translation followed the critical edition of the Pali *Mahāvaṃsa* text he had published for the Pali Text Society in 1908. The English translation was first undertaken by Mabel Bode and then amended by Geiger. The first translation into English of the *Mahāvaṃsa* was published by Turnour in 1837 by the colonial government of Ceylon.

2. See, for instances, the topics of many of the essays in Bardwell L. Smith, ed., *Religion and the Legitimation of Power in Sri Lanka* (Chambersburg, PA: Anima Books, 1978).

3. In some cases, academic careers were built on correcting or critiquing Geiger's work; Walpola Rahula's, *History of Buddhism in Ceylon: the Anuradhapura Period 3rd Century B.C.-40th Century A.D.* (Colombo, SL: M.D. Gunasena, 1956) and the many writings of G. C. Mendis are good examples of Sri Lankan scholars who mined the *Mahāvaṃsa* for reconstructing histories of Buddhism or cultural history in general.

4. See Steven Kemper's incisive study *The Presence of the Past* (Ithaca: Cornell University Press, 1991).

5. H. L Seneviratne notes that this mythic story is still ritually celebrated within the context of the *valyak* dance held annually at the Mahā (Viṣṇu) Devālaya in Kandy following the conclusion of the *asala perahara.* See his *Rituals of the Kandyan State* (Cambridge: Cambridge University Press, 1978), 102–108.

6. In point of fact, the Buddhist civilization in Sri Lanka appears to be the world's oldest continuous Buddhist culture.

7. Among many references, see in particular Nimal Prematillake, ed., *Hat Adiye Dehi Kapima* ("Cutting of the Lime in the Ritual of the Seven Steps") (Bandaragama, SL: Sisira Printers, 1987); K. D. Endiris de Silva, ed., *Vadiga Tantraya,* Part I (Kegalle, SL: Vidyakalpa Press, 1927), 15–16; Gananath Obeyesekere, *The Cult of the Goddess Pattini* (Chicago: University of Chicago Press, 1983), 103–105.

8. In Kandy, and at Gadaladeniya, Lankatilaka, Devinuwara, Hanguranketa, Dambulla, and Aluthnuwara.

9. See Archibald Lawrie, *A Gazeteer of the Central Province,* 2 vols. (Colombo, SL: George Skeen, Government Printer, 1898) 1: 127–29.

10. Richard Gombrich, *Precept and Practice: Buddhism in the Rural Highlands of Ceylon* (Oxford: the Clarendon Press, 1971), 177.

11. Excellent initial sources to ascertain an overview of the mythic personality given to Viṣṇu in late medieval Sinhala literature include L. D. Barnett, "Alphabetical Guide to Sinhala Folklore from Ballad Sources," *Indian Antiquary* 45–46 (1916–1917) and Hugh Neville, tr., *Sinhala Verse (Kavi),* ed. P. E. P. Deraniyagala (Colombo, SL: Ceylon National Museums Manuscript Series, vols. 4–6.

12. See Senaret Paranavitana, *The Shrine of Upulvan at Devundara.* Memoirs of the Archaeological Survey of Ceylon, Vol. VI. (Colombo, SL: The Ceylon Government Archaeological Department, 1953), 18–59, wherein the author argues, in very abstruse fashion, for Upulvan's identity with the Vedic god Varuna. Obeyesekere, *Cult of Pattini,* 312–21, has demolished Paranavitana's argument and submits that Upulvan was either an indigenous Sinhala deity adapted in the same way that Indra became Sakka, or was an early adaptation of Viṣṇu from the beginning. M. B. Ariyapala, *Society in Medaieval Ceylon* (Colombo, SL: Department of Cultural Affairs, 1956), 187–90, suggests that Upulvan was either Krishna or Rama, the latter speculation supported by Anuradha Seneviratne in "Rama and Ravana: History, Legend and Belief in Sri Lanka," *Ancient Ceylon: Journal of the Archaeological Survey Department of Sri Lanka* 5 (1984): 221–36. A. D. T. E. Perera, "Upulvan, the Patron God of the Sinhalese: An Attempt to Rediscover the God's Identity Through Literary and Archaeological Evidence," *Vidyodaya Journal of Arts, Science and Letters* 4, 1 and 2 (1971): 88–104, argues strongly for the identification of Upulvan with the Mahayana *bodhisattva* Avalokitesvara, a view that seems substantiated on iconographic bases by Ulrich von Schroeder, *Buddhist Sculptures of Sri Lanka* (Hong Kong: Visual Dharma Publications, 1991). Obeyesekere, ibid., has a concise analysis of how aspects of Upulvan/Viṣṇu have been grafted on to the mytic career of Aluthnuwara Deviyo.

13. Dennis Ratwatte, the current *basnayaka nilame* ("lay custodian") of the Mahā (Viṣṇu) Devālaya in Kandy recently made available a gold plated *sannasa* (royal grant) in his custody which Prof. P. B. Meegaskumbura of the Department of Sinhalese at the University of Peradeniya has translated into English for the first time. In that *sannasa,* the god who is addressed is Sri Ramachandran, thereby indicating that at least at the time of the *sannasa*'s date (1709 C.E.), Rama, as Viṣṇu's *avatar,* was regarded as this centrally important *devālaya*'s presiding deity. Rama is also addressed as the deity presiding at the royally endowed Mahā (Viṣṇu) Devālaya in Hanguranketa in the early-nineteenth-century panegyric poem *Rama Sandesa* written during the reign of the last of the Kandyan kings, Sri Vikrama Rajasinha (1798–1815 C.E.).

14. See the second chapter of my *The Religious World of Kirti Sri: Buddhism Art and Politics in Late Medieval Sri Lanka* (New York and Oxford: Oxford University Press, 1996).

15. For an overview of the system of central rites constituting public religious life in Kandy and its surrounding environs, see my *Buddha in the Crown: Avalokitesvara in the*

Buddhist Traditions of Sri Lanka (New York and Oxford: Oxford Univesity Press, 1991), 176–201.

16. For a description of the wanton desecration and destruction of this temple, see Paul E. Pieris, *Ceylon–the Poruguese Era* (Colombo, SL: Colombo Apothecaries Co., 1913), 238–41.

17. For an excellent study of how the Buddha has been regarded within Hindu tradition, including the perception that he is one of Viṣṇu's avatars, see Lal Mani Joshi, *Discerning the Buddha* (Dehli: Munshiram Manoharlal, 1983).

18. A good example is M. M. J. Marasinghe, *Gods in Early Buddhism* (Kelaniya, SL: University Sri Lanka, Vidyalankara Campus, 1974).

19. In the *Digha Nikaya* the Buddha compares ritually invoking the gods to commanding a stone to float on water.

20. The *Sigalovada Suttanta* of the *Digha Nikaya* is a particularly apt example in terms of the manner in which the Buddha advises lay followers to abandon efforts aimed at worshiping the gods of the four directions and the zenith and nadir in favor of cultivating wholesome social relations with various sets of people, including family, teachers, etc. For a powerful argument asserting the superiority of a religion without God at its focus, see Gunapala Dharmasiri, *A Buddhist Critique of the Christian Concept of God* (Antioch, CA: Golden Leaves Publishing, 1988).

21. Ariyapala, *Society and Culture,* 185, notes how the thirteenth century *Saddharma Ratnavaliya* admonishes the people to give up worship of Viṣṇu and Siva. Vidagama Maitreyi Thera, an eminent royal preceptor in the fifteenth century was a famous rival and critic of Sri Rahula Thera, the great grammarian and poet who is recognized as having sanctioned the worship of the gods and the practice of ritual magic. Kitsiri Malalgoda's brief account in *Buddhism in Sinhalese Society 1750–1900* (Berkeley: University of California Press, 1976) describes how an anti-Viṣṇu sentiment accompanied the formative years of the Amarapura monastic sect in Sri Lanka.

22. Prof. P. B. Meegaskumbura of the Department of Sinhalese at the University of Peradeniya suggests that there is a long history of elite monks in Sri Lanka who have resisted an acceptance of deities within Buddhist religious life, but that deity veneration in general has been accepted as a cultural norm throughout Sinhala cultural history.

23. Charles Hallisey, "Roads Taken and Roads Not Taken in the Study of Theravāda Buddhism," in *Curators of the Buddha,* ed. Donald Lopez (Chicago: University of Chicago Press, 1995), 31–61, notes how Sri Lankan scholars embraced Western scholarly analyses, particularly those of T. W. Rhys Davids, in the late nineteenth and early twentieth centuries.

24. Though Dharmakirti seems to have been "imbued with Mahayana ideals," Godakumbura notes that "one also sees in him a profound hatred towards the Saivites who have been gaining power in the country and spreading their ways of life and religious

practices." C. E. Godakumbura, *Sinhalese Literature* (Battaramulla, SL: Department of Cultural Affairs, 1955), 91–92.

25. For instance, the scathing attacks of Vidagama Maitreya Thera on *brāhmaṇical* practices during the Kotte period. See Ariyapala, *Society and Culture,* 182–83.

26. In the spring of 2000, a new Sinhala political party, Sinhala Urumaya, was founded to protect the interests of the Sinhalese community from being overrun by the Tamils, Muslims, and Christians. Buddhist monks have been deeply involved in the establishment of this new political party.

27. Rajpal Abeyanayake, "He Cuts Down Gods, Real and Imagined," *The Sunday Times,* January 17, 1999, 5.

28. Ibid., October 10, 1999, 6. In this interview, Ven. Soma charges that someone is hiding an inscription by King Saddhatissa which grants these lands to the Sinhalese temple. He says the land grant was last seen in the 1920s and that when it is rediscovered it will prove who really owns those lands.

29. Ibid., November 14, p. 15.

30. Kumbhakarana (an alias), *The Sunday Times,* September 5, 1999, 12.

31. *Sunday Times,* June 20, 1999, 14. I doubt that Abeyanayake is aware of the irony of his last sentence! It is very interesting to note that in the months following the articles by Kumbakarana and Abeyanayake that the *Sunday Times* enlisted Ven. Soma to write his own column entitled "Reflections." These columns ran for about two months before they stopped. Most of them were simply uninspired excerpts from Soma's boilerplate *dhamma*-talks and contained little controversy on political issues.

32. April 16, 5. The *Sunday Leader* was closed down in late May 2000 for allegedly violating draconian censorship laws put into effect as the war situation on the Jaffna peninsula deteriorated in April.

33. Whose mother is Sirima Ratwatte Bandaranaike (the world's first woman prime minister in 1960) and whose father, S. W. R. D. Bandaranaike, was elected prime minister by a resounding vote in 1956 (on a platform of "Sinhala-only" and Buddhism as the religion of the nation) only to be assassinated in 1959 by a Buddhist monk.

34. The nephew of J. R. Jaywardene, president of Sri Lanka from 1977–1989.

35. President Kumaratunga's grandfather was the longtime *basnayake nilame* of the Mahā (Viṣṇu) Devālaya in Kandy and the Aluthnuwara (Dädimunda) Devale. The post is currently held by Mr. Dennis Ratwatte, the president's uncle and Deputy Minister of Defense General Anuruddha Ratwatte's older brother.

36. Ven. Soma, "Reflections . . . ," *The Sunday Times,* November 7, 1999, 14.

37. Ibid., August 22, 1999, 13.

38. Ibid., October 31, 1999, 15.

39. Ibid., January 17, 1999, 5.

40. Lucien Rajakarunanayake, *The Sunday Observer,* June 4, 2000, 5.

41. Ruth Jansz, "Religious Star Wars," *The Sunday Times,* June 6, 1999.

42. Rajpal Abeynayake, "TV Demi-God and the Star-Crossed Leaders," *The Sunday Times,* June 20, 1999, 14.

43. Dennis Ratwatte's version of the story is corroborated by the manner in which the story was reported in by *India Today* in its January 17, 2000, issue.

44. During the course of field work at the Mahā (Viṣṇu) Devālaya in Kandy and at the Aluthnuwara Devālaya, I came to know that the deputy defense minister is indeed an ardent patron and frequent visitor to both *devālayas,* not surprising owing to the fact that his family has been deeply involved in the administration of both places for generations.

45. *Sunday Times,* August 15, 1999, 15.

SEVEN

LOCALIZING LINEAGE

IMPORTING HIGHER ORDINATION IN THERAVĀDIN SOUTH AND SOUTHEAST ASIA

Anne M. Blackburn

INTRODUCTION

SSAY ADDRESSES questions about the processes through whi st communities and institutions come to be localized and acce within the context of their development. Specifically, I use ıt of monastic institutional formation in eighteenth-century Sr nt of orientation for thinking about the historical processes inv cessful importation of monastic lineages within Theravādin So ast Asia. I ask, in effect, what makes it possible for a monastic ed from one part of the Buddhist world to another through *upa* me accepted as locally authoritative and congruent with local gs of Buddhist "tradition." Why, for instance, did the higher orc t to Sri Lanka from Arakan in the seventeenth century fail to ta island while the higher ordination introduced from Ayutthay nth century succeeded unmistakably?

account begins with a brief sketch of the circumstances in whic ic order called the Siyam Nikāya was established in Sri Lanka du nth century. I then comment on the challenges of localization f rs of the new order, and discuss a series of activities undert

Nikāya monks that combined to create a perception of the order
han foreign and as "traditional" rather than innovative. After a b
of these activities, I suggest that the Sri Lankan case offers a moc
we might study the importation of monastic lineage in Southe
ly this model in a preliminary way to two moments in Southea
st history.

THE RISE OF THE SIYAM NIKĀYA

mid-1700s there were no monks with higher ordination in Sri
time the Sri Lankan sangha was fraught with tension betwe
ic groups: those known as *gaṇinnānse*s (literally, "members of a
nd those who modestly called themselves the Disciplined O
amagama). Although the *gaṇinnānse*s had not received *upasam*
sen to give up this monastic status, they played many of the ro
xpected of monastics. Performing rituals for protection and
;, they were also preachers. As temple incumbents they look
lands and other property (including manuscript collections) a
nes served as teachers. Leaders among the *gaṇinnānse*s possess
e economic and political power in the Kandyan Kingdom, wh
utonomy in the island's central region despite increasing pressu
tch East India Company.

d by a novice monk named Välivița Saraṇaṃkara (1698–1778), t
d Ones campaigned for the reintroduction of *upasampadā* to Sr
utheast Asia and challenged the authority of *gaṇinnānse* monks.
criticisms of their *gaṇinnānse* brethren were charges that the latt
re to monastic disciplinary rules, causing the deterioration of th
mmunity in Sri Lanka. Leading monks among the *gaṇinnānse*s fe
ower of the Disciplined Ones, who had begun to attract the su
*aṇinnānse*s resident in important temples and to win the suppo
in the central region of the island. In this context *gaṇinnānse*s clos
urt charged the Disciplined Ones with impropriety in their turn
se led by Saraṇaṃkara of failing to show respect for senior *ga*
Backed by the reigning king of Sri Lanka's central Kandyan Ki
aya Narēndrasiṃha (r. 1739–1747), they thus contrived the exil
ned Ones from the Kandyan capital during the early 1740s.

the late 1740s, however, and in large part because of the Dis
kill as poets and disputants in the sophisticated performance cu
dyan Court, the novices and would-be monks led by Saraṇaṃ

⁷-1780), the Disciplined Ones became powerful enough to ga
: for the reintroduction of higher ordination from Southea
arrived from Ayutthaya to perform *pabbajjā* and *upasampad*
for Sri Lankan novices and *gaṇinnānses* in 1753. This marked t
:t of a new monastic order in Sri Lanka, which was called the
in recognition of its origins and,[2] in all likelihood, to distingu
dination tradition from those imported from Arakan in the p
:[3] Many *gaṇinnānses* initially resisted the rise of the Siyam Nikāy
loss of temple property and powerful incumbencies. Howeve
ıonks opposed to the new order eventually entered its ranks t
ordination since it was clear by the 1770s that the Siyam Nik
› stay as the central locus of Sri Lankan monastic power and w

THE CHALLENGE OF LOCALIZATION

lebratory histories of the Siyam Nikāya composed during th
century by authors sympathetic to the new order understandab
: order's smooth progress to dominance of the Sri Lankan s
er, when one looks carefully at the land and social capital held
Nikāya's *gaṇinnānse* predecessors and rivals, it is clear that th
rise to power could not have proceeded without considerable
'his is borne out by the record of the first *upasampadā* in which
ıl *gaṇinnānse* monks received higher ordination before long-s
rs of Saraṇaṃkara. This apparent attempt to neutralize the opp
gaṇinnānse leaders is reflected also in early monastic appoir
the Malvatu and Asgiri Vihāraya hierarchy.[6]

.e conflicted and combative state of the Sri Lankan sangha dur
also finds reflection in the polemical descriptions of *gaṇinnānse*
:ommon to Siyam Nikāya monastic biographies and histories.
the historical introduction to a monastic regulation promulgate
'the Siyam Nikāya's formation reads:

> he *sāsana* . . . declined gradually until our time when not a single monk
> ined in all of Lanka [and only] a few novices remained. Of these novi
> rt from some who were modest and liked discipline, the remaining maj
> . . . engaged in various improper activities such as trade and agriculture,
> ved villages and lands for royal service and studied reviled sciences that w
> hibited by the Buddha, such as astrology, medicine and *yakṣa*-sorcery. T
> :e mixed up with kin groups [rather than monastic groups] and cared

competitive context, in which the survival of the Siyam Nik upon its ability to galvanize the sustained support of as many ble, as well as that of the king and other lay benefactors, it was order to articulate its claim to legitimacy and authority in t‹ ıddhist traditions.[8]

LOCAL HISTORIES

d have been plausible, in these circumstances, for Siyam Nikāy efend the order's claim to authority within the sangha on the g Siamese *upasampadā* tradition was in fact the continuation of hala ordination traditions established earlier in Southeast Asia. ; however, the monastic histories composed by those connecte Nikāya failed to make any such claim. Siyam Nikāya monks ar ers had reason to be wary of claims to authority framed prim f re-importation, of course. Such claims would have diminisl e between members of the new order and many *gaṇinnāns* ordination lineage (though lapsed) could also have been describ orted local tradition. In any event, Siyam Nikāya supporters m ze the order's claim to authority within the local context by m of overlapping arguments, in discourse and in practice, for the ity with selected earlier Sri Lankan monastic traditions.

am Nikāya claims to serve as proper leaders of the sangha wer intelligible through the composition of narratives that pla Nikāya's formation squarely within a longer account of the Sri history. This was articulated in terms of religious decline and arratives, which we find in *vaṃsa* form as well as in monastic ıch as *Saṃgharājasadhucariyāva* and in monastic regulations, he tention away from the Siyam Nikāya's foreign *upasampadā* as s often innovative approach to monastic education and adm From the perspective of these histories, the Siyam Nikāya was one of a series of agents acting to sustain the Buddhist *sāsana* ım time possible, rather than as an agent of change.[11]

e illusion of continuity between the Siyam Nikāya and earli ic institutions was also sustained by the new order's insistence ated in a long-standing tradition of forest-dwelling monasticis elling or *araññavāsī* monks, as their name suggests, were ass style of monasticism that emphasized the distance between ic life as well as involvement in distinctive ascetic practices.

ons,[12] the *araññavāsī* designation was a prestigious one, crystalliz values of Buddhist monasticism with great efficiency. With t time, the idea of forest-dwelling monasticism acquired a rich orical associations. Particular monastic figures became emblem āsī monasticism as did specific types of educational practi l performance. Among the most important names connecte āsī monasticism were Dim̆bulāgala Kasyapa (fl. twelfth centu lāgala Medhaṃkara (fl. thirteenth century). Because of the c tween *araññavāsī* monasticism and substantial reorganizations conducted by kings Parākramabāhu I and II, *araññavāsī* monl y associated with disciplinary purity and knowledge of all thı f the *tipiṭaka*.[13] After the thirteenth century, because of the sc eft by the *araññavāsī* monks of the Dam̆badeṇi Period, forest-d icism was associated especially with prose preaching texts *(b* in Sinhala and Sinhala commentaries or *sannaya*s written esj ıoritative Pāli works.[14]

sociations between the Siyam Nikāya and Sri Lanka's earlier *ara* were forged through textual representations of desirable mon as through choices made with respect to textual and ritual prac nd advisory letters composed by the Siyam Nikāya's fo ṇkara, forest-dwelling monasticism was consistently promote 'his comes through clearly, for instance, in the emphasis on *ara* sm that characterizes several chapters of Saraṇaṃkara's comp *ısaṇgrahaya* and in *Sārārthadīpanī*'s frequent assimilation of all m orest-dwelling monasticism.[15] Saraṇaṃkara went farther still, u regulation composed by the famous thirteenth-century *ara* Medhaṃkara as the root text for his own disciplinary guideline am Nikāya leaders also invoked the legacy of forest-dwelling l phere of monastic practice. Siyam Nikāya monks made use of of text and ritual long associated with *araññavāsī* monasticism ı the study of Pāli language and the provision of access to *tipiṭa* ı Pāli and Sinhala commentarial traditions, the education prov ım Nikāya created a practical pedagogical link between the new prestigious model of learned Sri Lankan monasticism dating deṇi Period. Such similitude is also visible in the move made by monks to privilege the composition of commentarial and con (especially those appropriate for use as preaching texts), first p the Dam̆badeṇi Period *araññavāsī* monks.[17] In this regard, tl commentaries, so important to the Siyam Nikāya's educatior

constructing a stark disjunction between types of protectiv
ɜ, early monks of the Siyam Nikāya staked a further claim tc
vith local *araññavāsī* monasticism. Saraṇaṃkara's composi
ɪdīpanī, a commentary on the *paritta* texts contained in th
a, was modeled explicitly on a Daṁbadeṇi Period *paritta* comn
ed by an *araññavāsī* monastic scholar.[19] *Sārārthadīpanī* thus con
ment through composition, and indirectly through ritual prac
f the Siyam Nikāya as heir to an earlier forest-dwelling lineage
tandem with a clear proscription of other protective ritual p
sorcery and astrology, which were described as recent expres
rate monasticism.[20]

cause of the role played by *araññavāsī* monks in two substantial
ıs of the Sri Lankan sangha that occurred during the twelfth aı
centuries the connection forged between the Siyam Nikāya anc
lwelling monastics through textual and ritual practices endov
with an element of borrowed authority as reformist monks. Alt
e shown at length elsewhere,[21] members of the Siyam Nikāya
ponsible for substantial innovations within the sangha rather t
forward reintroduction of patterns of conduct characteristic oı
ic traditions on the island, identification with an earlier *araññaı*
lped to disguise this innovation. Moreover, because identificati
er *araññavāsī* lineage delicately cloaked Siyam Nikāya monks
of sangha reformism, Siyam Nikāya criticisms of their *gaṇinnān*
an element of moral authority they would not otherwise have
her choices made by the early Siyam Nikāya leadership made it e
and lay patrons alike to view the order as an agent of renewal ratl
gent of change. For instance, all of the *sīmā,* or monastic ritual
tablished in the first years of the order were erected on the site c
ldhist temples, and often at temples with a long and celebrated h
ult all of the new order's most important ritual transactions occı
ically and locally dense symbolic context that communicated the
he guarantor of local "tradition." Saraṇaṃkara and his colleagues
ıg selectivity with respect to Siamese Buddhist practices also, whi
sophisticated understanding of the arguments for lineage and aı
through Buddhist symbolic forms. As G. Vijayavardhana and P.
bura have shown in an important study of communication b
ınd Ayutthaya, leaders of the Siyam Nikāya rejected styles of ima
n and decoration favored by the Siamese embassies and sought a
e *saṇgharāja* in Ayutthaya for their favored Lankan style of *paritta*

This curriculum altogether ignored the system of monastic ex
tablished in Ayutthaya.[24] The hierarchy of monastic offices used i
ıay have provided inspiration to early leaders of the Siyam Nikā
a comprehensive and centralizing scheme.[25] However, Siyam
preferred to create an independent, local, administrative systen
replicate the Ayutthayan model.

LOCAL LANGUAGE

ır I have suggested that the Siyam Nikāya's rapid rise to a pos
.nce within the Sri Lankan Buddhist community was due in sig
the skill with which members of the order presented it as con
ıe island's earlier monastic traditions, creating a local history
der through a series of connected expressions in discourse and i
ıis impression of continuity was achieved despite the fact t
Nikāya had its roots in an imported tradition of higher ordinaı
ːd after a period of considerable rupture within the Sri
[26] Despite the circumstances of its origins, by the 1770s the ne
ːd a decidedly advantageous and locally coherent pedigree.
.e response of Siyam Nikāya monks to the challenge of localiz
also, I am inclined to believe, in their striking preference for
ıf composition. Eighteenth-century monastic biographies,[27] as
nanuscript collections,[28] reveal that Siyam Nikāya monks were
with the translation of authoritative Pāli texts and with the com
ala commentaries for texts from the Pāli *tipiṭaka* and *aṭṭhakath*
ssion of *tipiṭaka* textual traditions through local language genres
been a matter of greater concern to Siyam Nikāya monks thar
ıonastic community on the island since the earliest centuries
Nikāya monks were, as I have already indicated, indebted to
and—especially—Daṁbadeṇi monks for certain prose genres an
ial styles, they far outstripped them in comprehensive attention
ties. Among eighteenth-century compositions of this sort we fi
nslations of major works such as the *Milindapañha* and *Vimān*
compendia comprised largely of material drawn from the Pā
Visuddhimagga, monastic handbooks *(baṇa daham pot)* containi
.nslations and commentaries of Pāli disciplinary and *sutta* te
ıl commentaries on favorite Pāli *sutta*s composed for independ
ı. The composition of bilingual texts and translations was one
methods through which Siyam Nikāya monks demonstrated th

e Siyam Nikāya's preference for compositions that transmitted
Pāli textual traditions in local language forms was almost certai
t of several influences. There is evidence that Catholic mission
n the island during the seventeenth and eighteenth centuries i
position of Sinhala-language preaching and catechetical texts,
pendia composed of biblical extracts, for the Catholic fathers a
ed) converts.[30] Välivița Saraṇaṃkara's youth and early leadershi
amāgama occurred at a time when Catholic priests found consi
ith the Kandyan King Narēndrasiṃha.[31] Catholic devotional a
preferences were thus a visible and audible presence in Saraṇa
ite Kandyan milieu. It is therefore not impossible that Siyam
nces in textual production were in part a response to the incre
presence of Sinhala Christian texts in the Kandyan Kingdom.
e intensity of Siyam Nikāya interest in Sinhala-language com
nslation, however, and the attention paid to such compositio
hies and historical narratives written to support the new order
se linguistic choices were important to the order's self-definit
ey were understood by Siyam Nikāya monks and their suppo
authority intelligible within the local Buddhist context. When
ction with evidence of the Siyam Nikāya's early patronage
n Court and of the new order's monastic curriculum, it is cl
Nikāya monks approached study of the *tipiṭaka* and the produ
nguage and bilingual texts based on the *tipiṭaka* as a particular
rm of learned display.[32] In addition to the role played by such
s in the construction of links to a local *araññavāsī* lineage, they
v order squarely within an encompassing history of the *sāsa*
dge of Pāli required for the composition of such texts allowe
monks to present themselves as monks conversant with pan
textual authorities, responsible to the original authority of *bu*
d prepared to protect the vitality of the Buddhist *sāsana*.[33] At t
owever, these forms of composition underscored the order's c
the life of the *local* Sri Lankan *sāsana*, a commitment unders
the mediation of *buddhavacana* through Sinhala for the bene
mmunity.[34] As translators and commentators writing in and pr
the Sinhala medium, the first generation of Siyam Nikāya mo
emphatically local textual tradition that influenced the charact
Buddhist practice throughout the nineteenth century. Throu
ive discourse on monasticism and their textual and ritual pra
onks made clear their view that the success of the *sāsana* in Sri

:nany aspects of the Siyam Nikāya's formative period were, of
to the specific circumstances of eighteenth-century Kand
there are broader lessons to be learned from the localization pı
:ussed. A recapitulation of my argument thus far may be helpf
ıerging Siyam Nikāya faced considerable opposition from thei
redecessors on the island. *Gaṇinnānse* monks existed comfort
ɔrk of local and kingdom-wide patronage arrangements tha
disturbed easily by an upstart monastic movement. The res
by monastic establishment and court patrons alike to the Disc
eveals that the establishment of a new *upasampadā* lineage on
ıd with it a far-reaching new system of monastic administrati
ıge, was far from a guaranteed success. That the Siyam Nikāy
ıinate the monastic culture of eighteenth-century Sri Lank
o the ability of its early monks and supporters to connect t
ɔ the island's earlier prestigious monastic traditions and to an e
local understanding of the *sāsana*'s history. Through a series c
; arguments, made through strategic representations of the nev
rivals as well as other textual and ritual practices, Siyam
gained for themselves a crucial line of symbolic continuity to
ɔcal understandings of prestigious monasticism.[36]

.e successful establishment of an imported monastic lineage c
South and Southeast Asia required that monks connected w
ıeage win and sustain the attention of powerful lay patrons,
the king was typically the most important. In order to sustain sı
:, and to exercise command over resources and position in the
to-day activities within the monastic community itself, monl
with the new lineage had to be recognized as plausible sources
within the sangha. The circumstances of the Siyam Nikāya's
suggest that the attainment of sustained external patronage an
within the sangha depends upon several linked achievement
:al models and methods are required to accommodate an in
within a locally intelligible teleology, representating the impor
an agent of reform or revival, rather than a harbinger of cha
ıe time, a locally acceptable history must be created for the in
, linking it to monastic traditions already accorded prestige wit
uddhist culture. The development of such a local history is li
hrough a variety of Buddhist practices operating simultaneous

:s. Here I understand textual practices broadly enough to incl
made to compose, copy, and transmit texts, as well as to prot
genres through curriculum. By ritual practices I mean the pres
scription of specific ritual forms, as well as the establishment
on the location and style of performance.

LOOKING TO SOUTHEAST ASIA

odel of localization based on the Siyam Nikāya case places cert
evidence from Buddhist Southeast Asia in an intriguing new p
e brief discussion that follows is necessarily preliminary in nat
on the work of other scholars. It is my hope, however, that it
for further research on the historical processes involved in the
nd domestication of monastic lineages. I shall focus on events i
n in Lān Nā but note in passing that the period of King Dhamr
Pegu (1472–1492) deserves further study from this perspectiv
s striking, given the association between local-language and b
res and the Siyam Nikāya's rise, that William Pruitt has traced
ce to a Burmese *nissaya* text to the reign of Narapatisithu ir
–1210).[38] A *nissaya* is a commentary-translation of a Pāli text
were often composed for texts from the Pāli *tipiṭaka,* manuscr
also contain *nissaya*s for a variety of non-*tipiṭaka* texts including
works. When composed for *tipiṭaka* texts, they could treat a
racted directly or texts that made smaller sections of the *tipiṭak*
ccessible. Like the *sūtra sannaya* genre discussed earlier with re
anka, *nissaya* texts typically circulated with the Pāli root text,
on of local language access to Pāli texts.[39]

e period of Narapatisithu's reign was, of course, a time of
for Burmese literary and inscriptional production.[40] However,
n of events during the reign of Narapatisithu suggests that the
of the Burmese *nissaya* genre may be related to localization p
sort described above. This period saw the arrival of the Mor
a and his companions from Sri Lanka.[41] Chapata's criticism of
ic disciplinary practices deepened existing fractures within the
His insistence that all monks in agreement with him receive r
n marked the importation of a new monastic lineage to Pagan
ces were high at the time of Chapata's arrival is clear from M
Thwin's account of Narapatisithu's "purification" and reorganiz
gha.[43] *The Glass Palace Chronicle*'s description of Chapata and his

m thus inclined to view Chapata's monastic venture as a succe:
seek signs that the successful importation of ordination from Sr
d at least some of the elements proposed in my earlier model.
I suggest that the rise of *nissaya* production in twelfth-century
apparent preference given to *Vinaya* texts in early *nissaya* proc
ted to Chapata's rise,[46] and that the genre was favored by the
connected with his imported lineage. *The Glass Palace Chronicle*
the textual preferences of Chapata and his fellow monks off
for this view, describing Chapata as someone who had "stuc
Pitakas and the commentaries, and when he had mastered tl
to return to Pagan" and noting that Chapata's companions were
ali, commentaries and subcommentaries."[47] Shin Rahula, one
nion monks, is later associated with the *Khuddasikkhā,* the text
earliest *nissaya* for which Pruitt reports a reference.[48]

other words, the production of *nissaya*s might be read as evid
practice symbolically significant as well as pedagogically impo
iscussion of the successful localization of Chapata's higher ord
n, based on the model I have suggested, would also require
study of the Burmese chronicle and *thamaing* traditions.[49] My l
Pagan moves from evidence of textual production to suggest tl
f other elements in a process of localizing lineage. For Lān
historical narratives likely to have played a role in the loca
es modeled above. On the basis of these narratives, I suggest
r related evidence in the spheres of textual and ritual practice.

vid Wyatt has noted that the character of political and religio
in Southeast Asia changed substantially during the thirteenth
t such changes were reflected in an increasingly rich corpus
les subsequently produced within the Tai states.[50] The textual
eenth-century Lān Nā bears out Wyatt's views on Tai chronicl
t reveals an unprecedented local interest in the composition of
ratives relating to the history of the sangha in that region and i
ms with which the Lān Nā city-states had dealings. Here I refer
to the well-known *Jinakālamālī* (sometimes called the *Jinal
aṃ)* composed in Pāli, as well as the *Tamnān Mūlasāsanā Wat P
Tamnān Mūlasāsanā Wat Suan Dok,* both composed in Thai Yi
narratives devote considerable attention to monastic ordinatio
the region and, in particular, to events relating to the arrival
ed lineages (directly or indirectly of Sri Lankan origin) in the
ourteenth and fifteenth centuries. The first lineage was brough

Udumbaragiri (Dimbulagala) *araññavāsī* lineage, was associat
an Dok given to him by the king. In approximately 1430, dur
f King Sam Fang Kaen (r. 1411–1442) and with royal support,
eage reached Chiang Mai. Led by Lān Nā monk Medhaṃ
mbhira (sources vary), and accompanied by two Sri Lankan
yed for some time at Wat Pā Daeng in Chiang Mai but resid
outside the city.[52] Predictably, tensions arose between the two l
re expressed primarily in terms of disciplinary differences.[53] M
Daeng lineage were clearly in ascendance by the time o
āja (r. 1442–1487). They were appointed to the key posit
ru and Saṇgharāja, and received substantial royal support for m
including Wat Pā Daeng, which became the lineage's center f
rituals. The later sections of *Jinakālamālī* indicate strong royal
Pā Daeng lineage, which appears to have retained the highest
ic appointments of the period.[54]
ggest that the *Jinakālamālī* and the *Tamnān Mūlasāsanā Wat P*
he importance of historical narratives to the imported Pā Dae
d that their composition played a role in naturalizing the Pā
rise to power. While a closer examination of the tropologi
cal logic expressed by these texts is required to substantiate th
briefly note several pieces of evidence lending support to m
. The author of the *Jinakālamālī*, Ratanapañña Thera, lived fo
Cedī Cet Yod, a temple important to the Pā Daeng lineage and
nurādhapura-derived *bodhi* tree planted during Tilokarāja's reig
sed at least the text's colophon from Wat Pā Daeng.[56]
e density of the text's references to the lineages of Wat Suan D
Daeng is striking, as is the fact that such references occur as a
ts highly charged within a contested monastic community. Th
oyal patronage for temple construction, the establishment of *sī*
formance of large-scale ordination ceremonies. Such character
k increase the odds that the *Jinakālamālī* was written in at leas
to lineage-based historical argumentation. Moreover, the struc
's two concluding points, which focus on Pā Daeng monastic
suggest that the author's understanding of significant chronol
ced by his identity as a monk in the Wat Pā Daeng lineage.[57]
e *Tamnān Mūlasāsanā Wat Pā Daeng,* while almost certainly co
Pā Daeng in Chiang Tung to the northeast of Chiang Mai, pre
t of contested monasticism decidedly in favor of the Wat Pā
account gives Ñāṇagambhīra central billing, describes mona

west from Chiang Tung.[58] The colophon is striking in its
n to lineage identity.

ages, endowed with virtue and wisdom, who seek the righteous way
owledge, consider and read carefully, memorize orally and by heart, w
vn and practice for the continuation [of the tradition] the Mūlasās
ught from Rohana by Ñāṇagambhīra, so that the religion will not be
gered and deteriorate. . . . This *tamnān* must be placed in every *wa*
ryone will know the teachings of the Buddha. . . . The monk who is
ned in the *sāsanā* of Ñāṇagambhīra, a Siṇhalarattārāma Order, and who d
practice seriously, will become indolent and will not prosper. . . . The
, I who have religious knowledge have spoken these words to the monk
re generations.[59]

the very existence of the *Tamnān Mūlasāsanā Wat Suan Do*
the same period,[60] suggests that accounts of the past and cont
went hand in hand in Lān Nā as elsewhere in the Buddhist wo
as I have suggested, it is correct to interpret the *Tamnān Wat P*
Jinakālamālī in relation to the successful localization of an in
, the texts themselves provide rich clues for the reconstructio
guments made in the symbolic sphere of ritual practices. Mo
he contentious and learned character of the monastic culture
by these texts, we should expect to discern arguments related
the sphere of textual practices as well. In the light of eviden
nth-century Sri Lanka and twelfth-century Burma, scholars of
ns might attend to the possibility that the popularity of *vohan*
s,[51] in addition to the *tamnān* genre already mentioned, is in so
l to life of the monastic lineage.[62]

NOTES

the ideas presented below were first broached at the International Assoc
t Studies Conference in Lausanne, Switzerland. I wish to thank the Univ
arolina for travel support. For comments on earlier versions of this essay
re due to: Katherine Bowie, John Clayton, Richard Gombrich, Charles
lt, and Donald Swearer.

This section briefly recapitulates the account given in Anne M. Bla
Learning and Textual Practice in Eighteenth-Century Lankan Monastic
on: Princeton University Press, 2001), esp. chs. 2–3.

Kandyan Kingdom was willing to support the introduction of higher or
eral parts of Southeast Asia. Indeed, an embassy was sent to Pegu in 17
k thwarted this mission. See Lorna Dewaraja, *The Kandyan Kingdom of S
782* (Colombo: Lake House, 1988), 99–102; see also K. Goonewardene
he Twilight Years and Its Triangular Relations with the V.O.C. and Sri
Lanka Journal of the Humanities 6, 1–2 (1980):1–47; compare *Cūlavaṃsa,* e
Geiger (London: Pali Text Society, 1980), 98: 88–93. However, G. Vij
d P. B. Mīgaskumbura argue that Saraṇaṃkara and his early follow
monastic traditions in particularly high esteem, seeing the Siamese sangh
pure and undivided, *Siyam-Śrī Laṃkā Āgamika Sambhandanā* (Colombo:
ayō, 1993), xlii. It is interesting to note that Tibboṭuvāvē Buddharakk
he *Mahāvaṃsa* chapters composed during the eighteenth century and p
ūlavaṃsa, describes Ayutthaya as site eventually selected for the impor
rdination (98:91–92; 100:62–163), but later uses the term *Rakkhaṅga* in
be a reference to monks recently arrived from Ayutthaya (99:25–26); cf.
r., *Cūlavaṃsa* (Oxford: Pali Text Society, 1992), 257. This shifting nome
reflects Buddharakkhita's awareness of political shifts in mainland South
takeover of Ayutthaya by Burmese forces.

Though *gaṇinnānses* lacked the numbers to conduct higher ordination
anese line, some may have countered dismissive comments by the Di
th reference to Arakanese *paraṃparā*. Since most extant accounts of eig
events were composed from the perspective of Siyam Nikāya supporters, i
iscern *gaṇinnānse* attitudes toward lineage and their place in monastic con
at the nineteenth-century monastic lineages introduced from Southeas
Siyam Nikāya hegemony were named after the regions of ordination orig

For instance: the eighteenth-century chapters of *Mahāvaṃsa* (esp. 100:
ājasadhucariyāva (esp. 23–29), *Saṃgharājavata* (esp. v. 170–194), and
as promulgated during the reign of Kīrti Śrī Rājasiṃha, Nandasena R
kāvatas (München: Kitzinger, 1971), 96–98.

Gaṇinnānse monks controlled monastic buildings as well as the lands a
l for their maintenance through grants by the laity, of whom the king
portant. Rights to incumbency and associated labor and properties were
d by *gaṇinnānses* bound through familial ties. This system of property dist
atened—at least initially—by the establishment of a new monastic line
iple incumbencies. For details on land grants and inheritance systems,
The Kandyan Kingdom. Gaṇinnānse monks also served the royal court in se
some of which were extremely lucrative, see Dewaraja, *The Kandyan K*
Kobbäkaduvē Gaṇe Baṇḍāra is a striking (and perhaps extreme) case in
Dewaraja, *The Kandyan Kingdom,* 174. On *gaṇinnānse* activities, see
Vācissara, *Saraṇaṃkara Sangha rāja Samaya* (Colombo: Y. Don Edwin et a

kīrti and Tärūlē Dhammaratana (Colombo: Madhyama Saṃskṛtika Arā
8, 85.

Ratnapala, *The Katikāvatas,* 97. See also *Saṃgharājavata* (53–70) and *S*
riyāva, 14–19.

Several arguments have been articulated to explain the initial interest
iplined Ones by kings Śrī Vīraparākrama Narēndrasiṃha, Śrī Vijaya Rā
i Śrī Rājasiṃha. See, for instance, Dewaraja, *The Kandyan Kingdom,* a
Holt, *The Religious World of Kīrti Śrī* (New York: Oxford University Pres
pare Blackburn, *Buddhist Learning.* Whatever the reasons, members of
od to gain little devotional or political benefit by supporting a monasti
ld not articulate its authority and purity in a locally coherent idiom.

On which see, for instance, N. A. Jayawickrama, *The Sheaf of Garlan*
f the Conqueror (London: Pali Text Society, 1978), xvi–xvii.

For a more thorough treatment of this point see Blackburn, *Buddhi*
4.

On the possible life span of the Buddhist *sāsana* and narratives written
of its decline, see Jan Nattier, *Once Upon a Future Time* (Berkeley: Asian
s, 1991).

B. Sannasgala, *Siṃhala Sāhitya Vaṃśaya* (Colombo: Lake House, 1964)
.

Ibid., 76–79, 122–24.

Ibid., 126.

On *Sārārthasaṇgrahaya* see further Sannasgala, *Siṃhala Sāhitya Vaṃśaya,*
rthadīpanī see further Sannasgala, *Siṃhala Sāhitya Vaṃśaya,* 406–408, an
uddhist Learning, esp. chs. 6–7.

Ratnapala, *The Katikāvatas,* 93–100; cf. 44–64.

The importance of Daṁbadeṇi Period literary models for Siyam Nikāy
gested to me separately by Charles Hallisey and P. B. Mīgaskumbura.

On this commentarial genre and its importance to the Siyam Nikāya,
ckburn, *Buddhist Learning.*

Sannasgala, *Siṃhala Sāhitya Vaṃśaya,* 406–407; Blackburn, *Buddhi*
5.

See *Saṃgharājasādhucariyāva* (14), *Saṃgharājavata* (v. 80), and Ratnap
tas, 60, 96–97, 99. The numerous non-*paritta* protective texts contained
ipt collections such as the British Library's Hugh Nevill Collection stror

Blackburn, *Buddhist Learning*.

See Holt, *The Religious World of Kīrti Śrī*, Marie Gatellier, *Peintures mura*
cole Kandyenne, XVIIIe–XIXe siècles (Paris: Ecole Française d'Extrême-
nd *Mahāvaṃsa* (99–100).

Vijayavardhana and Mīgaskumbura, *Siyam-Śrī Laṃkā Āgamika Samb*
e correspondence over *paritta* chant suggests that, in addition, to the linea
ons in *kammavācā* recitation discussed by François Bizot, *Les traditions de l*
'u Sud-Est (Göttingen: Vandenhoeck and Ruprecht, 1976), protective r
e played a role in monastic self-identification in South and Southeast Asi

S. J. Tambiah, *World Conqueror and World Renouncer* (Cambridge: Ca
ty Press, 1976), 203–204.

I am grateful to Charles Hallisey for this observation. On the system
ra see Tambiah, *World Conqueror and World Renouncer*, 179–183.

On the character of the Sri Lankan sangha between the Daṁbadeṇi Pe
of the Siyam Nikāya the most interesting and useful source is Sannasgala,
'aṃśaya.

Of which the most striking in this regard is *Saṃgharājasādhucariyāva*, f
of which see Blackburn, *Buddhist Learning*.

See, for instance, C. E. Godakumbura, *Catalogue of Cambodian and Bur*
pts (Copenhagen: The Royal Library, 1983), and K. D. Somadasa, *Catalo*
will Collection of Sinhalese Manuscripts, 7 vols. (London: Pali Text Society
Library, 1987).

See Sannasgala, *Siṃhala Sāhitya Vaṃśaya*, 391–507, Somadasa, *Catalog*
will Collection of Sinhalese Manuscripts, and Blackburn, esp. chs. 3–5.

S. G. Perera, *Life of Father Jacome Gonalves* (Madura: De Nobili Press

Dewaraja, *The Kandyan Kingdom*, 77–79, 102–103.

Important evidence for the relationship between learning and patronage
onative texts compiled by Archibald Lawrie, *A Gazateer of the Central*
Colombo: George J. A. Skeen, Government Printer, 1898), some of w
d by Holt, *The Religious World of Kīrti Śrī*. For a fuller analysis of th
approach to learned display, especially in the context of the Kandyan C
rn, *Buddhist Learning*, esp. chs. 3 and 5.

This point is indebted to Steven Collins, unpublished manuscript, "Pa
-8.

s *Vimānavastu* teaching is a teaching as deep as a great ocean. . . . Thus, if [somec e to think, "I will elucidate the meaning, translating the meaning of the Pāli into ! ," it would be like someone trying to empty the water of the ocean with the she ustard seed. However, it is profitable—not useless—to satisfy someone with ev(;le gem after they've seen a great mine of gems. . . . Similarly . . . to preach with e line and to listen to preaching and so reach *nirvāṇa* are causes of mundane and su] ıdane benefit. Therefore, for the benefit of good and faithful people who underst ⁄ Sinhala . . . I present this explanation of the *Vimānavastu* in brief, translated into ıala language. (*Vimānavastuprakaraṇaya,* ed. Telvattē Sīlananda [Colombo: Jīnālal ;s], 3–4.

Blackburn, *Buddhist Learning,* ch. 4.

I use the term *strategic* in the sense developed by Pierre Bourdieu, who (nbers of a community naturally draw on a shared *habitus* to maximiz(t do not require self-conscious efforts to overcome an opponent, *Outline ractice,* trans. Richard Nice (Cambridge: Cambridge University Pres: !–87, 214 n.2.

See Maung Htin Aung, *A History of Burma* (New York: Columbia U)67), 101, and Michael Aung-Thwin, *Pagan* (Honolulu: University o1)85), 145–46.

William Pruitt, *Étude linguistique de* nissaya *birmans* (Paris: Ecole Françai)rient, 1994), 18.

C. E. Godakumbura, *Catalogue of Cambodian and Burmese Pāli Ma*: echert et al., *Burmese Manuscripts Part 1* (Wiesbaden: Franz Steiner Verla; ıraun and Daw Tin Tin Myint, *Burmese Manuscripts Part 2* (Wiesbade Verlag, 1985); and Heinz Braun, *Burmese Manuscripts Part 3* (Stuttgaı /erlag, 1996) describe a range of *nissaya* texts though from a much later

Maung Htin Aung, *A History of Burma,* 51–52.

Pe Maung Tin and G. H. Luce, *The Glass Palace Chronicle of the Kings* ı: Oxford University Press, 1923), 128.

Maung Htin Aung, *A History of Burma,* 54.

Aung-Thwin, *Pagan,* 140, 149–50, 205, 234 n. 41.

"Now the chief Uttarajiva the elder died and was buried before Cha d his fellows reached Pagan. So when they arrived they went to the c d worshipped there. Thereafter Chapata the elder spake to the elders, l saying, 'Masters, our teacher Uttarajiva the elder visited the island of Ce ed the duties of the Order in one accord with the Ceylonese monks. A must perform the duties of the Order in union with the monks dw ut now Burmese monks control them. We will not perform the duti‹ ·ith these Burmese monks.' So the five monks of the Order who had co performed their duties apart. And king Narapatisithu caressed and rega :asure these five noble elders. He caused a raft of boats to be put togeth ıwaddy, and thereon many novices were ordained monks. Thus they m ›urse of time till there were many sects of the Order." Pe Maung Tin aı *ıe Glass Palace Chronicle,* 144–45.

Aung-Thwin, *Pagan,* 140, 149, 205.

Pruitt, *Étude linguistique de* nissaya *birmans,* 19.

Pe Maung Tin and G. H. Luce, *The Glass Palace Chronicle,* 143.

Pruitt, *Étude linguistique de* nissaya *birmans,* 145.

On which see Pe Maung Tin and G. H. Luce, *The Glass Palace Chroni‹*

David Wyatt, *Thailand* (New Haven: Yale University Press, 1984), 40–

Donald K. Swearer and Sommai Premchit, "The Relationship Betv ıs and Political Orders in Northern Thailand," in *Religion and Legitiı Thailand, Laos, and Burma,* ed. Bardwell L. Smith (Chambersburg, PA .978), 22–25.

Swearer and Premchit, "The Relationship Between the Religious and in Northern Thailand," 26–29. See also Sommai Premchit and Dc "A Translation of *Tamnān Mūlasāsasanā Wat Pā Daeng,*" *Journal of the Sia* ›77): 73–110, pp. 85–92, and Jayawickrama, *The Sheaf of Garlands,* xx 136–38.

Swearer and Premchit, "The Relationship Between the Religious and n Northern Thailand," 27.

See Jayawickrama, *The Sheaf of Garlands,* 148–49; 159–86; and see A. , ed., *Jinakālamālī* (London: Luzac and Company, 1962), 111–19 and 12

Jayawickrama, *The Sheaf of Garlands,* xlvi.

See Jayawickrama, *The Sheaf of Garlands,* 185, and Buddhadatta, ed., 3.

The text's apparent initial conclusion follows a major ordination cerem ɔn of a high-ranking monk at Wat Pā Daeng (in 1518–1519). The event 'ollows the appointment of a new Saṇgharāja and Rājaguru at Wat Pā I ere I follow Jayawickrama's assessment of the text's construction, xxvii–› y Buddhadatta, ed. *Jinakālamālī,* 103–19.

Premchit and Swearer, "A Translation of Tamnān Mūlaṣāsasanā Wat Pā

Ibid., 109.

Swearer and Premchit, "The Relationship Between the Religious and
n Northern Thailand," 21.

Louis Finot, "Recherches sur la litterature Laotienne," *Bulletin d*
d'Extrême-Orient 17(1917): 1–219, p. 175.

For evidence of these genres in Siamese and Thai Yüan literatures, see t
not, "Recherches sur la litterature Laotienne," as well as the catalogue by
Catalogue des manuscrits en Pāli, Laotien et Siamois provenant de la]
ıagen: The Royal Library, 1966).

EIGHT

PREACHER AS A POET

POETIC PREACHING AS A MONASTIC STRATEGY IN CONSTITUTING BUDDHIST COMMUNITIES IN MODERN SRI LANKA AND THAILAND

Mahinda Deegalle

Even if monks preach *Budubaṇa* all the time
And people listen to it all the time
In terms of character and behavior
We are still in the forest.

—Rambukana Siddhārtha Thero,
Saṃsāre Api

PROSE OR VERSE? Which is more appropriate for Buddhist preaching? This question of the most appropriate literary "form" for Buddhist preaching raises the central concern that has challenged both the practitioner and scholar to rethink the nature of modern Buddhist preaching traditions in Sri Lanka. The traditional understanding is that the Buddhist preacher, being a monk, has nothing to do with music, singing, and dancing; the seventh of the ten precepts for a young novice prohibits such indulgences.[1] For a *bhikkhu,* watching a performance involving dance, singing, and instrumental music is a *dukkaṭa* (minor) offense;[2] for a nun, it is a *pācittiya* offense that requires ritual confession.[3] In this disciplinary context, how can Pāli recitations in verse *(gāthā),* and in particular, Sinhala poems *(kavi),* be accommodated? What are the limits of this stipulation for modern Buddhist religious practices? What is its impact on modern preaching styles? In general, there is an overwhelming consensus among believers and scholars that Buddhist preachers do not sing because they are not supposed to put the Buddha's words into musical tone.[4]

However, anyone who is familiar with Sri Lankan Buddhist religiosity is aware that in Sri Lanka monks not only chant Buddhist *sutta*s in Pāli prose in the *paritta* (protection) rituals, but also recite Pāli verses and sing poems in Sinhala as a part of Buddhist liturgies, whether as *Bodhi Pūjā* or a religious sermon.[5] Some modern monks such as the Venerable Rambukana Siddhārtha even compose popular songs *(sindu)* on secular and religious themes for popular singers;[6] popular vocalists such as Victor Ratnāyaka and Edward Jayakodi sing his songs. In addition to these modern innovations and developments, the most popular modern preacher who employed Sinhala poems for the liturgy associated with the Bodhi tree is the late Venerable Pānadurē Ariyadhamma (d. 1986). More than any other monk in this century, he encouraged the young to get into the habit of using Sinhala *kavi* (poems) for Buddhist liturgies. He composed Sinhala poems which he chanted melodically, giving them an aesthetic and religiously emotional tone. Like the Thai Buddhist preacher Phayom, he also had a strong desire that his poems and Buddhist liturgy would attract the young and compete with films and popular songs.

Because Ariyadhamma's style of preaching and his devotional liturgy have been adequately examined by others,[7] this essay examines a poetic movement that predated Ariyadhamma's innovation: for the active use of Sinhala verse for sermon and liturgy existed even before the appearance of Ariyadhamma on the Sri Lankan religious scene. While addressing the issues surrounding monastic involvement with poetry and the active use of poems as a part of Buddhist liturgy, this paper explores the way "poetry" has been used by a modern preacher as an efficient means of communicating Buddhism to a modern audience in the twentieth century. The poetic preaching *(kavi baṇa)* that I discuss here is not a devotional liturgy like Ariyadhamma's *Bodhi Pūjā*. Rather, it is a full-fledged Buddhist sermon. In every sense of the word, as a religious genre, it stands within the modern understanding of a Buddhist sermon. Its distinct feature is that unlike traditional preaching, the preacher uses Sinhala poems with occasional prose explanations to elucidate the teachings of the Buddha. After describing the religious work of the late Venerable Siyambalangamuvē Gunaratana, who founded the modern poetic genre of preaching in Sri Lanka, I will compare his poetic contribution to preaching with that of the modern innovative Thai Buddhist preacher, Phayom. My purpose is to demonstrate the way that two modern preachers in two Theravāda societies constitute a sense of community and religious affiliation as they struggle to establish themselves against the normative monastic authorities.

There is no doubt that the *kavi baṇa* is the most recent monastic innovation in the field of preaching in modern Sri Lanka. The Sinhala term *kavi baṇa* is rendered here into English as "poetic preaching." As a generic term, in modern Sri Lanka, it is quite often used to refer to the innovative style of preaching that began in the mid-1950s. As a religious genre, its origin lies within the monastic sphere. Unlike other preaching movements, the founder of this style of preaching has been identified; credit is given to the late Venerable Gunaratana for the original introduction of this preaching style, and to his immediate pupils for its adoption and propagation. Today this style of poetic preaching is widespread, going beyond its original fraternity affiliation with the Rāmañña Nikāya, which was established in 1864.

One advantage of examining this modern religious phenomenon is that as a devotional and an artistic movement its proponents, its expansion, and its influence on later generations of preachers can be identified and investigated with considerable certainty. As a religious innovation, this preaching style had a deliberate and clear purpose. Through this style, the founder wanted to popularize Buddhist teachings in post-Independence Sri Lanka; it aimed at strengthening Buddhist values and virtues among ordinary people in urban as well as in rural areas. As a Buddhist revival response, it had as its explicit purpose the constitution of strong Theravāda lay communities in the wake of the Buddha Jayanti celebrations in 1956.

Given this post-Independence socioreligious background, this essay traces the gradual development of the style of poetic preaching by examining the life of the charismatic poetic preacher Gunaratana, the religious content of his poetic preaching, and the way this new preaching genre was adopted into the twentieth-century preaching style.

THE PRECURSORS OF MODERN *KAVI BAṆA*

It is difficult to determine the exact beginnings of the use of poetry to disseminate Buddhism; it is much harder still to identify the original use of poetry as a preaching tool. However, certain precursors that perhaps influenced the modern innovations in poetic preaching in Sri Lanka can be identified through the study of the vast corpus of Sinhala literary works. The Buddhist literature of Sri Lanka included both prose writings and collections of poetry. From the early Dam̆badeṇi Period (1232–1284), Sinhala prose literature dominated the religious and literary scene. However, from time to time, monks as well as lay persons composed poetry having Buddhist themes as subject matter. In general, for literary inspiration, most writers of the medieval period turned to collections of Buddhist narratives. One medieval poet, the author of the *Siyabaslakara,* captured this literary tendency stating explicitly "if it is poetry, its subject matter should be *Buddhacarita* ['the life of the Buddha']."[8] As a result of this religious orientation and literary preoccupation, existing Sri Lankan literature contains a large collection of poetry that elucidates the virtues of the Buddha, his life, and his teachings.

Beginning from the late Anurādhapura Period (*c.* 301–1029 C.E.), Sinhala authors had composed poems celebrating the virtues of the Buddha. In certain periods, poetry became the popular literary genre of religious expression. Prolific authors in their poems used religious narratives in elucidating the value structure of the Buddhist community. In comparison with previous writings, one witnesses a strong tradition of poetry related to Buddhist sermons during the Kōṭṭē Period (1411–1597 C.E.). This new genre of Buddhist writings in verse became a distinctive feature of this period. These collections of poetry functioned as sermon books that had the explicit purpose of educating lay and monastic members in religious matters through the cultivation of morality and wisdom.

Though Sinhala verse had developed since the late Anurādhapura Period, it was not until the Kōṭṭē Period that verses were used to write an entire preaching story. The following Buddhist poems illustrate well the incorporation of Buddhist narratives into poetry. They accomplished a recorded success in composing poems to explain values, concepts, and Buddhist doctrines through narratives. The two masterpieces of the Kōṭṭē Period were Rāhula Thero's *Kāvyaśēkharaya* (1449) and Vättävē's *Guttila Kāvyaya* (1450–1460). While the former was based on the *Sattubhatta Jātaka,* the latter followed the narrative in the *Guttila Jātaka.* A close examination of the *Kāvyaśēkharaya*'s content shows that it was an epic as well as a Buddhist sermon in poetry.

Rāhula had written the *Kāvyaśēkharaya,* the second Sinhala epic, to fulfill the desire of King Parākramabāhu VI's daughter, the queen Ulakuḍaya. As the following verse (v. 22) well illustrates, she wanted to listen to *baṇa* in Sinhala verse:

utum me bisō	*sańda,*	This great queen invited me with delight
heḷu basini nisi pada	*bäńda,*	To compose a poem in Sinhala
kiyanuva baṇak	*sońda,*	To be preached as a wonderful sermon.
keḷen ārādhanā mana	*nańda*	

This monastic author's intention is explicit: it had been strictly a religious motivation—to write a *baṇa* in poetry. In this case, poetry had become only a vehicle in elaborating the teachings of the Buddha. Over and above the aesthetic pleasure derived from literature, the generation of religious sentiments through the elaboration of Buddhist doctrines received priority. Thus, this early work—the *Kāvyaśēkharaya*—played a dual role: a literary work of epic genre and a Buddhist work that functioned as a Buddhist sermon. In fact, evidence suggests that early Sinhala authors did not make a rigid division between the two genres, and their interests overlapped in writing as well as in the use of literature.

Though Rāhula wrote the *Kāvyaśēkharaya* following the rules that apply to an epic, it also bears the structure of a Buddhist sermon. When its epic features are eliminated, a Buddhist sermon emerges from it. The primary narrative of this work, the strategies that the author used to bind the listener to the text, and the descriptions that the author gave with regard to the dharma and righteous living support that it was intended as a sermon.

Vīdāgama's *Buduguṇālaṇkāraya* (1475) and *Lōvāḍasaṅgarāva* (1446) were not strictly based on one *baṇakathā* as were the above-mentioned two works; they also functioned as *baṇa* in poetry. While the *Buduguṇālaṇkāraya* was written to tell *Buduguṇa* (Buddha virtues) day and night, the *Lōvāḍasaṅgarāva* was composed in *sivupada* (quatrain) genre as a *baṇa*. They fulfilled the audience's desire to listen to *baṇa* in poetry. The production of these works during the Kōṭṭē Period demonstrates Sinhala readers' desire to read *baṇapot* in verse. This gave prominence to verse over prose writings. While prose was a characteristic feature of Sinhala literature of the early periods, verse writings gradually began to take its place as the popular literary form.

Though the preoccupation of giving sermons in poetry in the Kōṭṭē Period became less important in later times, some elements of this preaching got absorbed into the two-pulpit preaching that became popular in the late Kandyan Period (1707–1815). There is, however, an important distinction between this type of Sinhala poetry and the poetic preaching that I discuss in this essay. The poetic preaching that I discuss here consists of Buddhist sermons, strictly speaking. In this poetic preaching genre, poetry is only a vehicle for preaching, as Buddhism was a vehicle for Sinhala literary works of the early periods.

MONK AS A POPULAR POET: GUNARATANA'S POETIC PREACHING

Within the twentieth century, Buddhist preaching styles in Sri Lanka have gone through many phases and the exact changes that occurred in preaching styles are somewhat difficult to ascertain. Though this is not the place to discuss all the transformations, as an example of innovative phase Buddhist preaching, I have singled out the style of poetic preaching because of its influence on both monastic and lay practices. Poetic preaching has a social and religious function, and Buddhist preachers employed a variety of strategies and methods in popularizing Theravāda in rural areas. In examining these preaching activities, one can identify their strategies and innovations.

In modern Sri Lanka, as a style of preaching, *kavi baṇa* can be clearly distinguished from other types of preaching. In popularizing Buddhism, modern poetic preaching uses poems as a strategy. As a communication strategy, the *kavi baṇa* is effective in drawing the attention of the listeners and keeping them attentive throughout the sermon. The very use of poetry, the musical tone of the preacher, and rhythm serve to keep the audience attentive and interested in what is preached.

All sections of the Buddhist sangha in Sri Lanka have not yet completely absorbed this style of poetic preaching. As a style, it demands a variety of talents from the preacher. These factors prevent it from being absorbed by the entire hierarchy of the Buddhist establishment. Only pockets of young monks who have pleasant voices as well as an ability to compose poems have adopted the poetic preaching. Thus, the number of preachers who can give successful poetic sermons is quite limited.

The beginning of the modern style of poetic preaching can be documented with a considerable degree of certainty. As a style of preaching, it came into being as an exclusive creative enterprise of a group of monks headed by the late Venerable Siyambalaṇgamuvē Gunaratana (1914–1989). While the style of poetic preaching is closely associated with this monk's youth, his pupils are responsible for popularizing it. As a young progressive monk, in 1953 Gunaratana Thero began to preach *kavi baṇa*.[9] This was the time that Sri Lanka was preparing itself for the Buddha Jayanti celebrations. In a short time, his popular style of *kavi baṇa* caught the attention of young preachers as well as lay persons. Through four decades of continuous work and commitment, the late Venerable Gunaratana gave it its fundamental structure and shaped it as a form of religious instruction for the modern Buddhists in Sri Lanka.

A short introduction to the life of Gunaratana Thero will not be a distraction. On July 17, 1914, he was born into a Christian family in Siyambalangamuva (Yōdhagama, Rambukkana). Until Grade Eight (1919–1926), he pursued his early studies at a Christian school in Siyambalangamuva. Though he went to the temple in 1926, he did not receive novice ordination *(pabbajjā)* until 1928. In his ordination, his preceptor was Venerable Uḍunuvara Sārānanda. Sārānanda Thero, too, had an interesting religious profile. As a Buddhist missionary, living at Isipatana (1901), Benares, Sārānanda Thero had assisted Anagārika Dharmapāla (1864–1933) in constructing Mūlagandhakuṭi Vihāra. Further, he had taught Buddhism in Hindi for six months to the king of Nepal.[10]

Gunaratana Thero had his formal monastic education at Sirinivāsa Pirivena, Kaḍugannāva, from 1932–1942 where he earned the *panḍit* degree. In 1935, he received the higher ordination *(upasampadā)* at the Käḷäṇi River. Though he established several temples and monastic schools, his most distinguished contribution to Buddhist monastic education was the establishment of Sārānanda Pirivena, Peradeniya. Although Sārānanda Pirivena began with only eight students, in a short time the number of students had increased to three thousand by the early 1950s. To carry out these educational duties, Gunaratana Thero needed funds, and his new style of preaching assisted him in raising money for his religious works. As a pioneer of a new preaching style, Gunaratana Thero delivered the first sermon in poetry *(kavi baṇa)* in 1953, and continued to preach in poems until 1968.[11]

Through preaching, he cultivated both *śraddhā* (faith) and *bhakti* (devotion) in the hearts of his listeners. His distinct contribution was the preparation of a poetic sermon on the theme of the Buddha's death. His source was the *Mahāparinibbāna Sutta,* which records the events of the last three months of Gotama Buddha's earthly career. This devotional and pious sermon has left a lasting impression among Buddhist communities in Sri Lanka.[12] Within a short time, he was able to reach even remote villages. His poetic style and his very personality attracted the hearts of average people. His popularity as a preacher increased and his pleasant voice attracted many crowds. He received many gifts for his sermons including land, vehicles, and temples. For instance, the monastic school at Nārammala was a "gift that he received for the religious instruction" *(dhamma pūjā)* that he gave in the form of *kavi baṇa.*[13]

On February 9, 1980, Gunaratana Thero was appointed as the *Anunāyaka* (deputy chief) of Rāmañña Nikāya. At the Chamber Hall, in Kandy, the act of appointment was handed to Gunaratana Thero by the late Prime Minister Raṇasiṃha Prēmadāsa (d. 1993). On that occasion, Mr. Prēmadāsa invited him to recite a poem. Gunaratana Thero responded candidly with the following poem:

baṇa mańḍuvala di mahajanayā satuṭu koṭa
kavi kī namut mā poḍi avadiyehi siṭa
kolukama taruṇakama yana deka gevuṇu viṭa
baṇa pada misak oya kavi pada moṭa da maṭa?

In preaching halls, to please the public
From my childhood, I preached in poems.
But, at present, both manliness and youth are gone.
Except *baṇa pada,* what use are those *kavi pada* for me?

Gunaratana Thero transformed the pleasurable act of reciting poems *(kavi kīma)* into the act of preaching *(baṇa kīma)*. The modern poetic preaching that I discuss here in relation to Venerable Gunaratana and his successors is different in performance as well as in structure from the modern Buddhist preaching. It is also different from the sermon style of the early Sinhala literary works.

Characteristically, the use of poetry became the specific feature of *kavi baṇa*. In the traditional sermon, preachers used occasional verse quotations from texts such as the *Dhammapada* and prose quotations from other canonical texts to provide the setting for the sermon and further elucidate their points of argument. As the title of the genre suggests, though occasional prose explanations were added to the sermon in order to fill the gaps and to give clear instructions on the flow of the sermon, the most characteristic feature of this new style of preaching is the use of poetry to communicate Buddhist doctrines in the Buddhist pulpit. This very novelty attracted the attention of listeners.

The poetic preaching has a style similar to regular Buddhist sermons as delivered today in Sri Lanka: (1) The preacher begins with the administration of the five precepts and (2) recites the *dēvārādhanā* (invitation to deities); (3) Then he chants the *namaskārapāda* (formula used for paying homage), (4) and then begins the poetic sermon proper; and, (5) with the dedication of merit. The preacher devotes a considerable portion of the poetic sermon to explaining the benefits that listeners accrue through attentive listening. The poetic style of the preacher contains some dramatic elements; he uses poems and his musical tone like an actor or a professional singer to draw the attention of the listener to the sermon.

POETIC SERMON: THE MONK POET'S CONFLICTS WITH PREVAILING TRADITIONS

In order to show the complexities and tensions embedded in the *baṇa* tradition in Sri Lanka, I will relate the episodes that illustrate the social and religious obstructions that Gunaratana had to face in his innovation. This life story of Gunaratana's preaching career will illustrate the tensions that arise when an old tradition and its orthodoxy meet the challenges of reformation brought about by innovative members of the sangha.

In *kavi baṇa,* each poem is a quatrain often rhymed at the end of each line. The following two verses show the simple style Gunaratana adopted in making his poetic sermons understandable even to an ordinary person. In them, Gunaratana questions why it is wrong to preach in verse, given that the *tipiṭaka* contain texts such as the *Dhammapada* and the *Suttanipāta* that are exclusively in Pāli verse *(gāthā)*:[14]

kavikīmaṭa hon̆dada mehi hāmuduru *vanē*
yanuven hitana samaharu äti bavada *pen ē*
kaṇagāṭuyi ehema sitatot nodäna *ba ṇē*
saṇga säṭa namak kavi ahalalu rahat *unē*

Venerable Sir! Is it good (for a monk) to sing poems here?
There seems to be some who think like this.
It is sad if someone thinks like that without knowing *baṇa*.
It is said that sixty monks became arahants by listening to poems.

Buduhāmuduruvan dena lesa apaṭa *seta*
kaviyen desū baṇa Tun Piṭakayehi *äta*
karuṇak kiyami ē gäna yomu karanu *sita*
kavi vāsagam bē daya Budu baṇaṭa *näta*

To cause our welfare, the Buddha preached.
The Three Baskets *(tipiṭaka)* contain preaching in poems.
I will tell you a fact. Pay attention to it!
In Budu *baṇa,* there is no difference between verse and prose.

Here, Gunaratana attempts to extend to preaching in verse the privilege that had traditionally been assigned only to prose preaching. He does this by asserting that in the teachings of the Buddha, there is no difference between prose and verse because they are merely means of expression. His primary concern is to use a novel means of expression to teach the Buddha's teachings in the preaching. Gunaratana's *kavi baṇa* focused on doctrinal concepts such as karma, rebirth, dependent coorigination, nirvana, and Buddha biography.[15] In *kavi baṇa,* which lasts an hour or so, the preacher sings the poems rhythmically. This is an innovation in the preaching style, since in previous preaching rituals, the preacher did not sing Sinhala poems. Though the two-pulpit preaching since the eighteenth century included many sections with Sinhala poems, the two preachers did not sing any of those Sinhala poems; instead, the lay devotees sang them. This was perhaps because of the canonical injunction against monks' singing: "*Na bhikkhave āyatakena gītassarena dhammo bhāsitabbo*" (Monks! You should not preach the dharma in a lengthened musical tone). Glossing this *Vinaya* injunction, the late Venerable Pälänē Vajiragñāna Thero, who designed the modern sermon styles in Sri Lanka for radio preaching, stated that the Buddha had advised Buddhist monks not to preach in a long poetical tune appropriate for songs. They are not supposed to chant verses raising and lowering their voices according to various meters.[16] They should not use such a playful method for Buddhist preaching; indeed, a preacher who preaches in such a musical tone may not only commit an *äväṭ*

(P. *apatti*) but also may be subject to dangerous diseases. According to him, though the foolish may praise his preaching as excellent, even wise non-Buddhists may make fun of that preacher by blaming him for such acts. Further, such a preacher may bring unhappiness to deities and human beings who are gathered to listen to baṇa.

Gunaratana's innovative preaching despite canonical injunctions against using poetry in spreading *dhamma* as well as his family background, the Buddhist order to which he belonged, and his caste affiliations all brought about a tense environment. In a recent Sinhala publication, Gunaratana Thero remarks about the tensions and negative treatment that he received (from his environment in which he operated) as an innovative Buddhist preacher:

> Perhaps, in this century, there were no other Buddhist monks, who had suffered so much from social discrimination. When I went for preaching, sometimes, there was no preaching pulpit in the temple; at times, while there was a preaching pulpit at a corner of the hall, I was forced to preach sitting on a small chair. When I preach, there were times that I did not receive at least a *gilanpasa.*[17] One day, when I went to preach in a temple, a group of people invaded the temple; they attempted to chase me away without preaching; however, the people of the same village who were there did not allow their disturbances. I have a great deal of experience in facing such kind of earthly suffering.[18]

These remarks reflect a particular phase in poetic preaching. As Gunaratana suggests, innovation was not easy, especially in a country in which Theravāda Buddhism had lasted for centuries. In Gunaratana's comment, one can identify the problems that he was undergoing. From his own perspective, there was no other contemporary monk who was humiliated and punished for undertaking innovations in preaching. The discrimination in his case was both social and religious. On the one hand, he was not from a prominent monastic fraternity. On the other hand, he was challenging the prevalent tradition and the system that was familiar to both monastic and lay members. Humiliations that he faced in terms of preaching can be outlined. In Sinhala culture, the preacher is respected with utmost care. There are traditional rules in the culture that govern the conduct of the preacher. The most crucial symbolic feature of Buddhist preaching is the important place given to the preaching pulpit. The preaching pulpit elevates the preacher's influence. In his case, when he went to deliver poetic sermons, he did not find a pulpit prepared for him. Even in the cases where there was a preaching pulpit, instead of allowing him to preach from it he was given an ordinary small chair to sit and preach from. From the traditional perspective, this substitution was an insult to the preacher. The monk poet Vīdāgama Maitreya, the author of the *Lōväḍasaňgarāva,* captured the traditional respect associated with preaching as follows:

bima iňda siṭa kī baṇa *nāsannē*
vimativa uḍa iňda siṭa *nāsannē*
kämätiva k īvot *vimasāsannē*
ema veda sanga mok säpa *s ādannē*[19]

Sitting on the floor, do not listen to *baṇa* preached while standing.
Even with loss of memory, sitting on a higher chair, do not listen to *baṇa*.
If preached appropriately, listen with investigative mind.
Is it not that kind of listening which causes one the welfare in heaven and *nivan*?

This fifteenth-century monk poet has presented a glimpse of the traditional understanding of the nature of preacher, his audience, and the message. He emphasizes accurate reception and presents the suitable relationships among each part of the religious activity. The proper sitting posture of the preacher in a preaching pulpit, a location that is higher than everyone in the audience, is very important in Buddhist preaching traditions. It is one symbolic way of expressing respect to the Buddha and his message.

From this traditional understanding, one can understand Gunaratana's negative response. In the case of Gunaratana, the very denial of the preaching pulpit already available in the temple was an important symbol of rejection and refusal of his contribution. The preaching pulpit is the weapon of the preacher. If the pulpit is not given, the preacher is denied traditional respect and honor. While his opponents wanted to disrupt his preaching, even the people who talked with him seem to have done so without real appreciation. Gunaratana's case is an indication that modern popular preachers create controversies when they attempt to make innovations.

Gunaratana's critical comments about the life of Buddhists and the way some Buddhists reacted to different methods of preaching show how difficult it was for Gunaratana, as a popular preacher, to change the behavior of a particular class of Sinhala society that vehemently opposed the introduction of new styles of preaching. Though Sinhala people highly appreciate the preaching of the dharma, because of the stubbornness and reactions of some, certain popular preachers such as Gunaratana found it extremely difficult to preach the Buddha's words. As Gunaratana Thero records, though the honor and respect that Buddhist preaching demands from the audience were absent in some of his *kavi baṇa* audiences, negative characteristics such as jealousy had replaced virtues such as *mettā*, which were supposed to be cultivated in religious ceremonies.

In another respect, Gunaratana's case gives evidence sufficient to show the dynamism of the preaching tradition as well as the problems involved in popular preaching in Theravāda; Gunaratana's *kavi baṇa* helps us understand a preaching tradition that goes beyond any assumptions of uniformity in Theravāda preaching style. In addition, the *kavi baṇa* itself demonstrates that Buddhist preaching is a continuously unfolding tradition embracing novel genres as well as media; thus, as a tradition, *baṇa* can be conceived as "fluid" rather than fixed. As has already been demonstrated with reference to two–pulpit preaching, once the basic structure of a sermon is retained, the tradition itself leaves ample room for preachers to innovate and introduce new dimensions to religious discourse that can efficiently communicate Buddhist teachings.

COMPARING THE THAI BUDDHIST PREACHER PHAYOM WITH GUNARATANA

A comparison of the role of two Buddhist preachers shows that religious innovation is an interesting aspect of modern Buddhist preaching traditions. Both in Thailand and Sri Lanka modern preachers have introduced innovative methods to traditional styles of preaching. Whatever their religious and social contexts may be, preachers invent new religious strategies to meet the needs of their immediate communities. Precisely because of this innovation, Buddhism can exist as a religious system in the modern context.

However, as the following two cases demonstrate, religious innovations are not always accepted without significant opposition and obstacles. As in the past, modern preachers encounter obstacles to their innovative preaching whether in Thailand or Sri Lanka. In both countries, the opposition to innovation begins within the monastic community. Two recent examples of monastic resistance against the innovative preaching styles can be examined through the preaching career of the Thai Buddhist preacher Phayom and the Sri Lankan Buddhist preacher Gunaratana. While there exist similarities within their contexts, there are also differences in their styles of preaching. The responses that they had from their audiences are also significant factors.

During the 1970s, Thailand noted the birth of a new brand of preaching monks. Phayom Kalayano (b. 1949), a monk of the Mahanikai, the abbot of Wat Suan Kaew in Nonthaburi, became the most unconventional Thai Buddhist preacher.[20] His inspiration for a new style of preaching was born from his observation of society and its social concerns. While living at Buddhadasa's monastery, Suan Mokkhabalarama, in southern Thailand, he noted the daily activities of children in the neighborhood. Phayom's strength was that he understood the problems that people had in struggling with changes in economy and society. At the very beginning, he realized that to address these social issues he needed a new preaching style. He noticed the absurdity of rules that Thai monastic hierarchy had stipulated with regard to preaching. Rather than the traditional boring and dry monotonous sermons, he wanted to devise active and engaging sermons to keep the attention of the audience. Not limiting himself to ancient stories related to the Buddha's life and dharma, he began to draw stories for his sermons from new sources such as newspapers. He convinced the youth and Thai Buddhists at large that Buddhist sermons also can be timely and used for addressing modern problems. His ability to interpret old and new stories in understanding modern problems is one preeminent feature in his preaching style.

The cases of both Gunaratana and Phayom demonstrate well that being a popular Buddhist preacher is not an easy task today. Urban youth in both countries are driven by new technology and modern forms of entertainment. Preachers find it hard to convince an urban person to listen to a sermon. Films, television programs, videos, music tapes, CDs, and the like are readily available to young people, and traditional methods of entertainment, which were primarily religious in nature and served for folk and rural communities in traditional villages in the past, have lost their power and strength. In general, the expansion of popular culture in urban areas of Buddhist societies in South and Southeast Asia and the domination of Western cultural values among the youth do not encourage traditional religiosity. In short, traditional preaching in Theravāda societies is threatened. Today, even sermons that were primarily intended for cultivating detachment have to function as entertainment in order to retain the attention of easily distracted audiences. Most listeners feel that modern Buddhist sermons should be exciting in order to attract the youth; for the adults, their message should be relevant for their daily living; they should help resolve some of the problems that they are facing when they struggle with practical problems and social issues. More than ever before, this complex social context and its necessities create a greater demand on the preacher and his presentation of the Buddhist material.

In Phayom's case, the opposition between State Buddhism in Bangkok and local forms of Buddhist religiosity in local regions became the point of controversy. It is a battle between rational teachings of the Buddha preached in a civilized format and the devotional form of teachings couched in the folk tradition with humor and a relaxed attitude. Like all other regulations in the Thai sangha, the sangha authorities in Bangkok had prepared a "standard" for Buddhist preaching.[21] This standard is that the Thai sangha should deliver their sermons following Bangkok texts. The sermon should create a solemn atmosphere where the listeners listen quietly with the utmost respect. This emphasis on the style of preaching seems to be similar to the assumptions that developed in Sri Lanka in the context of Protestant Buddhism in the late nineteenth century. With increased pressure to present Buddhism as a rational and scientific doctrine, the elaboration of Buddhist teachings as rational became prominent. Ritualistic, devotional and ceremonial aspects of Buddhist preaching were undermined, and in both Sri Lanka and Thailand, Buddhist sermons were emptied of the ritual practices of villagers. In this process, perhaps, the large narrative literature, pious devotional tendencies, and entertainment from the dharma were neglected.

In Phayom's case, the innovation was that he dared to not adhere to this rigid standard. He gave priority to practical concerns of the modern society and used whatever efficient means to communicate Buddhist solutions to those problems. Phayom noticed that the youngsters of his neighborhood in the Chaiya District were addicted to watching shadow theater during the entire night.[22] Phayom wanted to produce sermons that could appeal to those youngsters. His concern was strictly religious; he wanted to direct the young who were driven to secular concerns and direct them toward more religious pursuits. With his rich oratory skills, Phayom was able to transform the traditional book-oriented preaching into a more attractive form of religious entertainment. His sermons were meant to be listened to; they were not meant to be read as the traditional sermon. His ability to use rhyme, his great sense of humor, and his courage to challenge the strict traditional authority of monastic establishments proved to be effective; the result was an attractive sermon style that could retain the attention of a large crowd comprised of both youths and adults. Furthermore, his sermons addressed the social problems that Thai society in general and the youth in particular were facing during the 1970s. Within a short time, through his innovative and popular preaching, Phayom became one of the most successful popular Buddhist preachers in modern Thailand.

Phayom's popularity as a modern preacher also brought criticism from his social environment. In particular, he was criticized for his improper sermon language, for the aspect of entertainment contained in his sermons directed toward teenagers, and as a preacher, for his relaxed attitude, which was quite different from the dignified air of the traditional preacher.

There are differences in the nature of the difficulties that Gunaratana and Phayom encountered in innovating new preaching styles. In Gunaratana's case, the obstacles were subtle; they did not come directly from the monastic hierarchy in Sri Lanka. In Phayom's case, however, the opposition came directly from the monastic authorities. Gunaratana had no public defenders within monastic or lay community who took his side. In the case of Phayom, however, at least one important Thai monk took Phayom's side and defended him: Nakhon Khemapali, the rector of Maha Chulalongkorn Buddhist University, came forward with a strong voice defending his preaching styles and providing timely and necessary spiritual support.[23]

In responding to the criticism against Phayom's use of "crude language," the rector advised the critics not to listen to it if it displeased them. His point is that there are people who can listen to that kind of language and that very language helps them to get back on the right track. Here the rector emphasizes the social role of Phayom's preaching. Phayom's preaching, which is "crude" from the point of view of some, is a medicine for others who are lost in the society. That very language and presentation help those who listen to him to conduct their lives in good ways; as religious instruction, it transforms their lifestyles by providing a vision. Thus, rather than worrying about the "means" and "methods" that various preachers use for preaching, one should focus more on the ends at which preaching is aimed, the regeneration of values in Thai urban society. In accordance with traditional Buddhist thinking, the rector also points out and acknowledges the diversity of listeners and their character types. Depending on the nature of the listener and his or her character, Phayom's sermon style has a role in modern Thai society. Even from the point of view of preachers, as the rector points out, it is "unrealistic to expect all monks to preach the same way."[24] The reality is, as the preachers vary, so do audiences and their expectations. From the rector's point of view, Phayom's preaching style has a place in Thai society, and such novel and timely preaching should be allowed to prosper.

When one reflects on these two responses of two Buddhist communities toward innovative preaching, one can note the differences as well as the similarities in the ways in which Theravāda societies respond to novel strategies. They demonstrate the challenges that modern societies face and the burden the preachers bear in fulfilling their religious roles as preachers when the entire social system is going in the opposite direction, bent on achieving worldly, secular, and materialistic goals.

In Thailand, the sangha authorities standardize preaching styles. This limits the potential of each preacher to create an innovative sermon. In contrast, in Sri Lanka there is no such monastic pressure on the preacher. It is increasingly clear, however, that there was a passive understanding of what constitutes a Buddhist sermon. With the work of Anagārika Dharmapāla[25] and Pälänē Vajiragñāna's radio sermons, the length of the Sri Lankan sermon was shortened to one hour. However, this was a standard left open to each individual. It was not a rule, and thus allowed for considerable individual variation. It did not obstruct the work of creative preachers. Though the content and style may change depending on the preacher, all have tended to follow an accepted style. These accepted styles in Thailand and in Sri Lanka have hardly considered the potential to use Buddhist sermon for destitutes. Rather, it was always used for the privileged and cultured, most often for the converted elderly audience, and only very rarely for young listeners. In the cases of Phayom and Gunaratana, one notices an extension of preaching to a wider audience that includes children. In particular, in the case of Phayom, it is clear that he deliberately used his sermons to educate and discipline the young children who were following unacceptable paths. To attract the youth to the dharma, Phayom had to devise new strategies and new sermons, new styles, new language that could appeal to his audience. Both Phayom and Gunaratana, in different ways, understood the needs of their societies and responded as powerful preachers with unique contributions. While they introduced new dimensions, they still retained the dharma as the heart of their message. Their purpose as preachers was to communicate the dharma in a more attractive way. This kind of revival in preaching emerges only with an understanding among many preachers of the necessity of making the sermon a vehicle of the society.

CONCLUSION

At the outset, this essay aimed at introducing the most recent innovations in Buddhist preaching styles in Sri Lanka and Thailand. In examining the modern poetic sermon style, I have discussed in detail the work of Gunaratana. I have shown that Gunaratana modified an already existing poetic tradition. His contribution was the use of an already existing Buddhist poetic tradition which began in the Kōṭṭē Period in an actual Buddhist liturgical context. He demarcated a social and religious location for the poetic sermon within the existing preaching tradition. By incorporating Buddhist poems into active preaching, he has shown a way that the large corpus of Buddhist poetry can be utilized in Buddhist services. In this process, he gave a new structure to the modern sermon. While he stayed within the one-hour limit placed on modern sermons by Vajiragñāna, he also showed ways to modify the style of Buddhist sermons to attract new audiences as well as to reduce the monotonous nature and boring quality of the traditional sermon. For the listeners, in general, poems and their musical and rhythmic recitation by talented preachers are more attractive than the mere prose sermon of the traditional type. Thus, Gunaratana's extensive use of Sinhala poetry of his own composition with occasional prose explanations has strengthened his preaching style and has given a broad basis and structure to the existing Buddhist sermon styles in Sri Lanka. If even the Buddha had refused monks' use of musical tone in preaching, he might disagree with Gunaratana's novel style, but Gunaratana's innovation has met some necessities of modern Sinhala society. In a similar way, the Thai Buddhist preacher Phayom fulfills important needs of modern Thai society though he became the target of opposition from monastic quarters of the contemporary Buddhist hierarchy for attempting to interpret the Buddha's message in constituting Thai Buddhist community feelings and identities. Using the sermon as a powerful religious weapon, Gunaratana has demonstrated ways that poetic preaching can be used positively in constituting Sinhala Buddhist communities in Sri Lanka along devotional and aesthetic lines, while Phayom has given religious inspiration and hope to the urban youth lost in the midst of capitalism and sensualistic trends in modern Thailand.

NOTES

The epigraph is taken from Rambukana Siddhārtha Thero, *Saṃsāre Api* (Singapore: Bauddha Bhāvanā Mādhyasthānaya, 1986) 31:

Budubaṇa kivuvat nirantarē
Budubaṇa äsuvat nirantarē
Gatiguṇa atin
Api tavamat vanantarē.

In this song, this monk poet has captured some contrary aspects in Sri Lankan Buddhist religiosity. As a custom, though Buddhist monks often deliver religious discourses and lay Buddhists listen to them with great enthusiasm, such religious instructions have done very little in the development of human character. This monk poet points out that the virtues learned in the temple through religious instruction have very little success in cultivating virtues and shaping the conduct and character of the people. According to him, Buddhists in Sri Lanka have failed in practice. In this song, the Sinhala term *Budubaṇa* means "the teachings of the Buddha." Because of the repetition in the first two lines of the original, I have presented here their general meaning rather than their literal translation.

1. *Nacca gīta vādita visūka dassanā veramaṇ sikkhāpadaṃ samādiyāmi* (Vin.I.83) "I take the precept of abstaining from dancing, singing, playing musical instruments, and seeing performances."

2. The *Vinaya* stipulates: "*Na bhikkhave naccaṃ vā gītaṃ vā vāditaṃ vā dassanāya gantabbaṃ yo gaccheyya āpatti dukkaṭassa.*"

3. Vin.II.107–108; Vin.IV.267.

4. Note the case of controversial six *bhikkhus (chabbaggiya)*. The public protested when they had begun to preach the dharma in musical tone. Responding to that the Buddha stated five disadvantages in reciting the dharma in musical tone *(pañcime bhikkhave ādinavā āyatakena gītassarena):* (1) one gets attached to the sound, (2) others get attached to the sound, (3) lay people perceive the style of preaching as inferior, (4) the preacher loses his (or her) concentration when he (or she) focuses on the tones and tunes of the recitation, and (5) public benefit decreases. However, among these discussions, one can also discover a thread of argument that encourages aesthetic treatment of the dharma. The Buddha had already allowed preaching the dharma in *sarabhaññu* style. It shows that there is no inherent problem in reciting verses according to their meter. The fundamental issue here is whether rhythmical recitation generates attachment. The attachment alone is rejected here as inappropriate. As long as preaching generates detachment and as long as monk's recitation produces freedom from lust, the verses can be accommodated in Buddhist recitations.

5. For Buddhist attitudes toward music, see Mahinda Deegalle, "Music: Buddhist Perspectives," in *Encyclopedia of Monasticism,* ed. William M. Johnston (Chicago: Fitzroy Dearborn Publishers, 2000). For the use of songs and other types of aesthetic elements in the preaching tradition of the Kandyan Period (1480–1815), see Mahinda Deegalle, "Marathon Preachers: The Two-pulpit Tradition in Sri Lanka," *Asiatische Studien: Études Asiatiques* 52, 1 (1998): 15–56.

6. First, a collection of the Venerable Rambukana Siddhārtha's Sinhala songs entitled *Saṃsāre Api* (1986, see above, n. 1) was published. Recently, two audio cassette tapes entitled *Samanala Kanda* and *Saṃsārē Gī Yātikā* (Nugēgoḍ: Singlaṇkā, 1992) have been released.

7. See H. L. Seneviratne and Swarna Wickremeratne, "Bodhipūjā: Collective Representations of Sri Lanka Youth," *American Ethnologist* 7, 4 (1980): 734–43; Richard F. Gombrich, "A New Theravādin Liturgy," *Journal of the Pali Text Society* 9 (1981): 47–73; Richard F. Gombrich and Gananath Obeyesekere, *Buddhism Transformed: Religious Change in Sri Lanka* (Princeton: Princeton University Press, 1988), 384–402.

8. *"peden budu sirita basin vat sirit."*

9. Neḷuvākandē Ñāṇānanda Thero, *Śrī Guṇaratana Lipi Saraṇiya* (Peradeniya: Siyambalaṇgamuvē Śrī Gunaratana Guṇānusmaraṇa Padanama, 1993), 6. See also the booklet prepared for the occasion of conferring the post of *Anūnāyaka.*

10. See Sārānanda's recent biography: Gāmiṇi Sēnādhīra, *Bahujana Hitāya* (Anurādhapura: Śrī Sārānanda Maha Pirivena, 2000), 94–106.

11. Candrasiri Palliyaguru (*Siṃhala Budusamayehi Nāṭya Laksāṇa* [Kaḍóavata: Candrasiri Palliyaguru, 1996], 83) had listened to a *kavi baṇa* delivered by Gunaratana Thero on October 21, 1968. He has documented it partially in the above-mentioned recent book. It is not clear why Gunaratana Thero stopped delivering *kavi baṇa* in 1968. Venerable Ariyadhamma seems to have adopted his style of recitation and serene manner of presentation into the *Bodhi Pūjī* in the 1970s.

12. When the Raja Raṭa Sēvaya of Sri Lanka Broadcasting Corporation began, Gunaratana Thero had the opportunity of delivering the first *dharma deśanā.* In that unique event he had delivered a *kavi baṇa* on the Buddha's death. When Gunaratana Thero himself passed away in 1989, to commemorate his contribution, on March 13, 1989, Sri Lanka Broadcasting Corporation rebroadcasted his *kavi baṇa* on the Buddha's *parinirvāna* (final cessation). As a very highly attractive sermon, it possesses a distinct style and responds creatively the question of the place music and recitation have within the Buddhist traditions. A comparison of this sermon with the chanting of Ariyadhamma demonstrates immediate influences on the development of a style of Buddhist recitation within Sinhala Buddhist preaching.

13. Ñāṇānanda Thero, *Śrī Guaratana Lipi Saraṇiya,* 6. I express my thanks to Venerable Kobbāvala Dharmapriya, pupil of Gunaratana Thero and the present principal of Śrī

Sīlavatī Pirivena, for allowing me to have a personal interview with him on August 7, 2000, at Sārānanda Pirivena, Peradeniya.

14. Ñāṇānanda Thero, *Śrī Guṇaratana Lipi Saraṇiya,* 23, 116.

15. Ibid., 23.

16. *'Ǝik v ū gī hañḍin noyek tālen äda äda usko ṭa nangana pahatkoṭa heḷana hanḍin lelava lelavā baṇa nokiya yutu."*

17. As a substitute for the term *te* (tea) in the original text, I have inserted here the commonly used term *gilanpasa* (P. *gilānapaccaya*), which is one of the four requisites of a Buddhist monk. It refers to soft drinks. As a custom, the devotees offer tea (or soft drinks) before the preacher starts delivering the sermon. By making such offerings, the lay Buddhists hope to accumulate merit (P. *puñña*). As reported here on some occasions, unfortunately, Gunaratana had not received any appropriate hospitalities. This was partly due to the lack of respect for him among his listeners.

18. Ñāṇānanda Thero, *Śrī Guṇaratana Lipi Saraṇiya,* 3.

19. Vīdāgama Maitreya, *Lōvāḍa Sangarāva* (Colombo: Department of Buddhist Affairs, 1984), v. 7.

20. A few books have been compiled in Thai outlining the life and preaching styles of Phra Phayom: *Thamma kap sinlapin āwusō* (1983) and *Yākhwāng . . . kū* (1991) and *Sinlapa hāng kānthamngān hai pensuk* (1997).

21. Kamala Tiyavanich, *Forest Recollections: Wandering Monks in Twentieth-century Thailand* (Honolulu: University of Hawai'i Press, 1997), 276.

22. Siri Tilakasiri has published a remarkable work on *The Asian Shadow Theater* (2000).

23. Tiyavanich, *Forest Recollections,* 277.

24. Ibid.

25. See H. L. Seneviratne, *The Work of Kings: The New Buddhism in Sri Lanka* (Chicago and London: the University of Chicago Press, 1999), 36–42, for a detailed examination of the implications of Anagārika Dharmapāla on the style of Buddhist preaching and monks' social work.

NINE

"FOR THOSE WHO ARE IGNORANT"

A STUDY OF THE *Bauddha Ädahilla*

Carol S. Anderson

THE *BAUDDHA ÄDAHILLA* is a small handbook of instruction for young Buddhists, written in Sinhala and distributed widely in a number of different editions and versions. The longest version is more than four hundred pages in a four by three inch format, and the shortest is a scant twenty pages in a three by two inch format with large print for children. The contents of all of the editions are quite similar: they detail precisely how a practitioner should visit a temple, and what they should do while they are there. They explain why the three refuges are important and provide more or less information on proper meditation. The shorter versions provide the texts alone with few explanations, where the longer versions include a great deal of commentary on why the practices should be undertaken. The text is designed for popular lay use. I have heard many stories about how both men and women received a copy of this text when they were young, usually around the age of seven or eight, when they were learning to read. At present the distribution and use of the manual is on the decline, in part due to the proliferation of devotional literature throughout Sinhala-speaking Sri Lanka during the last decade.

The title is a bit curious: *Bauddha* (or Buddha, as it is also used) is the Sinhala term for the Buddha, used adjectivally here as "Buddhist." *Ädahilla,* or belief, is a less familiar term in Sinhalese Buddhism than *śraddhā,* faith, but both terms evoke a similar sense of "believing in," or "having faith in" the

Buddha and his teaching. Despite the fact that the term seems like it is a contemporary term, one that emerged into common use during the colonial period, it appears in the *Pūjāvaliya* and other medieval Sinhalese texts. The irony embedded in the title is the fact that the handbook is not a statement of doctrine by any stretch of the imagination, but is a compilation of canonical, noncanonical, and commentarial sources on how one should *practice* as a Buddhist. The *Bauddha Äahilla* ennumerates different types of Buddhist practices, yet the title should be properly translated as "Buddhist Beliefs." This unwitting conflation of "belief" with ritual practices indicates that the author of the version we examine here had perhaps unwittingly recognized that the handbook would have a greater appeal if cast as a compendium of Buddhist doctrines, but in actuality, the handbook focuses on the Buddhist rituals that rest at the heart of Sinhalese Buddhism. For this reason, the *Bauddha Äahilla* is a highly useful point of entry into a study of the emergence of Buddhist lay practice in late nineteenth and early twentieth century Sri Lanka.

In scholarship that seeks to move beyond the orientalist model, the eighteenth and nineteenth centuries are cast as the period within which unprecedented change resulting from British colonial domination rapidly transformed indigenous notions of culture, community, and identity throughout South Asia. In Sri Lanka, this process has become known as Protestant Buddhism, which is commonly described as rationalist, textually based, and lay-oriented in terms of religious practices as well as in terms of authority. Anagārika Dharmapāla is recognized as the architect of Protestant Buddhism, as Obeyesekere observes: "He became a Protestant-Buddhist, a reformer of the Buddhist church, infusing that institution with the puritan values of Protestantism."[1] Very briefly, Dharmapāla created a new model for Sinhala Buddhist lay men and women, not only in terms of religious deportment but also in terms of daily dress, attitude, education, and behavior. The most important dimension of this new way of being Buddhist was the individual's own responsibility for his or her own salvation as well as for Buddhism itself. Different scholars, including George Bond, Gananath Obeyesekere, and Richard Gombrich emphasize different aspects of this period. Tessa Bartholomeusz highlights the creative and experimental tone of late-nineteenth-century Sri Lanka, while other authors seem to deplore, if not mourn, the processes by which Buddhism was reformed in the image of Protestant Christianity. Protestant Buddhism is virtually synonymous with the means by which Sri Lanka entered modernity, ushered in by its colonizers.

From one angle, the existence of a handbook entitled "Buddhist Beliefs" would seem to be a rather ubiquitous text that reflects this period of revival during which the character of Sinhalese Buddhism was reshaped into Protestant Buddhism. The *Bauddha Äahilla* at first glance supports the model of Protestant

Buddhism. But the content of the handbook does not lend itself to such a straightforward conclusion. Unlike Olcott's *Buddhist Catechism,* this book is not comprised of questions and answers about right beliefs—or even right views. It is a compilation of what to do and how to do it: it is a ritual manual, with explanations in case anyone has any doubts as to the efficacy of the practices.

I suggest that we need a more refined and nuanced examination of this handbook within the context of the rise of lay Buddhism in mid-to late-nineteenth-century Sri Lanka. Despite the title of the handbook, the fact that its content is a manual for ritual practice is a point not to be lightly dismissed. Furthermore, this handbook provides us with an excellent opportunity to explore the character of Sinhalese Buddhist lay practices, particularly in relation to monastic Buddhism, against the backdrop of the broad categories of reform, revival, and modernization. Toward this end, what follows are my initial observations of a more detailed study of the historical situation within which the handbook appeared and within which it continued to flourish throughout the twentieth century. My remarks are organized into four sections: a short overview of the contents of the handbook, the canonical and postcanonical sources employed, a discussion of the variety of editions, as well as the editors and compilers of the different editions and the distribution of the handbook. I conclude this paper by offering a different setting for the *Bauddha Äadahilla.*

RITUALS OF BUDDHIST BELIEFS

The handbook edited by Kiriälle Ñāṇavimala Thero (the first edition was published in 1955 by Gunasena's) opens with the Pāli text of the *namaskāra: namo tassa bhagavato arahato sammā sambuddhassa* (In the name of the Blessed One, arahat, the one who is fully enlightened). The refuges and the five precepts *(sil)* follow the *namaskāra.* The Pāli is printed in Sinhala script, the literal meaning of the phrases is provided in Sinhala, and a moderately lengthy commentary on the necessity of the phrases follows. This pattern continues all the way through the eight precepts, with detailed instructions on why it is important to take *sil,* how to approach a monk to ask for *sil,* or how to take *sil* if a monk is not available. There are longish explanations on why a lay Buddhist should take the eight precepts on *poya* day, and on the different divisions of the month into the quarters of the moon cycle. There is a short enumeration of the ten precepts at the end of this section.

There are a few interesting stories told in the discussion of the refuges and the precepts, as in the example of Queen Vessamittā, who was saved from execution by the fact that she had taken refuge in the Buddha, dharma, and the sangha along with the five precepts. The story unfolds on the battlefield, and Vessamittā realized that her husband, the king of Kosambī, had been killed. She was immediately captured and after an attempt to talk her captor out of executing her, the fuel stacked around her was set on fire. But the fire was "as a cool body of water" to the queen, and seeing this, her executor asked her why she was not burned. Her answer, as we might expect, was that she had taken refuge in the triple gem. There is no reference to this queen in the canon or in the commentaries, although her name does appear in the Hugh Neville manuscripts.

Another story tells how a student named Chatta was attacked and killed by robbers on his way to his teacher's residence. Because, however, he had taken the refuges and the precepts, he was reborn into Tāvatiṃsa heaven and all of his family became stream-enterers. This story is a late one in the canon, appearing in the *Vimānavatthu* and its commentary as well as the commentary to the *Majjhimanikāya*.

The second section describes different kinds of meditation, beginning with the recollection of the Buddha's good qualities, recollections of dharma, and of the sangha. It includes reflections on the body and concludes with reflections on dying; there are a total of twenty-seven different meditation topics, some of which are minor variations on others. Different types of worship—*vandana*—constitute the third section, including worship of the Buddha, dharma, and the sangha as well as the classic pilgrimage sites throughout Sri Lanka and different types of *pūjā*.

The fourth section is entitled *'Dharma Vibh āgaya,"* or "Investigations of Dharma." The topics include: the noble eightfold path, the seven noble riches—faith, virtues, modesty, caution, tradition, renunciation, and wisdom, the ten meritorious acts, and so on. Different kinds of *dāna* are described, as well as the merits of giving. This section ends with a detailed enumeration of different kinds of suffering, some of which are the familiar old age, birth, and death but some of which appear to be later supplements. This distillation of dharma is intriguing, insofar as it is a mix of canonical, commentarial, and more recent explanations of the teachings. Following the discussions of dharma is a short chapter on the *gihivinaya,* which contains the *Sihalovāda Sūtra* in its entirety. The final section is for the *paritta* ritual, and includes the *Mahāmaṅgala, Ratana, Karaṇīya-mettā,* and *Dhajagga Sūtra*s.

The shortest version of this text contains only the *namāskara* and the precepts, and runs about twenty pages in large type-set for young children. The longest is the one I have used here, which is the version edited by Kiriälle Ñāṇavimala Thero, and it is 434 pages long in a small typeface. I have seen at least four other printed versions, with printing dates ranging from the 1920s up through the 1990s; all are fundamentally similar. I have also located four *oḷa*-leaf manuscripts of this text, of varying lengths, dates, and orthography; I have been able to examine three at length. Of these four, two are quite similar to the long text compiled by Ñāṇavimala, although a good deal of the commentary that appears in the text is missing from the manuscripts, as are the *paritta sūtras* that appear at the end of Ñāṇavimala's handbook. Two of the printed editions include astrological material at the end that is omitted from Ñāṇavimala's edition. This is not a classical text in any sense of the word. The passages and verses are straightforward, and the commentary is rather mundane and graceless. There is no mention of other texts or sources. It is designed wholly for the lay practitioner, designed as a compilation of different kinds of practices: the refuges, precepts, meditation, worship, and *paritta.* The explanations of dharma are a loose compilation of classical teachings, although they reflect more closely the conglomeration of teachings that are filtered through classical Sinhala literature rather than the canonical and commentarial literature. For example, the eightfold path precedes any mention of the four noble truths. The ten meritorious actions and the ten de-meritorious actions are more important than a discussion of *anattā.* The classical categories of Pāli "theology" as transmitted through the academic study of Theravāda Buddhism drop away in this discussion of dharma; the section reads not as an introduction but more as a reminder of the salient points. Furthermore, in all of the discussions that I have had about this text with practicing Sinhalese Buddhists, no one remarked on this section. The overview of dharma receives, on the whole, little attention among readers of this text. The importance of the content of this handbook is not its style, rhetoric, or analysis: it is the description of the practices that make the handbook significant.

Even so, the handbook reflects the same attitude toward devotion that appears in medieval Sinhala literature described by Charles Hallisey: the Buddha is laden with honorifics, and the relationship established between the practitioner and the Buddha by the act of taking refuge alters the formal relationship between the supplicant and the distant Buddha.[2] It is not a coincidence that the handbook begins with the refuges and the precepts. The relationship established by taking the refuges establishes the Buddha as a protector, as a guardian, and as a guide. The Buddha remains the honored, omniscient one throughout the entire text. Contrary to Olcott's defense of the Buddha as an honorable man but not divine in his own *Catechism,* the Buddha in the *Buddha Äđahilla* is "the highest in the three worlds who is worthy of receiving offerings . . . in a very formal manner." The refrain of the *Dhammacakkapavattana-sutta* also appears: "There is no god, brahmā, or anyone else who is more exalted than He. The refuges are vested in anyone who worships and esteems his Buddha-qualities."[3]

This relationship is emphasized in the *Buddha Äđahilla,* where editors explain how and why the refuges are efficacious and how they can be, literally, broken. The Buddha's authority as the highest one in the cosmos makes the refuges and the precepts "work." On the other hand, if one has any doubt about the Buddha or if one has any "unwholesome regard" about the omniscient one, then one's act of going for refuge becomes defiled. Similarly, if one does not know the qualities of the Triple Gem, if one doubts those qualities, or if one confuses bad qualities for good, then one's refuge is violated.[4]

Four kinds of prostration are enumerated, and they provide an interesting glimpse into the reasons that one should take refuge. If one engages in the five-limb prostration to the Buddha when reciting the *namaskāra* and seeking refuge, there are four reasons for doing so. (The five-limb prostration means worshipping the Buddha first by kneeling, then by stretching out face down, touching both elbows and the forehead to the ground. This is sometimes understood to involve kneeling, bending over at the waist, laying both hands palm down on the ground and resting one's forehead on the back of the hands.) The first is recognizing that there is a kinship between the Buddha and his clan and the practitioner, thinking "he is a relative of mine." The second is out of fear—thinking that not worshiping such a powerful being as the Buddha will result in harm (an interesting variant on Pascal's wager!). The third reason for prostrating oneself is recognizing that "In the time when the Omniscient One was a bodhisattva, I studied the arts under him." The fourth reason is simply to regard refuge as a prudent resource in case of calamity or misfortune.[5] The authority of the Buddha as the highest being in the cosmos grants the refuges their efficacy, but the array of reasons for seeking refuge are scarcely the noble causes one might imagine. The altered relationship that Hallisey describes—recognizing the Buddha as "mine" or "ours"—is the first reason for prostrating oneself, but fear and good old common sense are equally valid reasons for bowing to the Buddha when going for refuge.

The Buddha and the world represented in the *Buddha Ädahilla* is the Buddha as *cakkavattin,* as wheel-turner, world-ruler, and omniscient one. He is not the logician of the debates, nor is he the seeker after enlightenment. He is the one who has turned the wheel, who has paved the path for others to follow. And he generously extends his protection to seekers who believe in him—not out of any "pure faith," but for whatever reason. All that follows in the *Buddha Ädahilla* is directed at cultivating and fixing that relationship, whether it is pilgrimage, meditation, or *paritta* rituals.

AN AUTHOR OF THE *BUDDHA ÄDAHILLA*?

The redactor of one of the *oḷa*-leaf manuscripts explains that it is a copy of the second part of a book that was printed in Koṭahena. This is an unambiguous reference to the earliest edition of this text that I have been able to find. The British Library houses a printed second edition that was edited by Mohoṭṭivattē Guṇānanda Thero; one biography provides 1889 as the date of the first edition. The second edition is dated in 1894, and both were printed on Guṇānanda's press at Dīpaduttārāmaya, the Sarvajña Press. *Oḷa*-leaf copies of the printed books were not uncommon, even in the early part of the twentieth century; they were a common means of circulating texts even on the outskirts of urbanized Colombo. Mohoṭṭivattē Guṇānanda wrote a variety of tracts, books, pamphlets, and published at least two newspapers during his lifetime. His temple in Koṭahena was at the center of the Buddhist revival, and he had long challenged Christian missionaries even before his success at the Pānadura debates in 1873.

Born in 1823 at Balapiṭiya at Mohoṭṭivatta (Migeṭṭuwatta), he was educated at home, under the tutelage of his uncle Danti Nayde Gurunnanse (Delath Andiris Mendis) who once wore the robes (that is, had trained to become a fully-ordained monk) and who was also highly skilled in reading *oḷa*-leaf manuscripts. Guṇānanda was ordained as a novice at the Subhadrārāmaya Purāṇa Vihāra when he was twelve, and his teacher was Balapiṭiya Gunaratne Thero. Some time later his father passed away, as did his teacher, and Guṇānanda disrobed and returned home. Through mutual friends, he was enrolled at what was to become Wesley College in Colombo where he learned English and Latin. After leaving the school over a dispute, he took a position at the *Ceylon Observer.* Maintaining a close friendship with his uncle, Sīnigama Dhīrakkhanda who was the chief incumbent at the Dīpaduttārāmaya Vihāra in Koṭahena, he took the robes once again after the death of his mother. Guṇānanda took his higher ordination in 1844 as a member of the Amarapura order in Balapiṭiya, although there is some question regarding his actual status. Richard Fox Young sides with testimony that Guṇānanda gave in court in 1883 that he was a novice, and suggests that perhaps Guṇānanda had once been an *upasampadā* monk but became a novice for the relative freedoms that that status provided.[6]

A few years before his ordination, Guṇānanda was assigned to the *Dīpaduttārāmaya* in Koṭahena under his friend and teacher Sīnigama Dhīrakkhanda. Guṇānanda continued to study informally with a variety of other teachers, including Hikkaḍuvē Sumaṅgala. His biographers describe how tireless his efforts in publishing and education were, in the over-laudatory language found in this genre: "A new light emanated from this temple owing to the untiring militant efforts and contributions of Venerable Guṇānanda Thero, extending gradually to the Islandwide Buddhist Revival Movement."[7] Despite the overblown rhetoric, Guṇānanda apparently established a printing press that was functioning in the early 1860s (Abhayasundara claims that it was running in 1857), and wrote many treatises, tracts, books, pamphlets, and a series of newsletters until his death in 1890. He was the champion of the debates at

Pānadura in 1873, and his name was widely recognized after that. Don David Hewavitarana, who would later become Anagārika Dharmapāla, was twelve years old when he heard Guṇānanda's speech at Pānadura.

Blavatsky and Olcott came to Sri Lanka in 1880 after hearing of Guṇānanda's success at Pānadura and worked closely with Guṇānanda for a short time after their arrival. However, Guṇānanda became suspicious about Olcott's motives. Abhayasundara (one of Guṇānanda's biographers) explains how Guṇānanda challenged Olcott on the misuse of funds raised for the Buddhist Education fund and how Guṇānanda had come to see that Olcott was "trying to teach distinguished monks and scholars instead of learning from them."[8] Young nicely characterizes the relative strengths of Guṇānanda and the Theosophists: Guṇānanda's strengths had always rested in the popular traditions of Buddhism—no one could "move the masses at a subconscious level like he could."[9] On the other hand, Young suggests, Blavatsky and Olcott were much better prepared to marshal resources at the lay level than was Guṇānanda. The Theosophists substituted lay leaders for monastic; Olcott explicitly excluded ordained monks from leadership positions in the Buddhist Theosophical Society. Prior to Dharmapāla's reconstruction of the devout lay Buddhist, then, Guṇānanda was addressing, inspiring, and teaching those Sinhala-speakers who no longer knew anything about Buddhism. In fact, the opening to one of the *oḷa*-leaf manuscripts of the *Buddha Äahilla* explicitly addresses itself to those "who do not know or who are ignorant about participating in *sil* and so on."[10]

As at least the earliest author of the *Buddha Äahilla,* Guṇānanda employed his knowledge of the Sinhala tradition, his purported familiarity with the monastic curriculum, and his oratory skills on behalf of Buddhism's defense. Young discusses at length the mentality of "beleaguerment" that seems to have characterized much of Guṇānanda's life. He took the responsibility of *damana* quite seriously, according to Young, and it was the attitude of beleaguerment that often motivated Guṇānanda's defense of the faith. Guṇānanda is recognized today—when he is remembered at all—for his invigorating and stalwart demeanor in public debate. The corpus of his writing that culminated in the *Buddha Äahilla* reveals a highly literate and well-trained writer of manuscripts and printed works. His other works included a tract entitled *Bauddha Prasna* (Questions Relating to Buddhism) that was published in 1887, in which he enumerated the Buddha's ten perfections instead of the Buddha's dharma.[11] Guṇānanda also edited and published three classical works in Sinhala, the *Kāvyaśēkharaya* (1872), the *Milindapraśnaya* (1876), and the *Pansiyapanas Jātakapota* (1881).

A close look at the Buddhism that Guṇānanda espoused shows that it was scarcely the rationalized Buddhism of the Theosophical Society. The *Bauddha*

Ädahilla is a classic example of Guṇānanda's emphases and interests: he emphasized knowledge of the rituals, the practices, and the variety of Buddhist acts that were intertwined with Sinhalese culture. Young's remark about Guṇānanda's *Bauddha Prasna* might also be true of the *Bauddha Ädahilla:* "He never got around to the Dhamma as such, because his interests did not lay in that domain: in his perspective, true Buddhists take refuge in the Buddha (and, of course, the Dhamma and Saṅgha), not a philosophy."[12] And that is the message of the *Bauddha Ädahilla,* that true Buddhists take refuge in the Buddha, meditate on and with the protection of the Buddha, and worship the Buddha.

Even though we have this evidence that Guṇānanda composed the *Bauddha Ädahilla* in the context of the Buddhist revival, it is common to attribute authorship of the handbook to more lofty periods of the past. For example, one well-known editor of the text was Kiriälle Ñāṇavimala Thero, who edited the version of the *Bauddha Ädahilla* that is most commonly found today. His first edition appeared in 1955. Ñāṇavimala was the author of many such texts, as well as treatises on many different aspects of Sinhalese Buddhism. In his introduction to his edition, Ñāṇavimala explains that the Dutch commissioned an elaborately bound and decorated volume and presented it to Kīrtī Śrī Rājasiṅha. However, one of his students cast doubts on this claim during an interview that I had with him—I learned that later in his life Ñāṇavimala was a less precise scholar than we might have wished—and I have found no other independent evidence to substantiate Ñāṇavimala's assertion about the age or origin of the handbook. Ñāṇavimala, like Guṇānanda, was highly trained; he edited many widely used editions of Sinhala literature. In terms of his popular writings, he was recognized for the proliferation of his works, if not necessarily his historical accuracy, particularly toward the end of his life.

During the course of my research, I have found that Ñāṇavimala was not alone in his desire to locate the *Buddha Ädahilla* in the distant and glorious past. Lay Buddhists and monks alike have insisted in informal conversations that this handbook "goes all the way back to the time of the Buddha." These claims seem to signal a desire to identify a history for this text that equals its popularity. The existence of *oḷa*-leaf manuscript copies of this handbook may stem from the same desire: if we can locate palm-leaf copies of the text, then certainly it must be a work with a revered history. The significance of this handbook, however, lies in its reputation and continued use throughout the twentieth century.

POPULARITY OF THE *BAUDDHA ÄDAHILLA*

As I noted above, the most popular version of the text is that edited by Kiriälle Ñāṇavimala, and it continues to be reprinted every few years by Gunasena

Printers in Colombo. I have seen stacks of this handbook, both in hardcover and bound in leather, for sale during May and June; it is a familiar gift for Vesak, the month during which the Buddha's enlightenment is celebrated. It is still being reprinted; during my last conversation with the manager of Gunasena's in 1998, he indicated that they would continue to reprint it as long as it sold—but he did note that sales had dropped off in recent years. The handbook was in its sixteenth printing in 1998, and each run was approximately 1,500 to 2,000 copies. It is reasonable to suggest that approximately 28,000 copies of the book have been sold since the mid-1950s by Gunasena's alone. In a country of roughly twelve million Buddhists today, that number is rather small: it seems that the popularity of the text outweighs the number of copies that were printed during the twentieth century. The text appeared to share the same popularity at the start of the century, as noted by Reginald Copleston, the Anglican Bishop of Colombo in 1908: "Most Buddhists who can read, at least in or near Colombo, possess a copy; and some of them who cannot read get it read to them."[13]

During the past three years since I have taken up this project, I have heard any number of stories about how people were given this book as children. When they first began to read, parents gave their children a copy to use as a guide to the proper recitations when visiting temples, doing one's evening devotions in the shrine at home, or when undertaking a more involved *pūjā* ritual. A glimmer of fond recollection appears in people's eyes when they describe how their grandmother or grandfather slept with the book under their pillow at night, and stored the book reverently in a nearby cabinet during the day. I have heard about how the *Bauddha Ädahilla* was used to ward off injury to infants and children by placing it in their cradles or their beds until they were four or five years old. A good friend's mother-in-law has described to me in detail how she gave each of her daughters a copy of the book when they were seven, and taught them how to recite the chants until they knew them by rote.

Often when I ask people about the handbook, they look at it like a long-lost friend, remarking about how long it has been since they thought of the book. One well-respected scholar told me how he had been approached by a member of the Premadasa cabinet to write a biography—never published—of the president that would be published in a small format, "exactly the same size as the *Bauddha Ädahilla,* so that people could carry it around in their pockets." In Colombo and its environs, the handbook is quite popular, and has been for the better part of the twentieth century, although more research is required to document this systematically.

These stories seem to reflect a different aspect of the book's importance. In these anecdotes, this book functions in a Sinhalese Buddhist community in much the same way that a Bible given to children at the time of their confirmation or first communion functions in Protestant or Catholic households. It is a gift, with a frontispiece in the book to record both the recipient and the donor. The stories I have heard about the efficacy of the book itself in warding off evil reflect the significance of the handbook as a commodity, similar in some ways to an amulet or charm—the text is significant because its religious teachings provide a source of protection for the bearer, not primarily because it is read, memorized, and acted upon. At the same time, the handbook *is* read, at least among some families, and the lines *are* memorized for use in ritual practice. It is my suspicion at this early date that there was a shift in how the text was used throughout the twentieth century. All of the stories I have heard about how the handbook was used to ward off potential harm to children and the elderly have been told to me by people in their sixties or seventies; people in middle age who tell me about the book have tended to emphasize the content of the book. Ironically enough, the earlier use of the book as a medium of protection would have been closer to Guṇānanda's ritualized Buddhism than the more recent emphases on the content of the book.

In the past decade, other Sinhala books on how to worship, meditate, and take the refuges have sprung up in large numbers and the *Bauddha Ädahilla* no longer stands alone. All of the stories about the handbook have been told to me by adults in their thirties or older; younger generations are perhaps familiar with the title of the book but not because they own or have owned a copy. Bookstores such as that at the Kälanīya Temple, Goḍage's, Gunasena's, and the Buddhist Cultural Centre in Nedimala sell countless children's books describing different types of Buddhist worship; what all of these books have in common is a focus on ritual practice. While books on different types of Buddhist literature are equally available, those that describe Buddhist worship are by far the more popular according to my interviews and conversations.

The *Buddha Ädahilla* is popular only among Sinhala-speaking families, and thus it occupies what I have come to consider a unique niche within Sri Lankan culture. Young has suggested, drawing on Obeyesekere, that the elite of Sinhala-speaking culture have adopted the rational and demythologized version of Buddhism spread by Olcott. In contrast, the popular, cosmological, Buddha-focused practices of the *Buddha Ädahilla* takes center stage among a certain strata of non-elite Sinhala-speaking people in the Colombo environs.[14] This Buddhism is closest to Spiro's notion of kammatic Buddhism, although that distinction requires closer scrutiny to be used accurately in this context, particularly in light of the arguments proposed in Gombrich and Obeyesekere's *Buddhism Transformed*. At any rate, this is a Buddhism that is not overly rational, although it does slip into the increasingly conservative forms of rationalized and crystallized Buddhism that have emerged in response to the civil war; nor is it predominantly spiritualized in the sense of the spirit religion described by Gombrich and Obeyesekere.

The type of Buddhism revealed in the pages of the *Buddha Ädahilla* is far more cultural, perhaps, than most studies of Buddhism recognize. At its core are the rituals of worship, the "ten good deeds" (generosity, morality, and so on), and proper attitude. It is equally aesthetic, with a great deal of attention placed on recognizing the proper rhythm of the chants and the demeanor instilled when listening to the words, whether on television, over loudspeakers at temples, or from a parent. Young encapsulates this traditional Buddhism very nicely in the conclusion to his article on Guṇānanda. He remarks that Guṇānanda had started a program offering free flowers to those who came to worship the Buddha at the temple in Koṭahena, in part as a form of protest against those "Theosophists [who] don't observe *sil,* light lamps, or offer flowers to the Buddha."[15] This core of *pūjā* exemplifies the Buddhism reflected in the pages of the *Buddha Ädahilla* .

LOCATING AND IDENTIFYING THE *BAUDDHA ÄDAHILLA*

I wish to place briefly this text in relationship to other movements of religious reform or revival in Sri Lanka and South Asia. Seeking answers to the question of what the genre of devotional Sinhalese literature looks like during this period is beyond the scope of this essay; suffice it to say, however, that both lay practice and devotion are central themes of Sinhala literature that date at least to the medieval period, as Hallisey has shown. Models for lay practice have been defined, constructed, and negotiated in dialogue with other religions, issues of ethnicity, politics, and the larger Indian subcontinent in Sinhalese literature at least since the tenth and eleventh centuries.[16] While I will not seek to define a specific genre for the *Bauddha Ädahilla,* it is useful to compare the text to similar types of literature first in South Asia, and then in Sri Lanka in order to determine the character of other types of religious reforms. Arguments in favor of the relevance of the category of Protestant Buddhism are weakened by the absence of comparisons of Sinhalese Buddhist reforms with reforms in Hinduism or Islam in South Asia during the same period.

The first parallel is found in the work of Arumugala Navalar (1822–1879) in Jaffna and in Madras. Born to a literate Śaiva family in a small village on the Jaffna peninsula, Navalar learned English in a Christian school while he spoke Tamil at home. As a young man, he was hired to teach Tamil and English in the Wesleyan Mission School in Jaffna, where he remained for eight years. Hudson remarks that Navalar came to define himself as a devotee of Śiva during this period of his life. When Navalar was twenty-six (in 1847), he began to preach on

Friday evenings, criticizing Christians and Śaiva priests alike and teaching others how to be properly Śaiva. With a colleague, Navalar left for Madras in 1849 to obtain a printing press from local supporters, and he established a press in Sri Lanka. He later established a second press in Madras, devoted to the same causes of education and publishing tracts on proper Śaiva devotion. When Navalar died in 1879, he had published some seventy-four works, among which were a children's primer, a treatise entitled "How to Worship in Śiva's Temple," and a "Śaiva catechism" of more than four hundred questions and answers.[17]

Rohin Bastin observes that there are similarities between Sri Lankan Buddhist and Hindu reformers, despite the fact that Navalar began his work nearly a generation before Buddhist reformers got underway. Most significantly, Bastin notes that both Hindu and Buddhist reformers sought to revive their religious traditions following centuries of Christian proselytizing, and thus the attempts of Christian missionaries to convert, taken together with their impact on education and on the rise of printed texts, "set the terms of revivalism in both the Hindu north and the Buddhist south."[18] Bastin also points out that relationships between Sinhala Buddhists and Tamil Hindus were cooperative and cordial in the 1870s and 1880s, since the more important adversary at that point was the British. (When Swami Vivekananda visited Anuradhapura in 1897, however, his public lecture was disrupted by protesting Sinhala Buddhists.) On the basis of this and other similarities, Bastin suggests that one might call the Hindu revival "Protestant" as well—but he opts not to employ this term in part because the foreign word neglects significant features of the Hindu renaissance.[19]

The most important feature about the use of the term *Protestant,* Bastin points out, is not the dimension elucidated by Max Weber, namely, some fundamental "Protestant ethic," but the fact that both Hinduism and Buddhism shared a similar intensification of lay religiosity during the period. If the dimension of secularization highlighted by the term is understood, then the term is a useful one. In the end, however, Bastin rejects the term for the Hindu revival because it projects a "false causality": neither the Buddhist nor Hindu revivals were dependent upon Protestantism, despite the significant impact it had on the religious revivals of nineteenty-century Sri Lanka.[20] Robert Bellah's remarks in 1963 on the need to take up broader issues involved in applying Weber's work to Asia ring particularly true, specifically in comparative context and with close historical research of the sort that Young has done.[21]

This point is born out when one considers the rise of Muslim reform as well. Catalyzed by the arrival in Sri Lanka during 1883 of the Egyptian nationalist 'Urābī (Arabi) Pasha (1839–1911), the Muslim revival was also characterized by increased lay devotion and increased use of religious texts.[22] 'Urābī was not the active leader of the Muslim revival that Dharmapāla was for the Buddhist movement, or that Navalar was for the Hindu movement. He was, on the other hand, a quiet and cautious man who was "particularly sensitive to the opinion of the colonial authorities"—but he was also a symbol around which the movement could coalesce. Similar to the Hindu and Buddhist movements, the Muslim revival first focused on education, although Muslim resistance to Christian schools set the task of Muslim education apart from both Hindu and Buddhist educational reforms. Like Hindu and Buddhist associations, the Muslim community also established societies to spread the study of English; Samaraweera suggests that the Hindu and Buddhist organizations served as models; for example, the Muslim Young Men's Association was established in 1910. Also in keeping with the Hindu and Buddhist revivals, the Muslim movement critiqued religious leaders and sought to democratize Islam. Samaraweera cites a review published in 1935: "[T]he community became mullah-ridden and men and women were led into a state of blissful ignorance in the name of religion."[23] Education, increased lay participation, and the establishment of lay organizations characterized the Muslim revival as well as the Hindu and Buddhist revivals; the *Bauddha Äahilla* was not the only text of its kind during the period by any means.

Several questions remain. First, to what degree is it useful to continue to call the Buddhist revival movement Protestant? This brief glance at the Hindu and Muslim movements reveals similar characteristics—education, challenges to religious leaders, growth of popular religious texts, and increased lay participation—both in numbers and in intensity. To what end, then, is it useful to separate the Buddhist revival from the Hindu or Muslim revivals? Furthermore, if we identify an increased lay participation for these movements, what does this look like? Does increased lay participation refer to a broader-based lay participation in terms of numbers, a substantive change in attitudes toward religious leaders, or some other as-yet-undefined form of religiosity? Particularly in light of Anne Blackburn's work, we need to be cautious about taking the challenges to monastic authority at face value.[24]

Second, we need to examine more closely the rise of nonelite groups in the Colombo area. Michael Roberts's work on elite formation is indispensable for a thorough understanding of the impact that colonialism had on shifting class and caste positions, but equally thorough research is needed to determine where the funds came from to support Guṇānanda's work in Koṭahena, and similar projects. I suspect that, despite what we suspect about the support of the elite for the Buddhist revival, the "middle class" (for lack of a more precise term) has played a central role in the support for the presses, and so on.

Third, from the perspective of the *Buddha Äahilla,* the revival movement focused on proper ritual behavior instead of rational belief. I suggest that the feature of rational belief that is so closely intertwined with the concept of

Protestant Buddhism requires closer and more nuanced analyses. For those who were taught how to behave in temples from the handbook, action was the proper vehicle to express one's ethnic and religious identity. If one behaved properly as a Buddhist, one *was* Sinhalese (recognizing that "all Sinhalese today are not Buddhist, all Buddhists in Sri Lanka are Sinhalese").[25] The third question, then, is the relationship between action and profession of belief in the late nineteenth century, particularly since rational belief is considered to be such a central pillar of Protestant Buddhism.

This final point is made clearer if we do return to the place and function of catechetical texts in religious history. The genre was inaugurated when Martin Luther published his *Enchiridion, or the Little Catechism* in 1529. His format was question-and-answer, and in his preface, Luther asks that his readers memorize the book: "I beg of you to adopt the present booklet I offer you, and to teach it, word for word, to your people. . . . Be faithful to that text, word for word, in such a manner that your hearers will be able to repeat it after you and to commit to memory."[26] This question-and-answer style remained popular among Protestants well into the twentieth century. Olcott's *Buddhist Catechism* is just such a series of questions and answers, designed to instill the reasons for proper belief and respect for the Buddha and Buddhism.[27]

Olcott's text is divided into simple sections: The Life of the Buddha, The Dharma or Doctrine, The Sangha, The Rise and Spread of Buddhism, and Buddhism and Science. Unlike Guṇānanda, Olcott poses many questions about Buddhism and provides answers. For example, in the first pages, he asks "What is Buddhism? Would you call a person a Buddhist who had merely been born of Buddhist parents?" Other questions deal with Pāli terminology, such as "what is a male lay Buddhist called?" In the section on the *dharma,* he asks doctrinal questions, such as "Upon what is the doctrine of rebirth founded?" Olcott's catechism is designed for those who seek answers about the doctrines and teachings of Buddhism; while he includes information on worship, that is a minor aspect of the *Buddhist Catechism.* In the preface to the thirty-sixth edition of the text (published in 1903), Olcott himself notes the fact that there is a gap between those who value his *Catechism* and Buddhist *bhikkhus*. He quotes an article from the *Theosophical Review* that calls upon "learned Buddhists of Ceylon" to "bestir themselves to throw some light on their own origins and doctrines." Olcott responded: "I am afraid that we shall have to wait long for this help to come from the Buddhist *bhikkhus*, almost the only learned men of Ceylon; at least I have not been able during an intimate intercourse of twenty-two years, to arouse their zeal. . . . [A]s I believe I have said in an earlier edition, I only consented to write *The Buddhist Catechism* after I had found that no *bhikkhu* would undertake it." Olcott's *Buddhist Catechism* was indeed published in 1881, twelve years earlier than Guṇānanda's

Buddha Äahilla, and has been translated into at least twenty languages (unlike the *Buddha Äahilla,* which has yet to be fully translated into English). Despite Olcott's protestations, however, the *Buddha Äahilla* was in circulation among Buddhist *bhikkhus* in Sri Lanka, but it was a very different text than Olcott required. To compare the *Buddhist Catechism* and the *Buddha Äahilla* as catechisms that, by implication, are legacies of Martin Luther's catechism does not address the radical differences between the two texts.

Guṇānanda's *Buddha Äahilla* was not a question-and-answer catechetical text, nor are any of the editions of the text at my disposal. It is a text of instruction, of explanation, and above all, a resource manual: there is nothing to be memorized except the Pāli passages. Entire chapters were not designed to be learned by rote, only the few verses and phrases that a devout Buddhist should recite when worshiping, visiting a temple, or on pilgrimage. The focus of the *Buddha Äahilla* lies in explanations of why one should practice in the proper fashion, not in explanations of why Buddhists believe as they do. By articulating what proper ritual Buddhist behavior is, Guṇānanda provided an explanation for Buddhist identity in a quintessentially Sinhalese style. This is one of the reasons that I find it difficult to continue to employ the terminology of "Protestant Buddhism." Despite an apparent similarity of form—the *Buddha Äahilla* appears to be a catechism, is given to children when they are young as a guide to proper religious comportment, and distills the essentials of Buddhism for interested readers—in the end, the handbook is not fundamentally about belief. In spite of its title, the handbook is a manual for proper ritual comportment and, as such, is a text that is thoroughly embedded within Sinhalese ritual practice.

NOTES

I would like to acknowledge the financial support I have received for this project from the AsiaNetwork Foundation (1997) and from the National Endowment for the Humanities, in the form of a summer stipend during 1998.

1. Gananath Obeyesekere, "The Vicissitudes of the Sinhala-Buddhist Identity through Time and Change," in *Sri Lanka: Collective Identities Revisited,* 2 volumes, ed. Michael Roberts (Colombo: Marga Institute, 1997), vol. 1, 375. This piece is a revision of an earlier article published under a similar title in a volume edited by George de Vos and Lola Romanucci-Rossi, *Ethnic Identity: Cultural Communities and Change,* published by the Mayfield Publishing Company in 1976.

2. Charles Hallisey, *Devotion in the Buddhist Literature of Medieval Sri Lanka,* Ph.D. dissertation (University of Chicago, 1988), 70–91. See also John Ross Carter, "The Notion of Refuge *(saraṇa)* in the Theravāda Buddhist Tradition," in *The Threefold Refuge in the Theravāda Buddhist Tradition,* ed. Ross Carter (Chambersburg, PA: Anima, 1982), 1–15.

3. Kiriälle Ñāṇavimala Thero, ed. *Buddha Äahilla* , 15th ed. (Colombo: Gunasena Publishing, 1990), 6.

4. Ibid., 7.

5. Ibid., 9–10.

6. Richard Fox Young, "Imagined Beleaguerment and the Self-Representation of Mohoṭṭivatte Guṇānanda," in *Sri Lanka: Collective Identities Revisited,* vol. 1, 181.

7. Vimal Abhayasundara, *Mohoṭṭivattē Śrī Guṇānanda Apadānaya* (Colombo: S. Godage, 1994), 518.

8.Ibid., p 524.

9. Young, "Imagined Beleaguerment and the Self-Representation of Mohoṭṭivatte Guṇānanda," 184.

10. *Buddha Äahilla, o ḷa*-leaf manuscript, University of Peradeniya Library, Sri Lanka, no. 277917. 50 leaves, five lines each side, approx. 6 x 35 cm.

11. Young, "Imagined Beleaguerment and the Self-Representation of Mohoṭṭivatte Guṇānanda," 186–87.

12. Ibid., 187.

13. Reginald S. Copleston, *Buddhism Primitive and Present in Magadha and Ceylon* (Colombo: Longmans, Green, and Co., 1908), 278. R. F. Young and G. P. V. Somaratna cite the same sentence in *Vain Debates: The Buddhist-Christian Controversies of Nineteenth-Century Ceylon* (Vienna: De Nobili Research Library, 1996), 208.

14. Gananath Obeyesekere, *Colonel Olcott's Reforms of the 19th Century and Their Cultural Significance* (Colombo: Ralph Peiris Memorial Lecture Committee, 1992), cited in Young, 187. See also Obeyesekere's more general discussion of Protestant Buddhism and rationality in Richard Gombrich and Gananath Obeyesekere, *Buddhism Transformed: Religious Change in Sri Lanka* (Princeton: Princeton University Press,), 13–15.

15. *Rivirăsa* (June 17, 1888), letter to the editor cited in Young, 188.

16. Hallisey, *Devotion in the Buddhist Literature,* 169–201.

17. I have drawn this information about Navalar in large part from Dennis Hudson, "Winning Souls for Śiva: Arumuga Navalar's Transmission of the Śaiva Religion," in *A Sacred Thread: Modern Transmissions of Hindu Traditions in India and Abroad,* ed. Raymond Brady Williams (1992; New York: Columbia University Press, 1996), 23–51. See also Dennis Hudson, "Tamil Hindu Responses to Protestants: Among Nineteenth Century Literati in Jaffna and Tinnevelly," in *Indigenous Responses to Western Christianity,* ed. Steven Kaplan (Albany: State University of New York Press, 1995), and "Arumuga Navalar and Hindu Renaissance Among Tamils," in *Religious Controversy in British India: Dialogues in South Asian Languages,* ed. Kenneth W. Jones (Albany: State University of New York Press, 1992), 27–51. Hudson has also translated a portion of "How to Worship at Śiva's

Temple" in *Religions of India in Practice,* ed. Donald Lopez Jr. (Princeton: Princeton University Press, 1995).

18. Rohan Bastin, "The Authentic Inner Life: Complicity and Resistance in the Tamil Hindu Revival," in *Sri Lanka: Collective Identities Revisited,* vol. 1, 390.

19. Bastin has a very nice discussion of the debates surrounding the term *Protestant Buddhism,* including John Holt's objections to the term and other rejoinders. He responds to Dagmar Hellmann-Rajanayagam's insightful article, "Arumuku Navalar: Religious Reformer or National Leader of Eelam," which appeared in the *Indian Economic and Social History Review* 26: 235–57.

20. Bastin, "The Authentic Inner Life," 416–18.

21. Robert N. Bellah, "Reflections on the Protestant Ethic Analogy in Asia," *Journal of Social Issues* 19 (1963): 52–60. It is worth noting, however, that Young and Somaratna explicitly reject a comparative approach to Hindu and Christian responses to Christianity in Sri Lanka, seeing only a superficial similarity between the two movements. Young and Somaratna, *Vain Debates,* 33.

22. Vijaya Samaraweera, "The Muslim Revivalist Movement, 1880–1915," in *Sri Lanka: Collective Identities Revisited,* 2 volumes, vol. 1, 293–321.

23. M. C. M. Kaleel, "The Progress of the Muslim Community in Ceylon, 1910–1935," *Serendib* 5 (May 1990): 1, cited in Samaraweera, 312.

24. For a brief overview of challenges to monastic authority in the late nineteenth century, see Tessa Bartholomeusz, *Women Under the Bo Tree,* Cambridge Studies in Religious Traditions, vol. 5 (Cambridge: Cambridge University Press, 1994), 24–41. However, in a paper presented at the South Asia conference at the University of Wisconsin-Madison in 1999, Anne Blackburn suggests that there is far greater continuity in monastic authority and education than has been previously considered in the nineteenth century. Anne Blackburn, "Reorienting the Buddhist Sāsana: Buddhist Education in 19th Century Sri Lanka," Twenty-eighth Annual Conference on South Asia at the University of Wisconsin-Madison, October 1999.

25. This requires more detailed attention, as Michael Roberts remarks in an editor's footnote to Obeyesekere's statement: What has happened to those Tamil Buddhists of the past? And what of those Tamils who have become Buddhist in the 1960s and 1970s? This is an issue that requires further attention. Obeyesekere, *Buddhism Transformed,* 382 and n. 39.

26. Joseph V. Tahon, *The First Instruction of Children and Beginners: An Inquiry into the Catechetical Tradition of the Church* (London: Sheed and Ward, 1930), 67–68. Cited in W. L. A. Don Peter, *Education in Sri Lanka Under the Portuguese* (Colombo: Colombo Catholic Press, 1978), 143, n. 75.

27. Henry Steel Olcott, *The Buddhist Catechism,* 45th edition (Adyar: The Theosophical Publishing House, 1970), preface to 36th edition.

TEN

INTERPRETIVE STRATEGIES FOR SEEING THE BODY OF THE BUDDHA

James R. Egge

IN THE CENTURIES following the Buddha's death, the most important focus for his worship was his bodily relics. Material and transient remains of a being believed to have attained final nirvana, the relics were nonetheless worshiped as being in some sense the living Buddha.[1] That seeing the relics could be an important part of this cult is succinctly expressed by Mahinda's statement in *Mahāvaṃsa,* "When the relics are seen, the Conqueror is seen."[2] But how did one see a relic? Relics were normally encased in *stūpa*s, hidden from view. Even if relics were displayed, as today at the Temple of the Tooth in Sri Lanka, one would likely see only a reliquary, and not the relic itself. Devotees therefore had to direct their vision to sacred objects such as *stūpa*s and bodhi trees. By the second century B.C.E., however, Buddhists adorned the precincts of these holy places with reliefs and other artwork visible to the eyes of the faithful. These marks provided a focus for the devotees' gaze, and showed the viewer how to understand and view the *stūpa* itself. Similarly, narratives about people seeing the living Buddha and marveling about his physical qualities taught their audiences how to perceive the Buddha's relics and *stūpas,* his physical body *(rūpakāya)* that remains in the world after his final nirvana.[3]

In this eassy, I show how some Theravādin canonical narratives and early Buddhist *stūpa* reliefs advance different ways of viewing the Buddha's body. Adopting categories from Stanley Fish, I refer to these ways of viewing as interpretive strategies, and to a group whose members share an interpretive strategy as an interpretive community.[4] I argue that different narratives present two distinct interpretive strategies for seeing the Buddha's body, and that different sets of reliefs present two analogous interpretative strategies for viewing his body. I further argue that if these interpretations are valid, then we can see an analogous development in the interpretive strategies these verbal and visual texts advance. I conclude with a brief discussion of the possibilities of locating historically the interpretive communities that constituted, and were constituted by, these texts and strategies.

VERBAL STRATEGIES

In this section I discuss three sets of texts from *Sutta Piṭaka* that represent significantly differing attitudes toward the Buddha's physical body. The first does not advance a particular understanding of the Buddha's body, but the other two present clear and distinct views. All of these texts focus on the Buddha's distinctive physical characteristics. To give some precision to my discussion of these marks, I employ Charles Sanders Peirce's categories of icon, index, and symbol. In brief, an icon is a sign that denotes its object by virtue of resembling that object; for example, a drawing or an onomatopoetic word. An index is a sign that denotes its object by virtue of being affected by its object; for example, smoke or a spontaneous smile (signifying fire and happiness respectively). A symbol is a sign that denotes its object by virtue of a convention; for example, a traffic signal or a numeral.[5]

The first set of texts I will discuss is a group of verses that appears at M II 146, Sn 548–567 and 570–573, and Thag 818–841. M and Sn frame these verses with a prose narrative and include some additional verses; that Thag lacks these prose and verse sections suggests that the verses common to these three passages represent an older version of the narrative.[6] In these verses, a Brāhmaṇ named Sela praises the Buddha for his glorious physical appearance, telling him that he possesses all the marks of a great man *(mahāpurisalakkhaṇa)* and that he ought to be a righteous king *(dhammarājā)* and a wheel-turning emperor *(cakkavattin)*.[7] The traits that Sela names are that Gotama is perfect in body, shining, well-born, lovely to behold, virile, tall, erect, and majestic, with golden skin, very white teeth, clear eyes, and a good face.[8] The Buddha replies that he *is* an unsurpassed *dhammarājā,* not in the sense of being a righteous king, but because he is a king of the dharma. He likewise claims that he is not a worldly *cakkavattin,* but a turner of the unsurpassed wheel of dharma.[19] After the Buddha dispels all Sela's doubts, he and his three hundred Brāhmaṇ followers take refuge in the Buddha, praising him and paying homage to his feet.

In this story, seeing the Buddha leads only indirectly to a recognition of his buddhahood. When telling his disciples about the Buddha, Sela asks rhetorically, "Having seen him . . . who would not have faith?"[10] Earlier in the narrative, however, Sela attains faith not immediately upon seeing the Buddha, but only after hearing the Buddha's words. This narrative thus does not reveal if or how seeing the Buddha by itself produces knowledge of his transcendent nature. When Sela interprets the Buddha's physical attributes as indices and icons of mundane greatness, as evidence of his noble birth and potential to become a great king,[11] the Buddha neither validates nor denies the Brāhmaṇ's statements, but instead contrasts the mundane attainments praised by Sela with the surpassing greatness of Gotama's buddhahood. Neither the Buddha nor the narrator explains why the Buddha possesses these physical traits, and neither states that these traits are evidence of his buddhahood.[12]

Our second set of texts, which includes the prose frame to the Sela story (M II 146 = Sn 102–112), *Brahmāyu Sutta* (M II 133–146), *Ambaṭṭha Sutta* (D I 88–110), *Mahāpadāna Sutta* (D II 1–54), and *Lakkhaṇa Sutta* (D III 142–179), represents the Buddha's bodily marks as reliable indicators that he is a great man *(mahāpurisa)* and therefore a buddha. These passages all include a paragraph that states that for one who possesses the thirty-two marks of a great man, only two destinies are possible: he will become either a world-conquering emperor endowed with seven wondrous jewels or a buddha.[13] Unlike text set 1, in which Sela takes the marks as evidence that Gotama is a great man who *could (arahasi,* Sn 552) become a world-conquering king, this paragraph states that a person endowed with the marks *will* attain the greatest mundane or transcendent end. Furthermore, in text set 2 the Buddha more or less explicitly validates this allegedly Brahmanical tradition of the marks of a great man and his alternative destinies.[14] Thus, while in text set 1 the Buddha establishes an analogy between universal kingship and buddhahood, in text set 2 Brāhmaṇs assert, with varying degrees of assent from the Buddha, that there exists a homology between these alternative destinies, and that a great man can and will choose between them.

The odd physical characteristics attributed to the Buddha in text set 2 are not transparent signs of the Buddha's beauty or strength; rather, they are arcane omens whose significance is known only by the Buddha and by Brāhmaṇs versed in Vedic lore. The thirty-two marks are given in *Brahmāyu Sutta, Mahāpadāna Sutta,* and *Lakkhaṇa Sutta* as follows: his feet have level tread; on the soles of his feet are wheels with a thousand spokes; he has long heels; he has long fingers and toes; he has soft and tender hands and feet; his hands and feet are net-like; he has high-raised ankles; his legs are like an antelope's; standing and without bending, he can touch and rub his knees with either hand; his genitals are hidden; his skin is golden; his skin is delicate and so smooth that no dust adheres to it; his body-hairs are separate, one to each pore; they grow upward, bluish-black like collyrium, growing in rings to the right; his body is divinely straight; he has the seven convex surfaces; the front part of his body is like a lion's; there is no hollow between his shoulders; he is proportioned like a banyan tree, that is, his height is equal to the span of his arms; his torso is evenly rounded; he has a perfect sense of taste; he has jaws like a lion's; he has forty teeth; his teeth are even; his teeth (or canines) are very bright; there are no spaces between his teeth; he has a divine voice, like that of a cuckoo bird; his eyes are very dark; he has eyelashes like a cow's; the hair between his eyebrows is white and soft like cotton; his head is like a turban.[15] The translation of a number of these items is uncertain, as many of these phrases do not appear apart from this list. However, unlike the traits named in text set 1, these attributes are not all self-evidently beautiful or desirable; many of them seem (to me at least) more monstrous than inspiring. Senart and Foucher are no doubt correct in suggesting that these marks must have originally been understood as signs predictive of a child's future destiny, and were only later interpreted as aspects of the Buddha's physical perfection.[16]

Most of the *sutta*s of text set 2, including the Sela frame story, *Ambaṭṭha Sutta,* and *Brahmāyu Sutta,* narrate similar encounters between the Buddha and a Brāhmaṇ in which the Buddha reveals the marks normally hidden from view—his hidden genitals and enormous tongue—in order to dispel the Brāhmaṇ's doubts about the Buddha's identity. In these stories, neither the Buddha nor the narrator ever affirms the tradition of the marks of a great man and his alternative destinies; rather, the Buddha uses this tradition as a means of getting the Brāhmaṇ to hear the transcendent dharma.[17] For example, upon seeing the marks, the Brāhmaṇ Brahmāyu reasons that since he is accomplished in the good of this life, he should instead ask Gotama how one may become a buddha. After the Buddha speaks five lines in response to his questions, Brahmāyu repeatedly kisses and caresses the Buddha's feet while stating, "I am the Brāhmaṇ Brahmāyu, O Gotama; I am the Brāhmaṇ Brahmāyu, O Gotama." The onlookers wonder at Brahmāyu's complete obeisance, and the Buddha recognizes Brāhmāyu's faith in him (M II 144). This display of devotion directed to the Buddha's body is a direct response to hearing the Buddha teach the dharma, not to seeing the marks.

The tone of these stories is polemical and even humorous: the Buddha demonstrates the size of his tongue by licking his ears and nostrils and then covering his entire forehead, thus perhaps mocking Brahmanical scruples regarding bodily purity. The Buddha reveals his hidden genitals by granting the Brāhmaṇ supernormal powers of vision; the perhaps scandalized author of *Ambaṭṭha* omits this detail.[18] A question by Brahmāyu reveals the upward displacement implicit in this strange episode: "Though called by a word of feminine gender, perhaps your tongue is a manly one?"[19] The Buddha's tongue is manly because it is large; the implication may be that the Buddha's sexual organ, although like his tongue hidden within his body, is similarly large and manly, and that the Buddha, although he restrains his sexuality, is nonetheless virile.[20]

Two *sutta*s of text set 2, however, explicitly affirm that the marks are reliable indices of a buddha's identity. In *Lakkhaṇa Sutta,* the Buddha himself teaches the tradition of the alternative destinies of a great man. Explaining that non-Buddhist sages *(bāhirakāpi isayo)* know the marks but not their karmic causes (D III 145), the Buddha describes at great length the past actions as well as the Brahmanical predictions associated with each mark. This *sutta* thus shows that the marks are, like the Buddha's attainment of awakening, products of his past actions; the marks are trustworthy signs that an ascetic is or will become awakened. This *sutta* therefore comes close to investing the marks with immediate transcendent significance; however, it does not distinguish the marks and karmic past of a buddha from those of a temporal *cakkavattin.* The marks thus point only ambiguously to a transcendent fulfillment.

In telling the story of the buddha Vipassī in *Mahāpadāna Sutta,* the Buddha goes a step further, implying that a buddha's marks show not only that he is a great man, but also that he embodies the dharma. Gotama's account of Vipassī's conception, birth, and infancy combine the tradition of the marks of a great man and his alternative destinies with another tradition, according to which a bodhisattva's destiny is clear from birth.[21] For example, in this other tradition, when a bodhisattva is born, he takes seven steps and proclaims that that is his last birth (D II 15). After describing each of the standard elements in the career of a bodhisattva, the Buddha proclaims, *'Dhammat ā esā,"* "This is the rule," or, "This is the nature of the dharma." A bodhisattva's life therefore embodies and exemplifies the Dharma even before he becomes awakened. In this context, the tradition of the alternative destinies takes on a different meaning. The Brāhmaṇs recognize that the child will become a world-conquering emperor or a buddha, but it is not really the case that two possibilities lie open to the child. It is already determined that the child will become a buddha; the apparent choice is only a function of the Brāhmaṇs' lack of knowledge. In other words, Gotama is not a buddha because he is a great man *(mahāpurisa)* who chose to become an ascetic; rather, he is a great man because he is a bodhisattva in his final existence. For the person who believes or knows that Gotama is a buddha, his marks, his body, and his bodhisattva career conform to and reveal the Dharma even prior to his awakening.

The third set of texts I will discuss consists of eleven stories from the *Apadāna* that refer to the thirty-two marks in descriptions of Gotama or of a previous buddha. In these stories, the physical characteristics of the buddhas reference not their status as great men (*mahāpurisa*s), but their transcendent buddhahood. The marks do not provide rational grounds for belief, as they do in many of the stories just discussed; rather, they produce immediate recognition of a buddha's greatness and elicit devotion to that buddha. Accordingly, seeing the marks leads to the conversions of Brāhmaṇs and non-Brāhmaṇs alike. Furthermore, because the marks function not as arcane symbols but as icons that reveal these buddhas' transcendent nature, the stranger of the thirty-two marks are rarely named in these stories.[22] Instead, the physical characteristics attributed to the buddhas, whether or not these marks are included in the list of thirty-two, are transparent signs of the buddhas' greatness.

That mentions of the thirty-two marks do not refer primarily to the tradition of the marks of a great man and his alternative destinies can most easily be seen in the five stories in which the convert is not a Brāhmaṇ, but a monkey, a farmer, a wealthy man, or a wealthy woman.[23] In these stories, the sight of a buddha endowed with the thirty-two marks evokes spontaneous expressions of devotion. For example, two *arhats* recalling past lives as monkeys (or foresters, *vānaro*) state, "I saw a buddha free of dust *[virājaṃ]* seated in the mountains. Seeing him, illuminating all directions like the king of sāl trees in blossom, endowed with marks and signs *[lakkhaṇavyañjan āpetaṃ],* I was happy. Uplifted, glad, joyful, elated, I placed three blue lotus flowers about his head."[24] The woman Sākulā similarly recalls seeing the Buddha in her present life, "Seated in a window I saw at the city gate the Sugata, blazing with glory, honored by deities and humans, endowed with the lesser signs and adorned with the marks *[anuvyañjanasampanna ṃ lakkhaṇehi vibhūsitaṃ].*[25] Uplifted and glad, I took pleasure in going forth [into ascetic life]; in a short time I attained arhatship." These responses to the marks exemplify the classical South Asian idea of *darśana* (Pāli *dassana,* literally "seeing"), an intuition of the object of worship by means of sight, rather than knowledge gained through rational reflection.[26]

Although the five stories about the conversion of Brāhmaṇs more or less explicitly reference the notion that Brāhmaṇs possess knowledge of the thirty-two marks, these stories, like those about non-Brāhmaṇs, primarily emphasize the converts' affective responses to the physical splendor of a buddha.[27] For example, in recalling a previous birth as a Brahmanical ascetic, Sāriputta describes seeing the buddha Anomadassī as follows:

> There I saw the fully awakened one, shining bright, pleasing to the mind.
> Like a brilliant blue water lily, an oblation-eating fire,
> A blazing lamp stand, a lightning bolt in a mass of clouds,
> Or a king of sāl trees in full bloom, the leader of the world, him I saw.
> This elephant is a great hero, a sage who removes miseries.
> Attaining this vision *[dassanam],* one sheds all miseries.
> Seeing this god of gods, I looked for the mark(s):
> "Is this or is this not a buddha? There, I see the one with vision!"
> Wheels with a thousand spokes are seen on the best of feet;
> Seeing his marks, I reached a conclusion regarding the Tathāgata. (Ap I 20)

(The future) Sāriputta then worships Anomadassī with a gift of eight flowers, and delivers a speech in praise of the buddha's omniscience that includes the statement, "Having attained a vision *[dassanam]* of you, they cross the stream of doubt" (Ap I 20). This is all in response to seeing a buddha, without hearing a single word of teaching. Mention of the canonical thirty-two marks (i.e., the marks as symbols) is anticlimactic, as Sāriputta recognizes the buddha's identity before looking for the marks. The only one of the thirty-two marks named here, the wheels on the buddha's feet, is one that may function as an icon of a transcendent referent, the wheel of dharma. Another story of a Brahmanical conversion names another of the thirty-two marks, the buddhas' golden skin, and this mark may likewise be understood as an index and icon of the buddhas' transcendent glory and not as an obscure omen (Ap II 398).

Strange marks are mentioned in one *apadāna,* that of Sela; however, this retelling of his story portrays Sela not as a cerebral doubter but as a quick and enthusiastic convert. When in the prose story Sela hears a report of the Buddha, he recounts to himself the tradition of the thirty-two marks and the alternative destinies that they foretell. The *Apadāna* omits this part of the story, and instead Sela states three times that joy arose in him on hearing the word *Buddha* (I 320). The *Apadāna* also adds to Sela's inquiry as to the Buddha's whereabouts that he wishes to worship the one who gives the fruit of asceticism. In addition, while Sela in the prose still doubts after seeing the Buddha's long tongue and hidden genitals and tests him further, in the *Apadāna* Sela is convinced upon seeing the marks and immediately becomes a monk together with his students.[28]

The *Apadāna*'s view of the marks as inspiring devotion is perhaps most developed in the story of Gotamī, the Buddha's aunt and foster mother, who even as an *arhat* at the end of her life worships the Buddha's body with its marks (Ap II 529–543). This story repeatedly refers to Gotamī and her followers worshiping the Buddha's feet and gazing at his body or face.[29] The narrator refers to the Buddha's body as "endowed with the 32 marks," and the narrator and Gotamī name a number of these marks: soft feet, feet marked with wheels, body like a mass of gold (i.e., golden skin), and feet with long heels and long toes. Other specific physical characteristics named—feet marked with goads and flags, feet like lotuses in bloom and shining bright like a new sun *(tarunādiccasappabhe),* feet with copper-colored nails—do not correspond to the thirty-two marks (vv. 39–43, 52, 137). All of these marks can be seen either as aspects of the Buddha's mundane splendor or as signs with potentially transcendent significance; in particular, the wheels, goads, and flags may suggest the Buddha's roles as turner of the wheel of dharma, tamer of persons, and leader of the world. The text makes explicit the significance of these marks when Gotamī echoes descriptions of the Buddha's feet as resembling the sun and bearing flags by stating, "I bow to the sun of men, the banner of the solar clan."[30] It is also noteworthy that almost all of the characteristics named describe the Buddha's feet; this fact suggests that the worship of the Buddha's feet that is so prominent in this text is not simply a conventional gesture of respect, but an act that is intensely focused on the physical particularities of the Buddha's body. Gotamī does realize that such devotion to the Buddha's physical body is ultimately unsatisfactory:

> This is my last vision of the lord of the world;
> I will never again see your face, the sign of immortality.
> My mouth will never touch your tender feet,
> O hero, best in the world; I go to extinction.
> Of what value is your face and body with things as they are?
> Every constructed thing is thus: uncomforting and transient.[31]

But how is it that Gotamī, an *arhat* who realizes the truth of impermanence, can desire and worship the Buddha's body at all? Clearly, in these *Apadāna* stories the Buddha's body with its marks stands for transcendent realities; in seeing or touching his body one gains a nondiscursive awareness of buddhahood, *nirvāṇa,* and the dharma.

Text sets 2 and 3 therefore present differing answers to the problem posed by text set 1: how do the Buddha's visible physical characteristics make possible a recognition of his buddhahood? The tradition of the marks of a great man and his alternative destinies in text set 2 posits a homology between mundane and transcendent attainments by asserting that a great man is capable of attaining earthly rule or supreme awakening. In this reading, the marks are indices and symbols of an essentially mundane status, that of being a great man who may or may not become a buddha. The *Mahāpadāna Sutta,* however, shows that the destiny of a bodhisattva is determined before his birth, and that his entire career, even before becoming awakened, conforms to and manifests the dharma; the marks are therefore indices of a Great Being's bodhisattvahood and symbols of his buddhahood. Text set 3 presents an iconic relationship between the mundane and the transcendent, as seeing a buddha's physical splendor can produce an immediate recognition of his transcendent nature. These individual *Apadāna* stories do not explain how or why a buddha's physical body effectively signifies its immaterial referent; however, the *Apadāna* as a whole (and *Buddhavaṃsa* upon which the *Apadāna* draws) presents a cosmic biography of the buddhas according to which they attain their final bodies as a result of their past bodhisattva vow and karmic actions. As in the *Mahāpadāna Sutta,* the Great Being's physical characteristics are indices of his bodhisattvahood, but unlike the *Mahāpadāna Sutta,* the marks are not only symbols, but also icons, of buddhahood.

VISUAL STRATEGIES

The beautiful reliefs that adorned the gates and railings of the great Buddhist *stūpa*s at Sāñcī, Bhārhut, and Amarāvatī provide us with another body of evidence about how some early Buddhist communities viewed the bodies of the Buddha and other Buddhist saints. The railing of Sāñcī's *stūpa* no. 2, which probably represents the oldest extensive *stūpa* decoration in existence, dates from about the second century B.C.E. and the reliefs from the other *stūpa*s date from about the first century B.C.E. through the third century C.E.[32] Although most previous scholarship has interpreted these reliefs as signs representing the dharma, nirvana, and buddhahood, this interpretation runs into difficulties especially with the reliefs of *stūpa* no. 2. I will argue that the texts discussed above suggest a more nuanced reading of the *stūpa*s' signs: that the marks of Sāñcī's *stūpa* no. 2 are, like the thirty-two marks discussed in text set 2, ambivalent symbols of auspiciousness, while the later reliefs function more like the physical qualities named in text set 3, as icons of the Buddha's transcendent nature.[33]

As Mireille Bénisti has shown, there is nothing distinctively Buddhist about the artwork of Sāñcī's *stūpa* no. 2; rather, its images, including human beings, animals, fantastic beings, and plants, represent traditional motifs common to the art of ancient India.[34] Marshall and Foucher associated some of the *stūpa*'s images primarily with events in the life of the Buddha, so that the tree stood for his awakening, the wheel for his first sermon, and the *stūpa* for his final nirvana. This system of interpretation breaks down with the birth of the Bodhisattva, which Marshall and Foucher argued was represented in the earliest art by the figure of a woman being bathed by two elephants.[35] This image has no obvious connection with stories of the Bodhisattva's birth, but is, as Coomaraswamy pointed out, a standard representation of Gajalakṣmī, a form of the goddess Lakṣmī (or Śrī) who personifies good fortune.[36] Lotuses and water pots, which appear often on the railing of *stūpa* no. 2, also represent Lakṣmī. Bénisti further notes that no aspect of the reliefs suggests the identification of trees as signs of awakening; however, trees were in ancient India venerated as deities or as the homes of *yakṣa*s and *yakṣī*s, spirits of fertility.[37] Bénisti argues that wheels do not signify the first sermon, but are simply the great solar symbols of the universal dharma (167). That the wheel primarily signifies mundane authority is shown by the fact that three images at *stūpa* no. 2, of a column on which lions support a wheel, resemble Aśoka's famous column at Sārnāth. As Snellgrove observes, Aśoka's wheel very likely primarily signified imperial rule, and only later came to represent the Buddha's teaching.[38] Furthermore, as the verse story of Sela illustrates, the primary reference of the term *cakravartin/cakkavattin* is to the political sphere, and the Buddhist notion of the wheel of dharma is a metaphorical extension of this idea.[39] Bénisti also argues that the single representation of a *stūpa* on the railing dates from the time when the gates of *stūpa* no. 1 were constructed, and thus the original decoration of *stūpa* no. 2 contained no representation of the Buddha's death. Finally, *stūpa* no. 2's railing also depicts symbols shaped like a small case omega that have often been identified as *triratnas,* symbols of the Three Jewels. However, as Bénisti has shown, no evidence supports this interpretation, and this motif is simply an auspicious mark.[40] The railing depicts other auspicious signs that lack specifically Buddhist significance, most frequently the *Śrīvatsa.*

To the puzzle of why *stūpa* no. 2 should be adorned not with distinctively Buddhist art but with commonplace symbols of auspiciousness, the tradition of the marks of a great man represented by text set 2 offers a possible solution. According to this tradition, the Buddha's marks symbolize his status as a great man destined to become a buddha or a *cakkavattin* king. The *Mahāparinibbāna Sutta* indicates that this is also the very meaning of burial in a *stūpa:* the Buddha states that a buddha's remains should be interred in a *stūpa* just as is done with the remains of a *cakkavattin* king (D II 142–143, 161). Text set 2 further points out that symbols of auspiciousness would have had different meanings for different viewers. Like the Brāhmaṇs in the stories who look for the marks of a great man, non-Buddhists viewing the awesome sight of a monumental *stūpa* may have read its marks as symbols of temporal auspiciousness and beauty. That the *stūpa*s with their marks could be so understood helps to explain how the otherworldly sect of Buddhism provided the unifying ideology for the first great South Asian empires, and why kings devoted great wealth for the *stūpa*s' construction. The auspicious marks on a *stūpa* guide one to see it as a locus of this-worldly power and blessing, and to view the Buddha within as a great man, an ascetic counterpart to the emperor. Persons of all sects could afford respect to such a monument, much as many South Asians today venerate the tombs of saints without acknowledging the exclusive claims of the traditions associated with those saints. On the other hand, these texts and especially the *Mahāpadāna Sutta* contend that on the body of an ascetic, symbols of auspiciousness indicate that one is not simply a great man, but a being who conforms to and embodies the dharma. Adherents of the Buddhist teachings may similarly have viewed a *stūpa*'s auspicious marks as signs of the Buddha's transcendent auspiciousness.

My hypothesis that Buddhists may have understood the marks adorning the railing of Sāñcī *stūpa* no. 2 as auspicious symbols similar to the thirty-two marks of a great man is supported by the *Kālingabodhi Jātaka* (no. 479), in which a Brāhmaṇ identifies by its marks a tree as a place where past buddhas attained awakening. The only mark named in this account is that the grass and creepers growing near the tree twist to the right *(padakkhiṇato āvattā* Ja IV

233); this sign resembles one of the thirty-two marks, that the hairs of a great man twist to the right *(dakkhiṇā vaṭṭakajātāni)*. Echoing claims made in the texts discussed above that knowledge of auspicious symbols is the province of Brāhmaṇs, the Brāhmaṇ explains, "We know by signs *[veyyañjanik ā]*, great king, but buddhas are omniscient. Omniscient all-knowing buddhas do not know by marks *[lakkhaṇena]*; we have book-knowledge, but buddhas know everything" (Ja IV 235).

In contrast to *stūpa* no. 2's conventional symbols of auspiciousness, the distinctively Buddhist reliefs on the gates and railings of *stūpa*s nos. 1 and 3 at Sāñcī and the *stūpa*s at Bhārhut and Amarāvatī function as icons of the Buddha's physical and transcendent qualities. These signs could have this double reference for the interpretive communities that created them because, as in *Apadāna,* the Buddha's physical body was thought to bear an iconic relationship to his buddhahood. Previous scholarship has recognized that signs such as wheels, trees, *stūpas,* thrones, columns, parasols, walkways (*cakrama*s), haloes, and footprints, which often form the focal point in reliefs depicting narrative scenes, suggest the presence of the Buddha by representing the transcendent referents of awakening, the dharma, and nirvana. We should note, however, that these signs also, and often primarily, signify physical and mundane realities. Such objects as footprints and thrones by their very forms suggest the body of the Buddha; thrones and parasols also denote kingship.[41] Trees, columns, and haloes may indicate the physical stature of the Great Being; this equivalence is suggested especially by the images at Amarāvatī that combine signs to form what Snellgrove calls a "symbolic body" of the Buddha.[42] That such signs may refer to the physical bodies of the buddhas is also indicated by textual sources, such as the *Apadāna* stories cited above that speak of the radiance of the buddhas' bodies or which liken them to trees. Similarly, the biographies of past buddhas in *Buddhavaṃsa,* after giving the height of each buddha, describe his appearance, usually likening him to some object such as a tree, a column, a mountain, the sun, the moon, lightning, a sacrificial pole, fire, or a circlet. Of course, many images of trees on *stūpa* railings do represent the trees under which buddhas attained awakening, as some inscriptions show. However, as Huntington argues, these images and inscriptions do not denote the concept of *bodhi* in general, but depict particular trees; these trees therefore suggest to the mind of the viewer the bodies of the past buddhas who sat under those trees.[43] These signs therefore all suggest the Buddha's transcendent qualities by first evoking his physical body. Even images of *stūpa*s denote primarily not the *parinirvāṇa* of the Buddha, but his continued bodily presence in the world after his death.[44] It is true that the wheel does not stand in any obvious iconic relationship with the Buddha's body; however, there is an iconic relationship between the mundane and transcendent referents of this symbol: as discussed above, the wheel stands for royal authority as well as the Buddha's dharma.

The best indication of how these signs were intended to be viewed is given by the reliefs themselves: the majority of scenes incorporating these icons depict people worshiping them. Alfred Foucher famously argued that these scenes represent events in the life of Gotama, whom Buddhists represented with abstract signs to avoid portraying him figuratively.[45] Against this view, Susan Huntington holds that a great number of these scenes represent not events in the life of the Buddha, but the worship of Buddhist objects and sites.[46] It may be that neither explanation is valid for all cases; nonetheless, common to both of these interpretations is the assumption that Buddhists used nonfigurative signs as objects of veneration. Foucher holds that in avoiding figurative images as objects of worship Buddhists simply continued Vedic practice (7–10); Paul Mus explains that Vedic religion had no need for figurative images because the presence of deities was mediated through objects such as fires, brick altars, and the soma plant.[47] It should not be surprising that Buddhists, who derived many cultic practices from Vedic ritual, similarly used nonfigurative signs as foci for religious practice.[48]

In these narrative scenes (whether depicting the original events or commemorations of them), buddhas are denoted by nonfigurative signs not from the time of their awakening, but from the time of their final birth. By contrast, illustrations of *jātaka* stories portray the Bodhisattva in his previous existences figuratively. It is therefore unlikely that, as Snellgrove suggests, Buddhists avoided representing the Buddha figuratively because he was believed to be in nirvana.[49] It is difficult to see why Buddhists would hold that the Buddha could not be figuratively represented when they believed him to be present in his relics and when early Buddhist texts draw attention to his physical appearance. It is more likely that Buddhists carved and venerated nonfigurative signs of the Buddha because they (following Vedic precedent) believed that such signs best evoked the bodily and immaterial aspects of the Great Being in his final birth.

Being artistic creations, these lithic signs are not, like the Buddha's body and relics themselves, indices of his bodhisattva vow and karma (rather, they index the karma of the donors); however, by evoking the body that came into being with his conception and birth, they function as icons of the Buddha's body and, thereby, of his transcendent nature. Because these nonfigurative icons represent the body of the Great Being from the time of his conception and birth, they cannot refer only to the perfections attained at the moment of awakening; rather, they reveal the body of the Great Being which throughout his life conformed to and revealed the dharma.[50] Like the glorious bodies (and physical characteristics) of the buddhas described in the *Apadāna,* these images make possible an intuitive perception of nirvana and the dharma. These images thus function as icons of buddhahood, and not, like the signs of *stūpa* no. 2 (and of text set 2) as auspicious symbols. In addition, while the auspicious symbols of *stūpa* no. 2 point to a larger symbolic body of the Buddha (the *stūpa*), the icons of the later reliefs by themselves evoke the Buddha's body in its totality. In so doing, they partly shift the devotee's attention from the *stūpa* as a whole to the individual icon, creating a tension between icon and relic. This tension perhaps stimulated the creation of freestanding images of the Buddha, which mediate this opposition by serving as both reliquary and icon.

STRATEGIES AND COMMUNITIES

If the interpretations proposed above are correct, then we see a parallel development in verbal and visual strategies, from symbols pointing ambiguously to the buddhas' this-worldly or otherworldly auspiciousness in text set 2 and Sāñcī *stūpa* no. 2, to icons manifesting the buddhas' physical bodies and transcendent nature in text set 3 and the later reliefs. We can hypothesize that this development reflects a shift in how some Buddhists viewed the body of the Buddha, and we can date this shift to the last centuries B.C.E. Huntington dates the railing of Sāñcī *stūpa* no. 2 to about 100 B.C.E., and the railing and gates of the Bhārhut *stūpa* to about 100 to 80 B.C.E., suggesting that the shift in artistic strategies took place around the beginning of the first century B.C.E.[51] Although dating the canonical texts is notoriously problematic, the *Apadāna* was probably taking shape at this same time. K. R. Norman writes that stories perhaps continued to be added to the *Apadāna* collection until the time of the text's redaction in the last quarter of the first century B.C.E., and Heinz Bechert argues that at least one section of the text probably dates from the first or second century C.E.[52]

A common origin for the *Apadāna* and the reliefs of Sāñcī, Bhārhut, and Amarāvatī has previously been proposed by Jonathan Walters, who holds that the same karmic soteriology informs both the *Apadāna* and the *stūpa*s' donative inscriptions.[53] Without rehearsing his larger argument, I will cite a few of his specific claims that support my thesis. Walters shows that donations of architectural elements to *stūpa*s figure prominently in many *Apadāna* stories, and that these stories describe these elements with terms that we otherwise know only from the epigraphs found at these *stūpa*s (171–72); these similarities indicate a specific historical connection between these texts. Walters also cites several *Apadāna* verses in which persons worship *bodhi* trees or *stūpa*s "as though face to face" *(sammukhā viya)* with the Buddha (190 n. 62). This expression indicates that the authors of the *Apadāna* regard seeing and worshiping the relics as tantamount to seeing and worshiping the living Buddha, and it conversely suggests that the *Apadāna*'s stories about seeing the Buddha are simultaneously about seeing his *stūpas*.

These texts therefore allow us to locate historically a widespread Buddhist interpretive community that produced both the *Apadāna* and the first great flowering of Buddhist art. This community participated in what David McMahan has characterized as "a wave of visionary literature and practice" that swept South Asia in the second and first centuries B.C.E.[54] McMahan argues persuasively that the development of writing played a crucial role in the development of this visual culture; I hope that this essay has identified the *stūpa* cult as another locus in which these developments occurred. Practices of seeing and worshiping the transcendent Buddha in his physical body began not necessarily with the production of figurative Buddha images, but with the emergence of interpretive strategies for viewing the Buddha's body in a new way.

NOTES

1. Gregory Schopen provides inscriptional and textual evidence to support this claim, and shows that from the second century B.C.E. on, inscriptions and texts frequently state that the Buddha's relics are infused with the virtues he gained through becoming awakened. "Burial *'Ad Sanctos'* and the Physical Presence of the Buddha in Early Indian Buddhism: A Study in the Archaeology of Religions," in *Bones, Stones, and Buddhist Monks: Collected Papers on the Archaeology, Epigraphy, and Texts of Monastic Buddhism in India* (Honolulu: University of Hawai'i Press, 1997), 126–28; idem, "On the Buddha and His Bones," in *Bones, Stones, and Buddhist Monks,* 154–57; idem, "Ritual Rights and Bones of Contention: More on Monastic Funerals and Relics in the *Mūlasarvāstivāda-vinaya,*" *Journal of Indian Philosophy* 22 (1994): 47–48.

2. *dhātūsu diṭṭhesu, diṭṭho hoti jino* Mhv 17.3.

3. The contrast between the Buddha's physical body and his transcendent "Dharma body" (Pāli *dhammakāya*) is a fundamental opposition in Buddhist thought. For a good overview of how the Theravādin tradition has treated this opposition, see Frank Reynolds, "The Several Bodies of Buddha: Reflections on a Neglected Aspect of Theravada Tradition," *History of Religions* 16 (1977): 374–89.

4. Stanley Fish, *Is There a Text in This Class? The Authority of Interpretive Communities* (Cambridge: Harvard University Press, 1980). In applying these categories to South Asian religious art, I follow the precedent of Richard H. Davis in his *Lives of Indian Images* (Princeton: Princeton University Press, 1999).

5. *Collected Papers of Charles Sanders Peirce,* ed. Charles Hartshorne and Paul Weiss (Cambridge: Belknap Press, 1960), vol. 2:247–49, cf. pp. 274–308.

6. In *Religious Giving and the Invention of Karma in Theravāda Buddhism* (Surrey: Curzon, 2002), I argue that in the mixed verse and prose compositions of the Pāli canon,

the verses often predate the prose in their present form. It may also be that the Sela story as found in M and Sn represents a combination of the verse tradition I discuss here with an independent prose tradition represented by *Ambaṭṭha Sutta* (D I 88–110) and *Brāhmayu Sutta* (M II 133–146), discussed below.

7. K. R. Norman argues that the term *cakkavattin/cakravartin* originally denoted the "possessor of a *cakra-vā ṭā*, i.e., the enclosure of the earth-circle." *The Elders' Verses I* (London: Pali Text Society, 1969), 241–42. The meaning of "wheel-turner" would therefore represent a reinterpretation of this term and not a scientific etymology. In Dhp 352, A II 35, and S V 158, a *mahāpurisa* is said to be a buddha, and *cakkavattins* are not classed as *mahāpurisas*.

8. *Paripuṇṇakāyo suruci sujāto cārudassano suvaṇṇavaṇṇo . . . susukkadṭho . . . viriyavā* Sn 548 (all references will be to Sn verse numbers in the PTS edition); *Pasannanetto sumukho brahā uju patāpavā* 549; *kalyāṇadassano . . . kañtanasannibhattaco . . . uttamavaṇṇino* 551.

9. For a discussion of the relationship between the mundane/royal and transcendent/ascetic orders in Theravāda, see "The Two Wheels of Dhamma: A Study of Early Buddhism," in *The Two Wheels of Dhamma: Essays on the Theravada Tradition in India and Ceylon*, ed. Gananath Obeyesekere, Frank Reynolds, and Bardwell L. Smith (Chambersburg, PA: American Academy of Religion, 1972), 6–30.

10. *ko disvā na-ppasīdeyya;* Sn 563, translated by K. R. Norman. In Sn 559 the Buddha states that it is difficult to obtain repeatedly a sight *(dassanaṃ)* of the buddhas. In Sn 561 and 563, the Buddha calls himself *brahmabhūto,* which could be translated as "having the nature of (a) Brahmā." The Buddha's use of this phrase could be understood as a claim to great temporal status and a confirmation of Sela's allegation that the Buddha is a *mahāpurisa*. However, other passages indicate that this phrase should be understood as a referring to the Buddha's attainment of awakening, and translated along the lines of "become *brahman*." In M I 111 = III 195 = III 224, the phrase *dhammabhūto brahmabhūto* is applied to the Buddha in connection with a discussion of the Buddha's vision and knowledge of the Dharma. In D III 84, the Buddha claims the titles *dhammakāyo, brahmakāyo, dhammabhūto,* and *brahmabhūto*. In the only use of the term *brahmabhūto* that I have been able to find in Brahmanical literature, *Baudhāyana Dharmasūtra* 2.7.22, *brahmabhūto* refers to a person who has attained the highest soteriological goal.

11. E.g., *sujāto, sujātassa* Sn 548, 549; *uttamava ino,* 551 may refer to the Buddha's social class or to his complexion.

12. Another passage that leaves indeterminate the significance of the Buddha's physical attributes is A II 35–37, in which a Brāhmaṇ sees the wheels on the Buddha's footprints. Thinking that these prints must have been made by a superhuman being, the Brāhmaṇ follows them to the Buddha. The Brāhmaṇ asks what sort of being the Buddha will be (is), and the Buddha replies that he will not be (is not) anything, because he is a buddha. The meaning of this exchange turns on the interpretation of the verbs, which are future in form. (See F. L. Woodward and E. M. Hare, *Gradual Sayings* (London: Pali Text Society: 1932–1936; reprint, Oxford: Pali Text Society, 1995–1996) vol. 2, 44,

n. 1.) I suggest that the best reading of this text takes the Brāhmaṇ's questions as present in meaning but with the connotation of "perplexity, surprise, and wonder" (A. K. Warder, *Introduction to Pali,* 3d ed. [Oxford: Pali Text Society, 1991], 55), and takes the Buddha's replies as future in meaning. The Buddha thus plays on the meanings of the future form to shift the Brāhmaṇ's attention from the Buddha's physical and mundane attributes to his transcendent attainments.

13. The career of a *cakkavattin* and the seven treasures are described briefly in these passages, and more fully in D 17 and 25. Verses expressing similar ideas appear in Sn 976–1031, which appears to have been added to Sn to provide a narrative frame for *Pārāyanavagga.* ("Pj II 575,2 calls these verses *vatthugāthā,* and says they were uttered by Ānanda *saṅgītikāle* (580, 29)¼. They are not commented upon in Nidd II, which possibly means that they did not exist at the time of the compilation of Nidd II, or were perhaps not regarded as being an authentic part of the text at that time." K. R. Norman, *The Group of Discourses, Volume II* [Oxford: Pali Text Society, 1995], 359). Sn 976–1031 resembles the prose stories of Sela, Ambaṭṭha, and Brahmāyu, in that in these verses Brāhmaṇs set out to see whether the Buddha possesses the thirty-two marks. However, in this version the Buddha does not reveal his hidden marks, but instead names the three marks possessed by the Brāhmaṇs' teacher. The Buddha therefore establishes his identity not by a display of the marks but by a show of omniscience. The Brāhmaṇs never investigate what they set out to find, and the Buddha does not endorse any beliefs concerning the thirty-two marks. In Sn 679–698 (which are also said to be *vatthugāthā* added by Ānanda at the First Council; Norman, *Group of Discourses,* 275), a Brāhmaṇ who has mastered "the marks and the mantras" predicts that the infant Gotama will become a buddha. The Brāhmaṇ had been told by deities that the prince was a bodhisattva, and the text does not say that the Brāhmaṇ identifies the boy by his marks. This passage also makes no mention of the tradition of the alternative destinies.

14. Brahmanical texts attest to belief in auspicious physical marks, but not (to my knowledge) to the tradition of the thirty-two marks presented in the Buddhist texts. For example, *Mahābhārata* 1 (7) 67:25–68:20 names a number of distinctive marks of a boy destined to become a *cakravartin,* including sharp, bright teeth and a large head. Of course, this passage may reflect the influence of the Buddhist tradition.

15. This list largely follows Walshe's translation of D II 17–19. Lamotte discusses differing interpretations of some of the marks and provides a bibliography in *Le Traité de la Grande Vertu de Sagesse* [Translation of *Mahāprajñāpāramitā śā stra* by Nāgārjuna] (Louvain-la-Neuve: Institut Orientaliste, 1981), 271–81. Three of the less remarkable of these marks—golden skin, erect posture, and very white teeth—are also named in the verse version of the Sela story. The Sela frame story and *Ambaṭṭha Sutta* name only the two marks that are not normally visible: the Buddha's enormous tongue and hidden genitals. Sn 976–1031 names the long tongue and hidden genitals, as well as the tuft of hair between the eyebrows. It may be that these three passages assume knowledge of the entire list of thirty-two; however, one reason for thinking that this might not be the case is that, as Walshe points out, it is difficult to imagine how the Brāhmaṇs could see that the Buddha has a perfect sense of taste (or, for that matter, a Brahmā-like voice). In *Brahmāyu Sutta,* however,

the Brāhmaṇs can without aid see all thirty-two marks except for the tongue and genitals. Ven. Bodhi addresses this problem by translating *passati kho* as "sees, more or less."

16. Alfred Foucher, *L'Art Gréco-Bouddhique du Gandhâra* (Paris: Éditions Ernest Leroux, 1918), 285–86. Rupert Gethin states that the thirty-two marks are "obviously not marks of the Buddha's ordinary body that we normally see;" however, the canonical Pāli texts give no indication that the marks are not features of the Buddha's physical body. Gethin, *The Foundations of Buddhism* (Oxford: Oxford University Press, 1998), 232, cf. 31.

17. The Buddha's failure to sanction this tradition is consistent with numerous passages in the canonical verses and prose that include the interpretation of marks (*lakkhaṇas*) in lists of Brahmanical practices to be rejected; e.g., Sn 360, 927, D I 9. This prohibition makes more remarkable the Buddha's apparent endorsement of this tradition in *Lakkhaṇa Sutta* and *Mahāpadāna Sutta.*

18. The phrase *kosohitaṃvatthaguyhaṃ* is usually rendered as "the genitals (lit. 'that which is to be hidden by a cloth') are enclosed in a sheath." However, because *kosa* can mean foreskin, this mark thus understood is hardly distinctive; in addition, this euphemistic interpretation of *vatthaguyha* is very strained. A more plausible interpretation is suggested by the reading *kośagatavastiguhyaṃ* in *Mahāprajñāpāramitāśāstra* 4.90, which could be rendered as "the genitals (lit., 'what is contained in the foreskin [or the scrotum]') are hidden in the abdomen." This text explains that the Buddha's genitals are like those of an elephant; see Lamotte, *Traité,* 274–75.

19. *Nārīsaha nāma savhayā? Kacci jivhā narassikā?* M II 143, translation by Bodhi.

20. Some manuscripts of Ap's retelling of the Sela story give further evidence that the Buddha's genitals have been viewed as being in some sense feminine. While the Burmese Chaṭṭha Saṇgāyana text says that the Buddha reveals his hidden genitals *'Iddhiyā,"* "by supernormal power," the manuscripts cited in the PTS text read *'Itthiy ā"* and *'Itthissa,"* "of a woman" (Ap I 321). For another interpretation of this strange mark, see Nancy Schuster Barnes, "Buddhism," in *Women in World Religions,* ed. Arvind Sharma (Albany: State University of New York Press, 1987), 259, n. 11.

21. This second tradition also appears in *Acchariya-abbhūta Sutta* (M III 118–124).

22. They are only mentioned in Ap's retelling of the Sela story, discussed below.

23. Ap I 277, 291, II 385–387, 508–510, 569–572. Also in this category would be Ap II 584, which refers to a buddha's feet as bearing wheels *(cakkalakkhaṇe).*

24. Ap I 277 and 291. Although the literal meaning of *virāja* makes most sense in this context, the figurative meaning of "free from passion" is suggested.

25. The earliest Pāli reference that I have been able to find to the *anuvyañjana* s forming a definite group of eighty marks is Mil 75, and the oldest Pāli enumerations of these eighty are from the Ṭīka literature; e.g., Mil-ṭ 17. Lists of the eighty marks appear much earlier in Sanskrit texts; see Edgerton, *Buddhist Hybrid Sanskrit Grammar and Dictionary,* s.v. *anuvyañjana* .

26. For some suggestive discussions of darśana in Buddhism, see Gregory Schopen, "Burial *'Ad Sanctos',*" 137–38, n. 9, and Paul Harrison, "Commemoration and Identification in the *Buddhānusmṛti,*" in *In the Mirror of Memory: Reflections on Mindfulness and Remembrance in Indian and Tibetan Buddhism,* ed. Janet Gyatso (Albany: State University of New York Press, 1992), 215–38.

27. Ap I 15–31, 316–322, 335–338, II 367–370, 398.

28. I 321. Ap thus completely omits the events included in the verses.

29. Worshiping feet: vv. 39, 42, 49, 52, 54, 91, 135, 137, 141; gazing at body or face: vv. 40, 49, 51, 136. The nuns worship Gotamī's feet in v. 7, and Ānanda is told to look at Gotamī in v. 67.

30. On a *cakkavattin* the same marks would suggest corresponding mundane functions. This is the only appearance of the expression *ādiccakula,* solar clan, in the canon; however, the Buddha is commonly called *ādiccabandhu,* kinsman of the sun.

31. Vv. 136–138, following Walters's translation with some alternative meanings. Jonathan S. Walters, "Gotamī's Story," in *Buddhism in Practice,* ed. Donald S. Lopez Jr. (Princeton: Princeton University Press, 1995), 132.

32. Susan Huntington dates the railing of Sāñcī *stūpa* no. 2 to about 100 B.C.E., while Mireille Bénisti places it in the first half of the second century B.C.E. Huntington, *The Art of Ancient India* (New York: Weatherhill, 1985), 62; Bénisti, "Observations concernant le stūpa no. 2 de Sāñcī," *Bulletin d'Études indiennes* 4 (1986): 165. This *stūpa* did not contain relics of the Buddha, but of ten *arhats* of the Mauryan period (*Art of Ancient India,* 62; Maurizio Taddei, "The First Beginnings: Sculptures on Stupa 2," in *Unseen Presence: The Buddha and Sanchi,* ed. Vidya Dehejia (Mumbai: Marg Publications, 1996), 77.

33. Many of the signs I discuss in the following paragraph are arguably icons rather than symbols; for example, the female form of Gajalakṣmī visibly represents the qualities of beauty and fertility. However, these signs do not visibly represent the auspiciousness of the *arhats* interred in the *stūpa,* and therefore, insofar as these signs refer to these *arhats,* these signs function as symbols, i.e., as conventional markers.

34. Bénisti, "Observations concernant le stūpa no. 2 de Sāñcī," 165–66.

35. Sir John Marshall and Alfred Foucher, *The Monuments of Sāñchī* (London: Probsthain, 1940; reprint, Delhi: Swati Publications, 1982), 96.

36. Ananda K. Coomaraswamy, "Early Indian Iconography [II. Śrī-Lakṣmī]," *Eastern Art* 1 (1929): 175–89.

37. Bénisti, "Observations concernant le stūpa no. 2 de Sāñcī," 167; Snellgrove similarly points out that trees were in India ancient signs of fertility and the *axis mundi.* Two scenes on the railing depict an *aśvattha,* the tree under which Gotama is believed to have attained awakening, surrounded by a railing. However, worship of the *aśvattha* is not distinctively Buddhist, and is attested even in two seals from Mohenjo Daro. In *Ka ha Upani*

ad 6.1 the *aśvattha* is identified as the sacred world tree. David L. Snellgrove, ed., *The Image of the Buddha* (Tokyo: Kodansha International / UNESCO, 1978), 40. Marshall and Foucher, vol. 3, plates 75 and 86. Ernest John Henry Mackay, *Further Excavations at Mohenjo-Daro* (Delhi: Government of India Press, 1938), vol. 1, 337–38, 351, vol. 2, plates XCIX, 686a and LXXXII, 1 and 2.

38. Marshall and Foucher, vol. 3, plates 74 and 82; Snellgrove, *The Image of the Buddha,* 24, 40.

39. K. R. Norman, *The Elders' Verses I* (London: Pali Text Society, 1969), 241–42.

40. Mireille Bénisti, "À propos du *Triratna,*" *Bulletin de l'École Française d'Extrême-Orient* 44 (1977): 43–81.

41. On the other hand, thrones and *cakramas* could be understood as representing sitting and walking meditation, and therefore otherworldly values.

42. Snellgrove, *The Image of the Buddha,* 40. For examples, see James Fergusson, *Tree and Serpent Worship: or, Illustrations of Mythology and Art in India in the First and Fourth Centuries after Christ* (2d ed. London: W.H. Allen and Co., 1873), plates LXVII, LXVIII, LXX, LXXI, LXXII, XCVIII.

43. Huntington, "Early Buddhist Art," 403. *Bodhi* trees are considered *pāribhogika* relics, or relics of use. This classification indicates that these trees derive their sanctity from their physical connection with a buddha. Another comparison of buddhas' bodies to trees is provided by one of the thirty-two marks, which specifies that he is proportioned like a banyan tree.

44. The elaboration of *stūpas* as cosmograms, which is evident as early as Sāñcī *stūpa* no. 1, also testifies to *stūpas'* this-worldly import. Huntington, *Art of Ancient India,* 92.

45. Alfred Foucher, "The Beginnings of Buddhist Art," in A. Foucher, *The Beginnings of Buddhist Art and Other Essays in Indian and Central-Asian Archaeology* (Paris: Paul Geuthner, 1917), 1–27. Foucher's hypothesis is generally referred to as aniconism.

46. Susan L. Huntington, "Early Buddhist Art and the Theory of Aniconism," *Art Journal* 49 (1990): 401–408; idem, "Aniconism and the Multivalence of Emblems: Another Look," *Ars Orientalis* 22 (1992): 111–56.

47. Paul Mus, *Barabuur: Esquisse d'une histoire du bouddhisme fondée sur la critique archéologique des textes* (Hanoi: Imprimerie d'Extrême-Orient, 1935), 1:62–63, 66.

48. Huntington ("Aniconism," 121) argues that because Buddhism was a non-Vedic or even anti-Vedic religious movement, Vedic practices are of little relevance for the interpretation of early Buddhist art. However, I demonstrate in the first chapter of *Religious Giving and the Invention of Karma in Theravāda Buddhism* that there were significant continuities between Vedic and Buddhist cultic practices.

49. Snellgrove, 23–24; Huntington argues against Snellgrove's interpretation in "Early Buddhist Art," 401. On the still-debated question of whether or to what extent

artists avoided making figurative representations of the Buddha, see among others, Huntington, "Early Buddhist Art," 401–402 and Ju-Hyung Rhi, "From Bodhisattva to Buddha: The Beginning of Iconic Representation in Buddhist Art," *Artibus Asiae* 54 (1994): 207–25.

50. This iconic semiotic even more clearly informs the production and use of Buddha images. One of the most popular ways of representing the Great Being shows him before the moment of awakening as he calls the Earth to witness to his karmic past. This image is an appropriate object for Buddhist devotion because even before his awakening the Bodhisattva embodies the Dharma.

51. Huntington, *The Art of Ancient India,* 62, 65. As noted above, Bénisti dates *stūpa* no. 2's railing to the first half of the second century B.C.E.

52. K. R. Norman, *Pāli Literature,* Vol. VII, fasc. 2 of *A History of Indian Literature,* ed. Jan Gonda (Wiesbaden: Otto Harrassowitz, 1983), 10–11, 90; Heinz Bechert, "Buddha-field and Transfer of Merit in a Theravāda Source," *Indo-Iranian Journal* 35 (1992): 102, 104.

53. Jonathan S. Walters, "Stūpa, Story and Empire: Constructions of the Buddha Biography in Early Post-Aśokan India," in *Sacred Biography in the Buddhist Traditions of South and Southeast Asia,* ed. Juliane Schober (Honolulu: University of Hawai'i Press, 1997), 160–92.

54. David McMahan, "Orality, Writing, and Authority in South Asian Buddhism: Visionary Literature and the Struggle for Legitimacy in the Mahāyāna," *History of Religions* 37 (1998): 264.

List of Contributors

Carol S. Anderson is Associate Professor of Religion at Kalamazoo College.

Anne M. Blackburn is Assistant Professor of Religion at Cornel University.

Mahinda Deegalle is Lecturer in the Study of Religions at Bath University College (UK).

James R. Egge is Assistant Professor of Religion at Eastern Michigan University.

Julie Gifford is a graduate student in the history of religions at the University of Chicago.

John Clifford Holt is Professor of Religion at Bowdoin College.

Jacob N. Kinnard is Assistant Professor of Religion at the College of William and Mary.

John S. Strong is Professor of Religion at Bates College.

Jonathan S. Walters is Associate Professor of Religion at Whitman College.

Liz Wilson is Associate Professor of Religion at Miami University (OH).

Index

Abeyanayake, Rajpal, 115, 119, 121, 122
Abhayasundara, Vimal, 177, 178
amulets. *See* practices, Theravāda Buddhist: protective
Anderson, Benedict, 2
Arnold, Sir Edwin, 86, 88, 91
art, Theravāda Buddhist
  and charismatic power of saints, 78–79
  as *dassana (darśana)*, 194–195, 202
  early Buddhist stūpa reliefs, 189, 197–201
  figurative elements in, 197–201
  icon, index and symbol in, 190
  purpose of, 189
  relationship to texts, 76–77, 189–202. *See also* texts, Theravāda Buddhist
  temple decoration, 27–28, 77, 78–79, 136, 189
  See also monasteries, temples and pilgrimage sites, Buddhist
Asaṃdhimittā. *See under* queens, Buddhist
asceticism. *See* practices, Theravāda Buddhist: ascetic
Aśoka Maurya. *See under* kings, Buddhist
astrology. *See under* practices, Theravāda Buddhist
Aung-thwin, Michael, 140
Ayutthaya. *See under* kingdoms and royal capitals, Buddhist
baṇa. *See* practices, Theravāda Buddhist: preaching
Banda, Gangalagoda, 109
Banerjee, Goroo Das, 95
Baptist, Egerton C., 12, 28, 30n.12
Bartholomeusz, Tessa, 172
Barua, B. M., 43
Bastin, Rohin, 183
Bechert, Heinz, 201
Beglar, J. D., 92
Behari, Bepin, 92, 93
Bellah, Robert, 183
Bénisti, Mireille, 197–198
bhavanā. *See* practices, Theravāda Buddhist: meditation
Bible, 181
Bihar, 87
Blackburn, Anne M., 184
Blavatsky, Helena, 178
Bodhgayā. *See under* monasteries, temples and pilgrimage sites, Buddhist
Bond, George, 172
Bongard-Levin, G. M., 42
Brahmāyu, 192
British Broadcasting Corporation (B.B.C.), 120
Buchanan, Francis, 87
Buddhaghosa. *See under* monks, Buddhist
Buddha Jayanti, 153, 156
Buddha, the. *See* buddhas: Gotama
buddhas
  Amitābha, 91, 94–96, 103n. 38
  Anomadassī, 194–95

buddhas (*cont.*)
bodhisattva destiny of, 193
Bodhi trees of, 199, 206–7nn. 37, 43. *See also* practices, Theravāda Buddhist: worship: of Bodhi trees
buddhahood as karmic institution, 25
Gotama
and *cakkavatti* kingship, 176, 190, 193, 195, 198
enlightenment of, 71, 85, 197
as focus of devotion, 175–76. *See also* practices, Theravāda Buddhist: worship: of the Buddha (*buddhapūjā*)
intimate community of, 14–15, 16, 18, 19, 21–22, 23. *See also* queens, Buddhist: Mahāmāyā; saints, Buddhist: famous *arahants*; sinners, famous: Devadatta; Śākyans
nonfigurative signs of, 197–200
orientalist conception of, 90, 175, 181–182
overflow karma of, 11, 19
parinirvāṇa and funeral of, 34n. 39, 108–109, 157, 189, 197, 198, 199. *See also* texts, Buddhist: in Pāli: *Mahāparinibbānasutta*
physical body (*rūpakāya*) of, 189–202
preaching of, 75, 81
relics of, 41, 77, 189, 202n. 1
as subject of Buddhist poetry, 153–155, 159
transcendent body (*dharmakāya*) of, 189–202, 202n. 3
as Viṣṇu avatar, 91–94, 95, 111, 119, 128n. 17
voice of. *See karavikā* bird
Kakusandha, 38n. 61
Kassapa, 35n. 49, 38n. 61
Konāgamana, 38n. 61
Metteyya (Maitreya), 10, 18, 19, 23, 35n. 43
numbers of, 26–27
omniscience of, 199
paccekabuddhas, 35n. 49, 37n. 57, 44, 45, 49, 51, 76
thirty-two marks of, 50, 191–202, 204–205nn. 13–18, 20, 25
karmic causes of, 193, 196
Vipassī, 193
Burma. *See* communities, Theravāda Buddhist; kingdoms and royal capitals, Buddhist; monasteries, temples and pilgrimage sites, Buddhist; monasticism, Theravāda Buddhist
Buultjens, Ralph, 114

Ceylon Observer (Colombo), 177
cakkavatti (*cakravartin*). *See* kings, Buddhist: *cakkavatti*
Chakravarti, Uma, 16
chants and chanting. *See under* practices, Theravāda Buddhist
chess, 41–42
Chiang Tung, 142–143
Christianity. *See* communities, Christian
cloth. *See under* practices, Theravāda Buddhist: giving
Colombo, 114, 115, 117, 119, 121, 126, 180, 184. *See also* communities, Theravāda Buddhist: urban vs. rural: in Sri Lanka
communities, Christian
missionaries and missionary schools, 123, 124, 138, 177, 182, 183, 184
Wesley College (Colombo), 177
Wesley Mission School (Jaffna), 182
in Sri Lanka, 117–19, 182–83
communities, Dalit Buddhist, 100
communities, Hindu
as constituted in relationship to religious others, 87, 99, 104n. 46
Brāhmaṇs 61, 86, 89, 93, 190–195, 197, 198
Giri lineage of Bodhgayā *mahants*, 85, 88–89, 91–96, 101–102n. 16, 106nn. 68, 71

Neo-vedantic, 97
reform movements in, 182–183
Śaiva
at Bodhgayā, 85, 87, 89, 90, 91–96. *See also* communities, Hindu: Giri lineage
in Sri Lanka, 182–183
in Sri Lanka conflict, 119–123. *See also* Sri Lanka: civil war in
Vaiṣṇava
at Bodhgayā, 85, 89, 90, 91–96, 102n. 31
in Sri Lanka, 113
See also deities; texts, Hindu; Vedic sacrifices
communities, Muslim, 111, 114, 118
reform movements in, 183–184
communities, Sarvāstivāda Buddhist, 64
communities, Theravāda Buddhist
assimilation of Vedic and Hindu patterns in, 63, 64–65, 108–126, 207n. 48
and caste, 113, 160
and class, 111, 123–126, 181, 184
and *communitas*, 86–87, 98–99
as constituted by karma, 9–39, 77
as constituted in relationship to religious others, 86–87, 89, 90, 96–97, 111, 117–123, 182
defining, 1–2
and deity worship, 111–113, 117–126. *See also* deities
and individual religious experience, 1
innovation in, 131–143, 151–167
as interpretive communities, 189–190, 201–202
local histories and, 107–108, 109, 134, 139–143
localization of, 131–143
multireligious conflict and
at Bodhgayā, 85–100
in Sri Lanka, 111–113, 117–123. *See also* Sri Lanka: civil war in
politics of. *See* karma: political; kings, Buddhist; kingship, Buddhist; political leaders and parties; queens, Buddhist; queenship, Buddhist
"Protestant Buddhist"
definition of, 163–164, 172–173
weakness of conceptual category, 182–186
reform movements in, 111–112, 136, 153, 158–162, 172, 177–179, 182–186
saints' impact upon, 80–82. *See also* saints, Buddhist
saṃgha. *See* monks, Buddhist; monasticism, Theravāda Buddhist; saints, Buddhist
as *sāsana*, 109, 121, 133, 134, 138, 139
Sri Lankan
origin myth of, 108–109
urban vs. rural
in Sri Lanka, 119, 156, 157
in Thailand, 163–164
See also Colombo; communities, Theravāda Buddhist: and caste; communities, Theravāda Buddhist: and class
See also practices, Theravāda Buddhist
Coomaraswamy, Ananda K., 197
Copleston, Reginald, 180
cosmology, Theravāda Buddhist
heavens in, 61, 62, 74–75, 79, 161
hells in, 22, 24, 45, 62, 76, 79
history of, 71, 79
and institutional routinization of saintly charisma, 79–80
"maps" of, 15, 72–77, 79–80
meditative insight and, 71, 72–77
Mount Meru in, 73
saṃsāra, 35n. 43, 71, 72
Uttarukuru continent in, 19
See also buddhas; deities; karma
Cunningham, Alexander, 89, 92

Daily Telegraph (London), 88, 89
Dalmia, Vasudha, 87, 99

dāna. See practices, Theravāda Buddhist: giving
Danell, William, 90
Daniel, Val, 16
deities
  Agni, 60
  Aluthnuwara, 110
  apsarās, 60–61
  in Buddhist thought, 112–113, 117–120, 123–126, 128nn. 17–22
  Brahmā, 119
  as constituted by karma, 118
  "deity-bashing," 61–63, 112–114, 123, 128nn. 21–22
  Dhataraṭṭha, 45
  Gangodawila Soma as, 115
  God, 25, 33–34n. 31, 117
  and justice, 125
  Kataragama *deviyo* (Skanda, Murugan) 110, 120–121
  Kuvera, 45–46
  Lakṣmī, 197
  nāgas, 73
  Sakka (Śakra, Indra), 57–58, 59, 62–65, 108–109
  Upulvan (Uppalavaṇṇa), 108–109, 110–111, 127n. 12
  Virūhaka, 45
  Virūpakkha, 45
  Viṣṇu
    at Bodhgayā, 86, 91–95, 102n. 31
    bodhisattva destiny of, 110, 125
    as "Minister of Defense" in Sri Lanka, 109–110
    images of, 92–94, 109, 121–123
    shrines of, 109, 110, 121–125, 127n. 13
    worship of, 98, 107–126
See also communities, Hindu; cosmology, Theravāda Buddhist: heavens in; practices, Theravāda Buddhist: deity cults
Dharmapāla, Anagārika. *See under* monks, Buddhist
dhūtaṅga. See practices, Theravāda Buddhist: ascetic
Dixit, Maduri, 115
Doctrines, Theravāda Buddhist
  co-dependent origination, 159
  Four Noble Truths, 175
  impermanence, 196
  karma. *See separate entry*
nibbāna (*nirvāṇa*). *See separate entry*
  Noble Eightfold Path, 174
  no-self, 175
  saṃsāra. See under cosmology, Theravāda Buddhist
  seven noble riches, 174
  ten meritorious acts, 174
D'Oyly, Charles, 90

education, Theravāda Buddhist. *See* monasticism, Theravāda Buddhist: educational practices and institutions of
Eelam, 116
Evans-Wentz, W. Y., 30n. 12

Fish, Stanley, 189
food purity, 57, 58, 62
Foucher, Alfred, 192, 197, 200
Freedberg, David, 78–79
Full Moon Day observances. *See under* practices, Theravāda Buddhist

Gayā, 89, 91
Geiger, Wilhelm, 107–108, 109, 113, 126nn. 1, 3
Giri lineage. *See under* communities, Hindu
giving. *See under* practices, Theravāda Buddhist
Godage Publishers, 180, 181
Gombrich, Richard, 16, 110, 172, 181–182
Gunaratana, Siyambalangamuvē. *See under* monks, Buddhist
Gunasena Publishing Company, 179–180, 181

Hallisey, Charles S., 175, 176, 182
heavens. *See under* cosmology, Theravāda Buddhist
Heesterman, J. C., 58, 65, 66, 70n. 23
hells. *See under* cosmology, Theravāda Buddhist
Hinduism. *See* communities, Hindu; deities; texts, Hindu; Vedic sacrifices
Holmwood, Herbert, 95
Holt, John C., 26, 27
Horner, I. B., 20
Hudson, Dennis, 182
Huntington, Susan, 199, 200, 201

Islām. *See* communities, Muslim

Jackson, Michael, 115
Jaffna, 115, 120, 182
Jayakodi, Edward, 152
Jesus, 111
Jones, John Garrett, 16

Käläṇi River, 157
Kandy. *See under* kingdoms and royal capitals, Buddhist
Kanthaka, 20
karavikā bird, 50, 55n. 50
karma
  agricultural metaphor for, 18, 57–58, 61, 62, 65
  and aspirations (*prārthanāva*), 9–10, 23–24
  bad
    bad results of, 10–11, 12, 13, 15, 19, 20, 22–23, 24, 76. *See also* cosmology, Theravāda Buddhist: hells in; sinners, famous
    vanquished by giving, 57–68
  as basis for deity states, 118
  and bio-moral status, 58, 62–63, 67–68
  and buddha-bodies, 193, 196
  as Buddhist presupposition, 10
  as field of merit. *See* karma: agricultural metaphor for
  good results of good, 10–11, 15, 18–19, 20–22, 23, 45, 74–75, 173–174, 200. *See also* cosmology, Theravāda Buddhist: heavens in; saints, Buddhist
  and kingship, 11–14, 19
  overflow, 11–12, 19–20
  political, 11, 12, 13–14, 15, 24–25, 30n. 12
  and queenship, 44–49
  "rebirth precursors," 9, 16
  of religions, 30n. 12
  seeds of. *See* karma: agricultural metaphor for
  social dimensions of, 9–39, 62, 77, 176
  sociokarma
    definition of, 11
    types of 11–12, 17–26
  transference of demerit, 12, 64–68
  transference of merit, 10, 12, 19–20, 158
Keyes, Charles, 16
King, Winston, 14
kingdoms and royal capitals, Buddhist
  Anurādhapura, 25, 38 n. 61, 183
  Arakan, 131, 133, 144n. 3
  Ayutthaya, 131, 133, 136, 143–44n. 2
  Chiang Mai, 142
  Daṁbadeṇiya, 134, 135
  Gampola, 113
  Kandy, 27, 109, 110, 113–114, 132, 136, 139, 157
  Lān Nā, 140, 141–143
  Pagan, 140, 147–148n. 44
  Pegu, 140
  Rangoon, 78
  Sukhothai, 141–142
kings, Buddhist
  Ajātaśatru, 41
  Aśoka Maurya, 25, 41, 42–49, 197
    children of. *See* Kuṇāla; saints, Theravāda Buddhist: famous *arahants*: Mahinda; saints, Theravāda Buddhist: famous *arahants*: Sanghamittā

kings, Buddhist (*cont.*)
Aśoka Maurya (*cont,*)
past lives of, 35n. 49, 37n. 57, 44
queens of. *See* queens, Buddhist: Kāluvāki; queens, Buddhist: Tiṣyarakṣitā; queens, Buddhist: Vedīsa-devī
as *bodhisattas*, 27
cakkavatti, 19, 27, 41, 190, 197, 203n. 7, 204nn. 13, 14
fourfold army of, 41
seven gems of, 42, 191
Devānampiyatissa, 35n. 49, 37n. 57, 38n. 61
Dhammazedi, 140
Duṭṭhagāmaṇi, 36n. 49
Ikṣvāku, 23
Kiki, 15
Kīrti Śrī Rājasiṃha, 27–28, 111, 114, 132–133, 145n. 8, 179
Kuenā, 141
Milinda, 22, 23, 24, 27, 35n. 49
Narapatisithu, 140, 148n. 44
Narēndrasiṃha, 111
Nayakkar dynasty of, 111, 113–114
Parākramabāhu I, 135
Parākramabāhu II, 135
Parākramabāhu VI, 154
Pasenadi, 36n. 52
Sam Fang Kaen, 142
Siṃhabāhu, 108
Śrī Vijaya Narēndrasiṃha, 132
Śrī Vijaya Rājasiṃha, 145n. 8
Śrī Vīraparākrama Narēndrasiṃha, 145n. 8
Suddhodana, 21
Tilokarāja, 142
Vijaya, 108–109
kingship, Buddhist
and karma, 11–14, 27–28, 30–31n. 6. *See also* kings, Buddhist: Aśoka Maurya: past lives of
as "family affair," 42–43
See also political leaders and parties; queenship, Buddhist
Kīrti Śrī Rājasiṃha. *See under* kings, Buddhist
Kumbakarna (pseudonym), 115, 121, 123
Kuṇāla, 49

Lala, 108
Lall, Nanda Kishan, 91–93, 98
Leoshko, Janet, 90
Luther, Martin, 185–186

Macpherson, George, 93
Macpherson, William, 95
Madras, 182–183
Mahākassapa. *See under* saints, Buddhist: famous *arahants*
Mahāmoggallāna. *See under* saints, Buddhist: famous *arahants*
mahāpurusa. *See* buddhas: thirty-two marks of
Malalasekera, G. P., 43
manuscripts, 137, 174, 177, 178, 179
Marriott, McKim, 57
Marshall, John, 197
Matale, 109
Max Müller, Friedrich, 90
McDermott, James P., 11–16, 24
McMahan, David, 202
meditation. *See under* practices, Theravāda Buddhist
Meegaskumbura, P. B., 136
merit-making. *See* karma; practices, Theravāda Buddhist
missions and conversion
Buddhist. *See under* practices, Theravāda Buddhist
Christian. *See* communities, Christian: missionaries and missionary schools
Mitra, Rajendralala, 89, 92
monasteries, temples and pilgrimage sites, Buddhist
Amarāvatī, 197, 199, 201
Asgiri Vihāraya, 133
Bhārhut, 197, 199, 201
Bodhgayā
as "Buddhist Jerusalem," 88, 90

Burmese at, 85, 87–88, 98, 99, 101n. 12
Dalit Buddhists at, 100, 105n. 62
ecumenicalism of, 85, 86, 97–100
history of Buddhist presence at, 87–89
Japanese at, 97–98, 105–106nn. 60, 64, 65, 68, 70
Mahābodhi Temple at, 85, 88, 91, 92, 93, 94, 96, 99–100
See also Arnold, Sir Edwin; communities, Hindu; monks, Buddhist: Dharmapāla, Anagārika; Okakura, Kakuzo
Bodhi Tree
at Anurādhapura, 38n. 61, 142
at Bodhgayā, 20, 49, 92
See also practices, Theravāda Buddhist: worship: of Bodhi trees
Daladā Māligāwa, 110, 189
Dambulla, 109
Devinuwara, 111
Dīghavāpi, 114
Dīpaduttārāmaya at Koṭahena, 176, 177, 182, 184
Gaḍalādeṇiya, 113
Käläṇiya Rājamahā Vihāraya, 181
Laṃkātilaka, 113
Mahāvihāra, 25
Malvatu Vihāraya, 133
Mathurā, 78
Mūlagandhakuṭi Vihāra, 156
Rājagaha (Rajgir), 60, 61
Sāṭcī, 197–201
Sārnāth, 197
Śrāvasti, 59
Subhadrārāmaya Purāṇa Vihāraya, 177
Takṣaśilā, 41
Wat Cedī Cet Yod, 142
Wat Pā Daeng, 142
Wat Suan Dok, 142
Wat Suan Kaew, 162
Wat Suan Mokkhabalārāma, 162
See also art, Theravāda Buddhist; monasticism, Theravāda Buddhist
monasticism, Theravāda Buddhist
adminstrative structures of, 134, 137, 139, 142
Amarapura Nikāya, 177
educational practices and institutions of, 134, 135, 136–137, 138, 157, 178
Buddhist Cultural Centre at Nedimala, 181
Maha Chulalongkorn Buddhist University, 164
Nārammala monastic school, 157
Sārānanda Pirivena, 157
Sirinivāsa Pirivena, 157
forest-dwelling (*araṭṭavāsī*), 59, 77, 134–136, 138, 142
gaṇinnānses, 132–134, 139, 144nn. 3, 5
legitimating discourses of, 134–143
lineages and pupillary succession in, 131, 134, 136, 139, 140, 141–142
Mahanikai, 162
material resources of, 133
monastic discipline (*vinaya*) and, 132, 133, 134, 135, 138, 141
music and, 151–52, 159–60
opposition to innovation in, 152, 158–162, 162–166
Pā Daeng lineage, 141–143, 148n. 57
Rāmañña Nikāya, 153, 157, 160
ritual boundaries (*sīmā*) of, 136, 142
rivalry within, 132–134, 136, 139, 140, 142, 160
saṃgha as one Theravāda community among many, 2
Silvat Samāgama, 132, 145n. 8
Siyam Nikāya, 131–140
Suan Dok lineage, 141–144
See also communities, Theravāda Buddhist; monasteries, temple and pilgrimage sites, Buddhist; practices, Theravāda Buddhist
monks, Buddhist
Ariyadhamma, Pānadurē, 152
Aśvaghoṣa, 90
Buddhadāsa, 162

monks, Buddhist (*cont.*)
Buddhaghosa, 15, 28, 50, 66, 67, 70n. 23
Chapata, 140–141, 147–148n. 44
Chatta, 174
Danti Nayde Gurunnanse (Mendis, Delath Andiris), 177
Devadatta. *See under* sinners, famous
Dhammapāla, 60
Dharmakīrti, 113, 128–129n. 24
Dharmapāla, Anagārika, 88, 90, 91–96, 97, 98, 103n. 39, 156, 165, 172, 178, 183
Dhīrakkhanda, Sīnigama, 177
Faxian, 78
Guṇānanda, Mohoṭṭivattē, 177–179, 182, 184
Gunaratana, Balapiṭiya, 177
Gunaratana, Siyambalangamuvē, 152, 153, 155–62, 163, 164, 165, 166
Kāsyapa, Diṁbulāgala, 135
Khemapali, Nakhon, 164
Lakkhana, 76
Maitreya, Vidāgama, 155, 160–161
Meḍhaṃkara, Diṁbulāgala, 135
Meḍhaṃkara (or Ñāṇagambhira), 142, 143
Ñāṇavimala, Kiriälle, 173–175, 179
Nyanaponika, 13, 25
Phayom Kalyano, 152, 162–166
Phra Malai, 76–77, 78–79
Rāhula, Toṭagāmuvē Śrī, 154–155
Ratanapañña, 142
Ratanapāla, Gamullē, 146–147n. 34
Sārānanda, Uḍunuvara, 156
Saraṇaṃkara, Väliviṭa, 114, 132, 135, 136
Shin Rāhula, 141
Siddhārtha, Rambukkana, 151, 152, 167n.
Sīlācāra, 11, 12, 30n. 7
Soma, Gangodawila, 114–126
Sumana, 141
Sumangala, Hikkaḍuvē, 177
Uttarajīva, 147–148n. 44
Vajiragñāna, Pälänē, 159, 165, 166
Vättävē, 154
Wachiriyan, 11, 12
Xuanzang, 78
See also monasticism, Theravāda Buddhist; saints, Buddhist
morality. *See* practices, Theravāda Buddhist: moral precepts; virtues, Buddhist: morality
Mus, Paul, 53n. 25, 200
music. *See under* monasticism, Theravāda Buddhist:monastic discipline (*vinaya*) and

Nandiya, 75
Navalar, Arumugala, 182–184
Nepal, 156
Neville, Hugh, 174
nibbāna (*nirvāṇa*), 10, 29, 146–147n. 34, 159, 161, 196, 200–201. *See also* buddhas: Gotama: *parinirvāṇa* and funeral of; buddhas: Metteyya (Maitreya); saints, Buddhist
Norman, K. R., 201
nuns. *See* monasticism, Theravāda Buddhist; saints, Buddhist: famous *arahants*

Obeyesekere, Gananath, 172, 181–182
Okakura, Kakuzo, 97–98, 105n. 64
Olcott, Col. Henry Steele, 97, 103n. 39, 173, 175, 178, 185–186. *See also* theosophists
ordination. *See under* practices, Theravāda Buddhist
Orientalists and Orientalism: 87, 89, 93, 107, 113, 172, 184

paccekabuddhas. *See under* buddhas
Pānadura debates, 177–178
Pali Text Society, 107
Parry, Jonathan, 58, 62–63, 65
Pasha, 'Urābī (Arabi), 183–184
Peirce, Charles Sanders, 190

Phra Malai. *See under* monks, Buddhist
pilgrimage. *See under* practices, Theravāda Buddhist
political leaders and parties
East India Company, 87
Elgin, Gilbert, 94
Elgin, Lord, 94, 103–104n. 41
Gandhi, Mohandas K., 99
Gordon, Sir Arthur, 89
Kumaratunga, Chandrika Bandaranaike, 115, 116, 117, 122, 129n. 33
Liberation Tigers of Tamil Eelam (L.T.T.E.), 31n. 19, 115, 116, 120, 122, 123. *See also* Sri Lanka: civil war in
Nehru, Jawaharlal, 86
People's Alliance (P.A.), 116
Prabhakaran, Velupillai, 116, 120. *See also* political leaders and parties: L.T.T.E.; Sri Lanka: civil war in
Premadasa, Ranasinghe, 120–121, 157, 180
Ramachandran, M. G., 122
United National Party (U.N.P.), 116, 120–121
Wickremesinghe, Ranil, 116, 120
Portuguese invasion of Sri Lanka, 111
poya. *See* practices, Theravāda Buddhist: Full Moon Day observances
practices, Theravāda Buddhist
ascetic, 59, 66–68, 135
astrology, 133, 136, 175
begging
as means of unburdening others' bad karma, 57–68
chants and chanting
devotional verses (*gāthās*), 151, 186
namaskāra, 158, 173, 176
protective (*paritta*), 109, 132, 136, 146n. 23, 152, 174, 175, 176
Triple Refuge (*tisaraṇa*), 86, 171, 173, 174, 175, 176, 179
See also practices, Theravāda Buddhist: deity cults; practices, Theravāda Buddhist: moral precepts; practices, Theravāda Buddhist: worship
deity cults
dēvārādhanā (invitation of the gods), 158
kapurālas (priests), 109, 124
santiya (blessings), 125–126
yātikā (ritual invocation), 109
See also deities; practices, Theravāda Buddhist: worship: of deities
Full Moon Day observances (*poya, uposatha*), 10, 107, 173
Vesak, 180
funerary rites, 66–67
giving (*dāna*), 10, 27, 44–49, 51, 57–68, 77, 174
of cloth, 44–46, 54n. 34, 59, 65–68
famous givers
Anāthapiṇḍika, 59
Sujātā, 67
See also kings, Buddhist: Aśoka Maurya; queens, Buddhist: Asaṃdhimittā
gilanpasa, 160, 169n. 17
"regifting," 60, 63, 69n. 5
liturgical. *See* practices, Theravāda Buddhist: chants and chanting; practices, Theravāda Buddhist: deity cults; practices, Theravāda Buddhist: worship
manuals for, 171–186
medicine, 133
meditation, 60, 171, 174, 175, 176, 179
jhāna states of, 74
and Mahāyāna and Pure Land visualization practices, 74
as productive of supernormal cosmological knowledge, 72–77
samādhi state of, 60
as source of distinctively saintly teaching, 81
merit-making (general), 10, 132. *See also* karma

missions and conversion, 64, 73–74, 79, 156, 193–195
moral precepts, 182
eight precepts, 173
five precepts (*pañcasīla*), 114, 118, 119, 158, 173–174
ten precepts, 173
ordination
lower (*pabbajjā*), 133, 156
higher (*upasampadā*), 131–134, 139, 142, 157, 177
pilgrimage, 10, 174, 176. *See also* monasteries, temples and pilgrimage sites, Buddhist
preaching, 10, 178
addresses social problems, 164
bad effects of inappropriate, 159–160
as fluid tradition, 162
of *gaṇinnānses*, 132
listening as meritorious act, 10, 147n. 34, 161
modern forms of
in Sri Lanka, 114, 115, 118, 151–162, 166–167, 178, 182
in Thailand, 162–167
musical, 157–60
of queens, 50–51
poetic, 151–167, 167n. 4
of saints, 80–82
of Siyam Nikāya monks, 138
texts for (*baṇa pot*), 135, 137, 154, 155. *See also* texts, Buddhist
traditional culture of, 158, 159–161, 162–166
prostration, 176
protective, 136, 145n. 20
amulets and charms, 77–79
Bauddha Ādahilla as, 180–181
See also deities; practices, Theravāda Buddhist: chants and chanting: protective (*paritta*); practices, Theravāda Buddhist: deity cults
seeing (*dassana*), 194–195, 201–202. *See also* art, Theravāda Buddhist
sorcery, 49, 67, 122, 133, 136, 144n. 20
Ten Perfections and, 27, 178, 182
worship
artistic representations of, 200
of Bodhi trees (*bodhipūjā*), 152, 189. *See also* monasteries, temples and pilgrimage sites, Buddhist: Bodhgayā; monasteries, temples and pilgrimage sites, Buddhist: Bodhi Tree; art, Theravāda Buddhist: figurative elements
of the Buddha (*buddhapūjā*), 10, 95, 174, 175–176, 179, 180, 182. *See also* buddhas
of deities (*devapūjā*) 121, 125. *See also* deities; practices, Theravāda Buddhist: deity cults
of the Dharma (*dhammapūjā*), 157, 174
of stūpas (*thūpapūjā*), 51, 77, 78, 189, 198, 200, 202
See also practices, Theravāda Buddhist: chants and chanting; virtues, Buddhist: devotion; virtues, Buddhist: faith
See also communities, Theravāda Buddhist; karma; monasticism, Theravāda Buddhist
Prasad, Rajendra, 99
preaching. *See under* practices, Theravāda Buddhist
Pruitt, William, 140, 141
pūjā. *See* practices, Theravāda Buddhist: worship

Queens, Buddhist
Asaṃdhimittā, 35n. 49, 37n. 58, 43–51
Cāmadēvī, 42
and cloth-giving, 44–46, 54n. 34
in chess, 42
as ideal Buddhist wives, 47–48
Kāluvākī, 42–43

Mahāmāyā, 21
Mahāpajāpatī Gotamī. *See under* saints, Buddhist: famous *arahants*
as merit-makers, 31–32n. 23, 45–48
sovereignty of, 47
Tiṣyarakṣitā, 49
Ulakuḍaya, 154
Vedisa-devī, 43
Vessamittā, 173–174
Empress Wu, 42
Ye-ses-mtsho-rgyal, 42
Queenship, Buddhist, 41–55

Rajakarunanayake, Lucien, 120–121
Rambukkana, 156
Ratnāyaka, Victor, 152
Ratwatte, Gen. Anuruddha, 117, 121, 123, 130n. 44
Ratwatte, Dennis, 122–123
Ratwatte (family) 117, 129n. 35
Ray, Reginald, 72–73, 77, 80–82
Reynolds, Frank E., 3, 6–7, 16, 26, 43, 71, 74
Reynolds, Mani B., 3, 43
Roberts, Michael, 184
robes. *See* practices, Theravāda Buddhist: giving: of cloth
Roy, Sanjit, 99
Rupavahini, 115

Saints, Buddhist
charisma of, 77–80
distinctively saintly teaching of, 80–82
famous *arahants*
Ānanda, 14, 20, 23, 32n. 24
Bhaddā-Kāpilāni, 15
Channa, 20
Kāluḍāyi, 20, 23
Mahākassapa, 15, 57–68
Mahāmoggallāna, 14, 23, 32n. 24, 71–82
and Phra Malai, 76–77
violent death of, 12, 74, 81–82
Mahāpajāpatī Gotamī, 15, 19, 21, 23, 195–196
Mahinda, 25, 43, 189
Moggaliputtatissa, 35n. 49
Nāgasena, 22, 23, 24, 27, 35n. 49
Nigrodha, 35n. 49, 37n. 57
Rāhula, 14, 15, 21
Sakula, 194
Sanghamittā, 43
Sāriputta, 14, 21, 22, 23, 32n. 24, 194–195
Sela, 190–195, 197
Soṇa, 147n. 44
Upagupta, 41
Uttara, 147n. 44
Yasodharā, 14, 15, 20
foremost disciples, 23, 37n. 55, 72. *See also* buddhas: Gotama: intimate community of
forest-dwelling, 72, 73, 77, 80
past lives of, 194. *See also* karma; texts, Buddhist: in Pāli: *Apadāna*
relics of, 77–78
supernormal powers of, 71, 72–74
as teachers, 72, 75, 80–81
See also buddhas; monks, Buddhist; monasticism, Theravāda Buddhist; *nibbāna* (*nirvāṇa*)
Śākyans, 25
slaughter of, 12, 20, 22, 36n. 52. *See also* sinners, famous: Viḍūḍabha
Samaraweera, Vijaya, 184
saṃgha, Buddhist. *See* communities, Theravāda Buddhist; monks, Buddhist; monasticism, Theravāda Buddhist
saṃsāra. *See under* cosmology, Theravāda Buddhist
Śānkarācārya, 97
Sāriputta. *See under* saints, Buddhist: famous *arahants*
Schober, Juliane, 16
Schopen, Gregory, 90
sermons. *See* practices, Theravāda Buddhist: preaching

Shils, Edward, 79
sil (*sīla*). *See* practices, Theravāda Buddhist: moral precepts; virtues, Buddhist: morality
sinners, famous
  Bandhula the Mallian, 13, 19, 23, 36n. 52
  Ciñcamānavikā, 24
  Devadatta, 14, 19, 21, 22, 24, 32n. 24
  Sundarī, 24
  Tiṣyarakṣitā, 49
  Viḍūḍabha, 12, 13, 19, 20, 22, 36n. 52
  See also cosmology, Theravāda Buddhist: hells in; karma: bad: bad effects of
Smith, Brian K., 64
Snellgrove, David L., 197, 199, 200
sociokarma. *See under* karma
Soma, Gangodawila. *See under* monks, Buddhist
sorcery. *See under* practices, Theravāda Buddhist
soteriology. *See* buddhas; cosmology, Theravāda Buddhist; doctrines, Theravāda Buddhist; karma; *nibbāna* (*nirvāṇa*); practices, Theravāda Buddhist; saints, Buddhist
Spiro, Melford, 16, 181
Sri Lanka
  civil war in, 113, 181–182
    and deity worship, 125–126
    Norwegian intervention in, 116–117
    See also political leaders and parties
  karmic institutions of, 38n. 61
  See also communities, Theravāda Buddhist; kingdoms and royal capitals, Buddhist; monasteries, temples and pilgrimage sites, Buddhist; monasticism, Theravāda Buddhist
Sri Lanka Broadcasting Corporation (S.L.B.C.), 168n. 12
Stevenson, Ian, 22
Stietencron, Heinrich von, 87, 99
Strong, John S., 17, 21, 24, 60, 78
stūpas. *See* art, Theravāda Buddhist: early Buddhist stūpa reliefs; buddhas: Gotama: relics of; monasteries, temples and pilgrimage sites, Buddhist; practices, Theravāda Buddhist: worship: of stūpas
Sunday Leader (Colombo), 115, 129n. 32
Sunday Observer (Colombo), 117
Sunday Times (Colombo), 115, 117, 119, 121, 122, 123, 129n. 31
Suriyabongs, Dr. Luang, 12–13

Tagore, Rabindranath, 97, 98
Tambiah, Stanley Jeyaraja, 77
Tamils, 113, 114. *See also* Sri Lanka, civil war in
temples. *See* monasteries, temples and pilgrimage sites, Buddhist
Tendulkar, Sachin, 115
Texts, Buddhist
  in Burmese
    donative inscriptions, 31–32n. 23
    Glass Palace Chronicle, The, 140–141
    nissaya texts, 140
    thaimang texts, 141
  for children, 180–181, 186
  in English
    Buddhist Catechism, 173, 175, 185–186
  manuscripts of, 137, 174, 177, 178, 179
  in Pāli
    Ambaṭṭhasutta, 191, 192
    Anāgatavaṃsa, 19, 25, 35n. 43
    Anguttaranikāya, 11, 13, 15, 20, 72
    Apadāna, 15, 17, 18, 21, 23, 193–197, 199–202
    Apadānaṭṭhakathā, 20
    *Aṭṭhakathā*s (in general), 137, 174
    Brahmāyusutta, 191
    Buddhavaṃsa, 15, 18, 19, 25, 196, 199
    Catubhāṇavāra, 136
    Dasavaṭṭhuppakaraṇa, 43, 44–45, 46, 47

Dhajjaggasutta, 174
Dhammacakkapavattanasutta, 175
Dhammapada, 158
Dhammapadaṭṭhakathā, 12
Dīghanikāya, 43, 191, 198
Dīpavaṃsa, 38n. 61
Extended (or *Cambodian*) *Mahāvaṃsa*, 43, 44, 48
Jātakas (in general), 14, 17, 18, 21, 26–27, 32n. 24
  Bhaddasāla, 12
  Guttila, 154
  Kālingabodhi, 198–199
  Kurudhamma, 11, 13
  Maṇicora, 11, 13
  Paññāsa, 16
  Sattubhatta, 154
  Vessantara, 27–28, 38n. 62, 39nn. 66–68
Jinakālamālī, 141–143
Karaṇīyamettasutta, 174
Khuddakanikāya, 15
Khuddasikkhā, 141
Lakkhaṇasutta, 191, 193
Mahābodhivaṃsa, 49
Mahāmangalasutta, 174
Mahāpadānasutta, 191, 193, 197, 198
Mahāparinibbānasutta, 32n. 26, 157, 198
Mahāvaṃsa, 25, 43, 44, 45, 107–109, 113, 189
Majjhimanikāya, 43, 190, 191
Milindapaṭha, 22, 27, 137
Papañcasūdanī (Majjhimanikāya-aṭṭhakathā), 50, 174
Paramatthadīpanī (*Udānaṭṭhakathā*), 60
Paramatthadīpanī (*Vimānavatthu-aṭṭhakātha*), 61–62, 63–64, 74–75, 174
Ratanasutta, 174
Saṃyuttanikāya, 15, 28
Sihalovādasutta, 174
Sumangalavilāsinī (*Dīghanikāyaṭṭhakathā*), 50
Suttanipāta, 158, 190, 191
suttas (in general), 137, 190
Theragāthā, 190
Tipiṭaka (in general), 14, 135, 137, 138, 140, 141, 158, 174, 189, 201
Tuṇḍilovādasutta, 32n. 26
Udāna, 60–61, 64
vaṃsa (genre), 134
Vimānavatthu, 74, 75, 137, 146–447n. 34, 174
Vinaya. *See* monasticism, Buddhist: monastic discipline (*vinaya*) and
Visuddhimagga, 66, 137
in Sanskrit
  Lalitavistara, 59, 67
  Mahāvastu, 76
  Mūlasarvāstivādavinaya, 58, 59, 64, 65
in Sinhala
  baṇa pot, 135, 137, 154, 155
  Bauddha Ädahilla, 171–186
  Buduguṇālaṇkāraya, 155
  Guttila Kāvyaya, 154
  Kāvyaśēkharaya, 154–455, 178
  Lōväḍasaṅgarāva, 155, 160–161
  Milindapraśnaya, 178
  Pansiyapanasjātakapota, 178
  Pūjāvaliya, 172
  Saṃgharājasādhucariyāva, 134
  sannasas, 127n. 13
  sannayas, 135, 140
  Sārārthadīpanī, 135, 136
  Sārārthasaṇgrahaya, 135
  Sinhala literature (in general) 109, 110, 153–155, 175
    Anurādhapura period of, 154
    Daṁbadeṇi period of, 135, 136, 137, 145n. 17, 153
    Kandyan period of, 155
    Kōṭṭē period of, 113, 154, 155, 166
    Poḷonnaruwa period of, 134, 137
  Siyabaslakara, 154

Texts, Buddhist (*cont.*)
in Thai and Thai Yṃan
Brapāṃsukūlānisaṃsaṃ, 59, 66
nissai texts, 143
Phra Malai Klon Suat, 76
Tamnān Mūlasāsanā Wat Pā Daeng, 141–143
Tamnān Mūlasāsanā Wat Suan Dok, 141–143
Trai Phum (Three Worlds According to King Ruang), 19, 30n. 6, 32n. 26, 43, 46, 47, 71
vohan texts, 143
translation into local languages, 137–138, 140–141
"visual texts," 189–190. *See also* art, Theravāda Buddhist
texts, Hindu
Agni Purāṇa, 92
Bhagavata Purāṇa, 92
Dharmaśāstras, 58, 61
Purāṇas (in general), 110
Vāyu Purāṇa, 92
Viṣṇu Purāṇa, 104n. 46
Thailand. *See* communities, Theravāda Buddhist; kingdoms and royal capitals, Buddhist; monasteries, temples and pilgrimage sites, Buddhist; monasticism, Theravāda Buddhist
theosophists, 178, 182. *See also* Blavatsky, Helena; monks, Buddhist: Dharmapāla, Anagārika; Olcott, Col. Henry Steele
Theosophical Review, 185
Trevethick, Michael, 97
Turner, Victor, 86, 98

upasampadā. *See* practices, Theravāda Buddhist: ordination

Varanasi, 62–63
Vedic sacrifices, 58, 60, 64–66, 200
Ver Eecke, Jacqueline, 43
Viḍūḍabha. *See under* sinners, famous
Vijayavardhana, G., 136
vinaya. *See* monasticism, Theravāda Buddhist: monastic discipline (*vinaya*) and
virtues, Buddhist
compassion (*karunā*), 29, 32–33n. 27, 61, 81–82, 118
devotion (*bhakti*), 157, 175, 192, 193, 194, 195. *See also* practices, Theravāda Buddhist: worship
faith (*śraddhā*), 89, 91, 157, 171, 176, 190, 192
generosity, 31n. 21, 176, 182. *See also* practices, Theravāda Buddhist: giving (*dāna*)
gratitude, 28
loving-kindness (*metta*), 28, 118, 161
morality (*sīla*), 173, 178, 182. *See also* practices, Theravāda Buddhist: moral precepts
Viṣṇu. *See under* deities
Vivekananda, Swami, 97, 183

Wach, Joachim, 71
Walters, Jonathan S., 201–202
Weber, Max, 14, 23, 24, 77, 79–80, 183
Wheel of Dharma, 47. *See also* art, Theravāda Buddhist: figurative elements in
White, David, 60
Woodward, Mark, 17, 26
Wyatt, David, 141

Young, Richard Fox, 177, 178, 182, 183

www.ingramcontent.com/pod-product-compliance
Lightning Source LLC
Chambersburg PA
CBHW020652230426
43665CB00008B/401